Books are to be returned on or
the last date below.

Sally J. Stevens, PhD
Harry K. Wexler, PhD
Editors

Women and Substance Abuse: Gender Transparency

Women and Substance Abuse: Gender Transparency has been co-published simultaneously as *Drugs & Society*, Volume 13, Numbers 1/2 1998.

Pre-publication REVIEWS, COMMENTARIES, EVALUATIONS . . .

"In these years of increased poverty, addiction, violence and incarceration for women, it is a welcome relief to have a book (edited by a woman) dedicated to the subject of women and substance abuse. Hopefully the efforts of Dr. Stevens will bring academic attention and research to the subject which will help shape policies so that more aid is extended to women. As a treatment professional responsible for the delivery of services to women for over a decade it is encouraging to finally see, in print, research findings and discussions that are reflective of the reality of what is occuring in the field. Substance abusing women have been on the waiting list too long in every area!"

Robin McGrath
Director of Women's Services
Desert Willow Project, NDRI
Tucson, Arizona

"Stevens and Wexler have assembled an exceptional volume of the patterns, correlates and consequences of substance abuse among women. Much of the work includes data from samples that are population-based, which increases the generalizability of findings to a large population of women. *Women and Substance Abuse* underscores the urgent need to increase efforts to recruit more women into drug abuse treatment, and to reduce the barriers that restrict women from enrolling. In describing the characteristics of substance abusing women, this volume also covers the intersecting epidemics of STDs, violence and HIV and addresses the importance of integrating gynecologic services and domestic counseling into prevention programs for women. As AIDS has become the 3rd leading cause of death among 25 to 44 year old women in the US, and the leading cause of death among minority women of that same age, there is an urgent public health need to target women for intervention studies that focus on reducing high risk behaviors. This compilation of studies describes what has worked, what could be improved and what direction is needed for the future.

The findings presented in this book are timely and comprehensive and indicate the devastating societal, medical and economic consequences of substance abuse. *Women and Substance Abuse* should be read by substance abuse researchers, as well as drug treatment counselors, primary care providers, health care administrators and policy makers.

Women and Substance Abuse is a wake up call for all investigators to do the hard work necessary to recruit and maintain women in studies, and to focus interventions on topics that are relevant to women. It is also a plea to the funding institutions to base funding decisions not only on a promise to enroll women but on actual success in enrolling women in research studies. Recruiting women–especially women with children, minority, substance abusing, out of treatment, HIV positive and incarcerated women–into research projects is a major accomplishment, and the authors must be congratulated for their extraordinary success in enrolling women in numbers great enough to be able to evaluate findings specifically related to gender."

Linda B. Cottler, PhD
Associate Professor
of Epidemiology in Psychiatry
Washington University School
of Medicine, Department
of Psychiatry, St. Louis, Missouri

Women
and Substance Abuse:
Gender Transparency

Women and Substance Abuse: Gender Transparency has been co-published simultaneously as *Drugs & Society*, Volume 13, Numbers 1/2 1998.

The *Drugs & Society* Monographs/"Separates"

Prevention Practice in Substance Abuse, edited by Carl G. Leukefeld and Richard R. Clayton

Multicultural AIDS Prevention Programs, edited by Robert T. Trotter II

Sociocultural Perspectives on Volatile Solvent Use, edited by Fred Beauvais and Joseph E. Trimble

Substance Abuse Prevention in Multicultural Communities, edited by Jeanette Valentine, Judith A. De Jong, and Nancy J. Kennedy

Women and Substance Abuse: Gender Transparency, edited by Sally J. Stevens and Harry K. Wexler

These books were published simultaneously as special thematic issues of *Drugs & Society* and are available bound separately. Visit Haworth's website at http://www.haworthpressinc.com to search our online catalog for complete tables of contents and ordering information for these and other publications. Or call 1-800-HAWORTH (outside US/Canada: 607-722-5857), Fax: 1-800-895-0582 (outside US/Canada: 607-771-0012), or e-mail getinfo@ haworthpressinc.com

Women
and Substance Abuse:
Gender Transparency

Sally J. Stevens, PhD
Harry K. Wexler, PhD
Editors

Women and Substance Abuse: Gender Transparency has been co-published simultaneously as *Drugs & Society*, Volume 13, Numbers 1/2 1998.

The Haworth Press, Inc.
New York • London

Women and Substance Abuse: Gender Transparency has been co-published simultaneously as *Drugs & Society*™, Volume 13, Numbers 1/2 1998.

The Haworth Press, Inc., 10 Alice Street, Binghamton, NY 13904-1580 USA

Cover design by Thomas J. Mayshock Jr.

Library of Congress Cataloging-in-Publication Data

Women and substance abuse: gender transparency/Sally J. Stevens, Harry K. Wexler, editors.
    p. cm.
    "Has been co-published simultaneously as Drugs & society, Volume 13, Number 1/2 1998."
    Includes bibliographical references and index.
    ISBN 0-7890-0386-4 (alk. paper).–ISBN 0-7890-0389-9 (pbk.)
    1. Women–Drug use. 2. Women–Substance use. 3. Narcotic addicts. 4. Narcotic addicts–Rehabilitation. 5. Drug abuse. I. Stevens, Sally J. II. Wexler, Harry K. III. Drugs & society (New York, N.Y.)
HV5824.W6W645 1998
362.29'082–dc21
    98-16153
    CIP

Dedicated to Evelyn Mae Walcott Stevens

INDEXING & ABSTRACTING

Contributions to this publication are selectively indexed or abstracted in print, electronic, online, or CD-ROM version(s) of the reference tools and information services listed below. This list is current as of the copyright date of this publication. See the end of this section for additional notes.

- *Abstracts in Anthropology,* Baywood Publishing Company, 26 Austin Avenue, P.O. Box 337, Amityville, NY 11701

- *Academic Abstracts/CD-ROM,* EBSCO Publishing Editorial Department, P.O. Box 590, Ipswich, MA 01938-0590

- *ADDICTION ABSTRACTS,* National Addiction Centre, 4 Windsor Walk, London SE5 8AF, England

- *ALCONLINE Database,* Centralforbundet for alkohol-och narkotikaupplysning, Box 70412, 107 25 Stockholm, Sweden

- *Applied Social Sciences Index & Abstracts (ASSIA) (Online: ASSI via Data-Star) (CDRom: ASSIA Plus),* Bowker-Saur Limited, Maypole House, Maypole Road, East Grinstead, West Sussex, RH19 1HH, England

- *Brown University Digest of Addiction Theory and Application, The (DATA Newsletter),* Project Cork Institute, Dartmouth Medical School, 14 South Main Street, Suite 2F, Hanover, NH 03755-2015

- *Cambridge Scientific Abstracts, Health & Safety Science Abstracts,* 7200 Wisconsin Avenue #601, Bethesda, MD 20814

- *Child Development Abstracts & Bibliography,* University of Kansas, 213 Bailey Hall, Lawrence, KS 66045

- *CNPIEC Reference Guide: Chinese National Directory of Foreign Periodicals,* P.O. Box 88, Beijing, People's Republic of China

- *Criminal Justice Abstracts,* Willow Tree Press, 15 Washington Street, 4th Floor, Newark, NJ 07102

- *Criminal Justice Periodical Index,* University Microfilms, Inc., P.O. Box 32770, Louisville, KY 40232

(continued)

- *Excerpta Medica/Secondary Publishing Division,* Elsevier Science, Inc., Secondary Publishing Division, 655 Avenue of the Americas, New York, NY 10010

- *Family Studies Database (online and CD/ROM),* National Information Services Corporation, 306 East Baltimore Pike, 2nd Floor, Media, PA 19063

- *Health Source: Indexing & Abstracting of 160 selected health related journals, updated monthly:* EBSCO Publishing, 83 Pine Street, Peabody, MA 01960

- *Health Source Plus: expanded version of "Health Source" to be released shortly:* EBSCO Publishing, 83 Pine Street, Peabody, MA 01960

- *Human Resources Abstracts (HRA),* Sage Publications, Inc., 2455 Teller Road, Newbury Park, CA 91320

- *IBZ International Bibliography of Periodical Literature,* Zeller Verlag GmbH & Co., P.O.B. 1949, d-49009 Osnabruck, Germany

- *Index to Periodical Articles Related to Law,* University of Texas, 727 East 26th Street, Austin, TX 78705

- *International Pharmaceutical Abstracts,* ASHP, 7272 Wisconsin Avenue, Bethesda, MD 20814

- *International Political Science Abstracts,* 27 Rue Saint-Guillaume, F-75337 Paris, Cedex 07, France

- *INTERNET ACCESS (& additional networks) Bulletin Board for Libraries ("BUBL") coverage of information resources on INTERNET, JANET, and other networks.*
  - <URL:http://bubl.ac.uk/>
  - The new locations will be found under <URL:http://bubl.ac.uk/link/>.
  - Any existing BUBL users who have problems finding information on the new service should contact the BUBL help line by sending e-mail to <bubl@bubl.ac.uk>.
  The Andersonian Library, Curran Building, 101 St. James Road, Glasgow G4 0NS, Scotland

- *Medication Use STudies (MUST) DATABASE,* The University of Mississippi, School of Pharmacy, University, MS 38677

(continued)

- *Mental Health Abstracts (online through DIALOG)*, IFI/Plenum Data Company, 3202 Kirkwood Highway, Wilmington, DE 19808

- *National Criminal Justice Reference Services*, National Institute of Justice/NCJRS, Mail Stop 2A/2277 Research Boulevard, Rockville, MD 20849-6000

- *NIAAA Alcohol and Alcohol Problems Science Database (ETOH)*, National Institute on Alcohol Abuse and Alcoholism, 1400 Eye Street NW, Suite 200, Washington, DC 20005

- *Personnel Management Abstracts*, 704 Island Lake Road, Chelsea, MI 48118

- *Psychological Abstracts (PsycINFO)*, American Psychological Association, P.O. Box 91600, Washington, DC 20090-1600

- *Public Affairs Information Bulletin (PAIS)*, Public Affairs Information Service, Inc., 521 West 43rd Street, New York, NY 10036-4396

- *Referativnyi Zhurnal (Abstracts Journal of the All-Russian Institute of Scientific and Technical Information)*, 20 Usievich Street, Moscow 125219, Russia

- *Sage Family Studies Abstracts (SFSA)*, Sage Publications, Inc., 2455 Teller Road, Newbury Park, CA 91320

- *Social Planning/Policy & Development Abstracts (SOPODA)*, Sociological Abstracts, Inc., P.O. Box 22206, San Diego, CA 92192-0206

- *Social Work Abstracts*, National Association of Social Workers, 750 First Street NW, 8th Floor, Washington, DC 20002

- *Sociological Abstracts (SA)*, Sociological Abstracts, Inc., P.O. Box 22206, San Diego, CA 92192-0206

- *SOMED (social medicine) Database*, Landes Institut fur Den Offentlichen Gesundheitsdienst NRW, Postfach 20 10 12, D-33548 Bielefeld, Germany

- *Sport Search*, Sport Information Resource Center, 1600 James Naismith Drive, Suite 107, Gloucester, Ontario K1B 5N4, Canada

- *Violence and Abuse Abstracts: A Review of Current Literature on Interpersonal Violence (VAA)*, Sage Publications, Inc., 2455 Teller Road, Newbury Park, CA 91320

(continued)

SPECIAL BIBLIOGRAPHIC NOTES

related to special journal issues (separates)
and indexing/abstracting

☐ indexing/abstracting services in this list will also cover material in any "separate" that is co-published simultaneously with Haworth's special thematic journal issue or DocuSerial. Indexing/abstracting usually covers material at the article/chapter level.

☐ monographic co-editions are intended for either non-subscribers or libraries which intend to purchase a second copy for their circulating collections.

☐ monographic co-editions are reported to all jobbers/wholesalers/approval plans. The source journal is listed as the "series" to assist the prevention of duplicate purchasing in the same manner utilized for books-in-series.

☐ to facilitate user/access services all indexing/abstracting services are encouraged to utilize the co-indexing entry note indicated at the bottom of the first page of each article/chapter/contribution.

☐ this is intended to assist a library user of any reference tool (whether print, electronic, online, or CD-ROM) to locate the monographic version if the library has purchased this version but not a subscription to the source journal.

☐ individual articles/chapters in any Haworth publication are also available through the Haworth Document Delivery Service (HDDS).

ABOUT THE EDITORS

Sally J. Stevens, PhD, is Research Associate Professor with the Southwest Institute for Research on Women (SIROW) in the College of Social and Behavioral Sciences at the University of Arizona in Tucson, Arizona. Dr. Stevens has received numerous large-scale federal grants to administer and research innovative drug treatment programs that serve pregnant women and women with children. She has also developed and implemented women-centered interventions that assist drug using women to reduce their risk of becoming infected with HIV. Dr. Stevens is widely published in the area of women's health, particularly health issues that encompass concerns of underserved, disenfranchised drug-involved women.

Harry K. Wexler, PhD, is Senior Principal Investigator at the Center for Therapeutic Research at National Development and Research Institutes, Inc., in New York, New York. Dr. Wexler serves on the editorial boards of substance abuse and psychological journals, has written numerous articles for scholarly publications, and has held appointments at major universities and positions in many professional organizations. A regular speaker at national conferences, Dr. Wexler also provides consultation for federal and state agencies in the areas of substance abuse and criminal justice. An accomplished research and clinical psychologist, he has achieved a national reputation in the areas of substance abuse policy, treatment, and research in the last 30 years.

Women
and Substance Abuse:
Gender Transparency

CONTENTS

Preface

The selected concerns and research findings presented in this volume pertain to issues involving women and substance abuse. The three papers that comprise the first section address drug use patterns and HIV risk behavior of female substance abusers. These papers provide enlightening information regarding drug use patterns and HIV risks of women from three cities: Rio De Janeiro, Brazil; Philadelphia, PA; and New Haven, CT. The authors conclude that given the intensity of drug use, the extent of HIV risk behavior, the high level of HIV seroprevalence, and the social context and forces within which the women live, there is a tremendous and immediate need to provide ethnic and gender specific concentrated harm reduction interventions including drug treatment.

The second section of this volume examines differences between women engaged in drug treatment and women who are not engaged in drug treatment. Additionally, a gender comparison identifying how women who enter treatment are different than men who enter treatment is included. These authors found significant differences on variables such as race, choice of drug, injection as a route of administration, HIV risk, and drug treatment history of women in versus out of treatment. Consequently, the authors conclude that harm reduction strategies must be tailored to meet the needs of these two different groups of women. Moreover, gender differences such as women reporting more daily use of cocaine, greater proportions of past and current physical and sexual abuse, and greater concerns about issues related to children were also noted. These differences indicate that harm reduction strategies and drug treatment interventions must be refined to fit the specific needs of substance abusing women.

Section three includes two topics of special concern for substance abusing women: sexually transmitted disease and incidents of violence. Gender differences in risk for gonorrhea infection were shown to differ between

[Haworth co-indexing entry note]: "Preface." Stevens, Sally J., and Harry K. Wexler. Co-published simultaneously in *Drugs & Society* (The Haworth Press, Inc.) Vol. 13, No. 1/2, 1998, pp. xvii-xviii; and: *Women and Substance Abuse: Gender Transparency* (ed: Sally J. Stevens, and Harry K. Wexler) The Haworth Press, Inc., 1998, pp. xvii-xviii. Single or multiple copies of this article are available for a fee from The Haworth Document Delivery Service [1-800-342-9678, 9:00 a.m. - 5:00 p.m. (EST). E-mail address: getinfo@haworthpressinc.com].

xvii

women and men. Risk factors for women included the trading of sex for money, being American Indian or Alaska Native, perceiving oneself as homeless, and trading sex for drugs. Results of this study may be particularly helpful in guiding public policy and public health interventions. Also helpful in developing public policy and interventions are the results from the paper on violence. While substance abusing women report frequently being the victim of violence they also report being the perpetrator of violence; treatment interventions must address both.

The fourth section looks at the role of physicians and prenatal care providers of substance abusing women. These studies explore whether physicians and prenatal care providers identify and address substance abuse and HIV with their clients. Conclusions from these authors suggest that medical settings often miss opportunities to provide prevention, referral and interventions that are clearly needed by substance abusing women. Moreover, drug treatment programs need to be multifaceted to include family planning, prenatal care, and parenting skills.

The final section of this volume addresses drug treatment strategies that may be particularly effective for addicted women. One of the papers discusses the development of a prison-based therapeutic community for women, while two papers examine the treatment effectiveness of long term residential treatment for women without children, pregnant women and women with children. Outcome data from these two papers supports the need for long term treatment and the inclusion of children in the treatment setting. The final paper discusses the economic impacts of clients before, during and after substance abuse treatment. Data from this important study supports the cost effectiveness of providing substance abuse treatment for women.

Sally J. Stevens, PhD
Harry K. Wexler, PhD

I. DRUG USE AND HIV RISK BEHAVIOR OF FEMALE SUBSTANCE ABUSERS

Drug Use and Risks for HIV/AIDS Among Indigent Women in Rio de Janeiro, Brazil

Hilary L. Surratt, MA
James A. Inciardi, PhD

SUMMARY. The PROVIVA project (*Projeto Venha Informar-se sobre o Vírus da AIDS*), funded by the National Institute on Drug Abuse and administered by the University of Miami School of Medicine, was established in 1993 for the purpose of developing and implementing a community-wide HIV/AIDS prevention effort in Rio de Janeiro, Brazil. Recruitment began in mid-1994 and the spe-

---

Hilary L. Surratt and James A. Inciardi are affiliated with the Comprehensive Drug Research Center, Department of Epidemiology and Public Health, University of Miami School of Medicine.

This research was supported by HHS Grant No. 5 UO1 DAO8510 from the National Institute on Drug Abuse.

[Haworth co-indexing entry note]: "Drug Use and Risks for HIV/AIDS Among Indigent Women in Rio de Janeiro, Brazil." Surratt, Hilary L., and James A. Inciardi. Co-published simultaneously in *Drugs & Society* (The Haworth Press, Inc.) Vol. 13, No. 1/2, 1998, pp. 1-12; and: *Women and Substance Abuse: Gender Transparency* (ed: Sally J. Stevens, and Harry K. Wexler) The Haworth Press, Inc., 1998, pp. 1-12. Single or multiple copies of this article are available for a fee from The Haworth Document Delivery Service [1-800-342-9678, 9:00 a.m. - 5:00 p.m. (EST). E-mail address: getinfo@haworthpressinc.com].

cific target groups included cocaine-using women and men in Rio's *favelas* (shantytowns) and "red light" districts. Study participants were obtained through standard chain referral and targeted sampling techniques, and through May 31, 1997 over 1,500 were enrolled in the project. This analysis focuses on the first 339 women recruited.

The women ranged in age from 18 to 62, with a median of 29 years. The majority were either black or multi-racial (*morena, parda, mulata, café com leite,* and other multi-racial designations), and almost all were of low socio-economic status. The HIV risk behaviors engaged in by these women during the 30-day period prior to interview included sex with multiple partners (17%), sex with an injection drug user (3.8%), injection drug use (4.1%), and anal sex (12.7%). In addition, also during the past 30 days, 70.8% had used cocaine either daily or several times a week and 81% reported no use of condoms. Finally, 95.6% of the women had never been in drug treatment, 28.9% reported exchanging sex for money, 10.3% reported exchanging sex for drugs, and 15.5% reported histories of one or more sexually transmitted diseases.

A total of 8.5% of the women tested positive for antibody to HIV-1. The HIV test results and risk behaviors, combined with the apparent lack of drug abuse treatment services suggest that cocaine-using women in Rio's *favelas* and red light districts are in need of concentrated services in the areas of HIV and other STD prevention/intervention, substance abuse treatment, and other risk reduction initiatives. *[Article copies available for a fee from The Haworth Document Delivery Service: 1-800-342-9678. E-mail address: getinfo@haworthpressinc.com]*

Although it would be difficult to predict the future course of the AIDS epidemic, The World Health Organization anticipates that the number of HIV-infected persons worldwide will reach 26 million by the year 2000, and that 90% of all AIDS cases will be diagnosed in developing nations (Berkley, 1993). Currently, women constitute more than 40% of those infected with HIV. In absolute numbers, over 7 million women are already infected, and another 1 million HIV infections were anticipated to have occurred in 1995 alone (World Health Organization, 1995). Although women in sub-Saharan Africa display the most elevated rates of HIV seroprevalence, those in Latin America are becoming infected in ever-expanding numbers (De Bruyn, 1992).

It is believed that HIV transmission began in Latin America almost simultaneously with that in the United States, affecting primarily gay and bisexual men and injection drug users. Since the late 1980s, however, many Latin American nations have experienced dramatic increases in the number of HIV infections acquired through heterosexual contact (Berkley, 1993). The rise in heterosexual transmission of HIV in Latin America has greatly impacted seroprevalence rates among women, given that male to female transmission is reported to be 24 times more efficient than female to male (World Health Organization, 1995).

In terms of reported cases of AIDS, Brazil ranks first among Latin American nations, and second in the world, surpassed only by the United States. Through November 1996, the Brazilian Ministry of Health National STD/AIDS Program had reported 94,997 cumulative AIDS cases (Brazilian Ministry of Health, 1996). In the late 1980s, the number of HIV-infected and AIDS symptomatic women in Brazil began to increase rapidly. Through 1987, for example, only 250 cases had been reported among Brazilian women, yet by late 1996 this number had risen to 18,320 (Brazilian Ministry of Health, 1996). Accordingly, the male to female ratio of AIDS cases dropped from 30:1 in 1985 to 6:1 in 1991 (Heise and Elias, 1995) to 3:1 at the close of 1995 (Brazilian Ministry of Health, 1996). Heterosexual contact is the major mode of transmission for females in Brazil (43.8%), followed by unknown causes (23.3%), injection drug use (19.6%), blood transfusions (7.2%), and perinatal transmission (6.0%). The actual number of AIDS cases in Brazil is likely underestimated and according to epidemiologists, the rate of underreporting may approach 100% (Goldstein, 1994). Especially troublesome is the underreporting of cases among women due to their lack of access to health care services and the belief of many physicians that "good girls do not get AIDS" (Hankins and Handley, 1992; Carovano, 1991).

The response of the Brazilian government to the AIDS epidemic has been far from adequate. Government inaction was notable as the AIDS epidemic was unfolding, with scare tactics being used as the most typical attempt at intervention rather than informational advertisements and proactive prevention programming. In fact, many campaigns actually neglected to report how HIV was contracted (Goldstein, 1994). Further, the vast majority of AIDS prevention/intervention efforts–in Brazil and elsewhere–have targeted injection drug users and commercial sex workers, to the exclusion of others at risk for HIV (Carovano, 1991; Campbell, 1990). As a result, many women who do not engage in injection drug use or prostitution do not perceive themselves to be at risk and may do little to change their behaviors (Campbell, 1990).

Despite the low perception of risk among the general population of women in Brazil, heterosexual contact with a seropositive sex partner continues to present a significant risk for contamination. In fact, the greatest need for AIDS education and intervention efforts may be among monogamous married and cohabiting women. For example, a study conducted in São Paulo–Brazil's largest city–found that just under half of all new AIDS cases among women were reported among those who were both married and monogamous (Heise and Elias, 1995). This rising seroprevalence rate might be explained in any number of ways. A 1995 study found the percentage of married or cohabiting Brazilian men reporting multiple sex partners in the past year to be approximately 20%, far surpassing that of men in the United States, Great Britain, and France (Caraël et al., 1995). Further, research in Rio de Janeiro found that *unprotected* insertive anal intercourse with male partners during a six month period was routine among men who identified themselves as bisexual. Just under 90% of these same men also reported unprotected vaginal sex with regular female partners in the same period (Heise and Elias, 1995).

The implications of these data for the spread of HIV among women in Brazil are evident, and when considered in the context of Brazilian cultural values they appear all the more troubling. As in many developing nations, the inferior social and economic position of women in Brazil elevates their risk for HIV infection. They are frequently denied both educational opportunities and the right to purchase or hold property (World Health Organization, 1995). This subordination increases women's economic dependence while lessening their negotiating power in personal relationships (World Health Organization, 1995; Carovano, 1991). For indigent women, subordination and risk would appear to be even more pronounced, particularly among those who engage in drug use as well. Within the context of these remarks, this analysis examines the drug using and HIV risk behaviors in a sample of indigent women recruited for HIV/AIDS prevention/intervention at the NIDA-funded PROVIVA project in Rio de Janeiro.

METHODS

The general purposes of the PROVIVA (*Pro*jeto *V*enha *I*nformar-se sobre o *V*irus da *A*IDS) project are to establish a community HIV/AIDS surveillance and monitoring system in Rio de Janeiro, Brazil, and to develop, implement, and evaluate a community-based HIV/AIDS prevention/intervention program for cocaine injectors and snorters, and transvestite prostitutes, in Rio's *favelas* (shantytowns) and "red light" districts. A secondary purpose is to generate an effective field-based HIV prevention program that can be utilized in other developing communities.

PROVIVA has been in the field since March 1994, and as of May 31, 1997, over 1,500 clients had been recruited, 339 of whom were women.

Eligible participants were those who were at least 18 years of age, were not in drug treatment or jail during the month prior to interview, and who reported cocaine use during the thirty days prior to interview. Project recruitment was conducted by indigenous outreach workers who were familiar with the target areas. Outreach workers located respondents in neighborhoods with high rates of cocaine use. Contacts were made on the street and in the *favelas* using standard multiple-starting-point snowball sampling techniques.

After informed consent was obtained, interviews were conducted with the clients using the Cooperative Agreement Risk Behavior Assessment (RBA), a standardized data collection instrument developed by scientists and funded investigators. Questions about drug use, sexual behavior, and health status were asked during an interview lasting approximately 1 hour, and respondents were paid the equivalent of US$10 for their time. Urine and blood samples were also collected. The characteristics, risk behaviors, and serostatus of the female clients for whom basic assessment and HIV data are available form the core of the analysis in this paper.

RESULTS

As indicated in Table 1, the 339 female respondents had a median age of 29 years, with the overwhelming majority (72.2%) under age 35. In terms of race/ethnicity, 38.9% identified themselves as black, 35.7% as "multi-racial" (mulata, parda, and morena), and 25.4% as white. Educational attainment was low, with 87.9% of the women completing 8 or fewer years of schooling, while only 6.5% had graduated from high school. Income data also indicate that the earnings of these women were extremely low. The median monthly income of the sample was $100 U.S., which is equivalent to a minimum wage rate of $0.63 per hour for a full-time job, as compared to the rate of $5.15 per hour in the U.S. Furthermore, only 14.5% reported income from a paid job, while 51.6% received support from a spouse or relatives. Interestingly, a substantial number of women reported sources of income outside of the formal sector of the economy. For example, 8.6% earned money from prostitution in the month prior to interview, and 33.6% reported income from odd jobs, which primarily included street vending.

Almost all of the cocaine-using women had histories of alcohol use (98.5%), and the majority had experience with marijuana (69.0%). Table 2 shows that in terms of sequential patterns of drug use onset, the first drug used was alcohol at a median age of 15 years, followed by marijuana and cocaine at age 18. During the past 30 days, 87.6% reported alcohol use,

TABLE 1. Selected Demographic Characteristics of 339 Cocaine Using Women in Rio de Janeiro, Brazil, 1997

	N = 339
Age at Interview	
18-24	28.1%
25-34	44.1%
35+	27.8%
Median	29.0
Race/Ethnicity	
Black	38.9%
White	25.4%
Multi-racial	35.7%
Education	
8 years or less	87.9%
Some high school	5.6%
High school graduate	6.5%
Monthly Income	
(In U.S. Dollars)	
Less than $100	49.9%
$101-$300	37.8%
$301+	12.4%

Note: Income data were collected as the number of minimum salaries, then converted into US$ using an average minimum salary of R$100 (Brazilian Reais) at an exchange rate of 1.00.

35.1% reported marijuana use, and *all* reported cocaine use. Only 9.7% of the sample reported a history of injection drug use, and even fewer (4.4%) had received any treatment for substance abuse. Drug use during sexual activity was not uncommon, with 38.1%, 14.7%, and 39.2% reporting alcohol, marijuana, and cocaine use, respectively, during sexual encounters in the previous month.

Of the 283 women recruited into the prevention/intervention program who consented to a blood draw, 8.5% tested positive for antibody to HIV-1.[1] As indicated in Table 3, the risk factors most related to HIV seropositivity included having ever exchanged sex for drugs, a history of any sexually transmitted disease, and having had vaginal sex with multiple partners in the last 30 days. A history of injection drug use was also

1. HIV testing was done by ELISA, with confirmatory testing through both Western Blot and Indirect Immunofluorescence Assay (IFA) procedures.

TABLE 2. Drug Use and Treatment Histories of 339 Cocaine Using Women in Rio de Janeiro, Brazil, 1997

	N = 339
Percentage Ever Using	
Alcohol	98.5%
Marijuana	69.0%
Cocaine	100.0%
Median Age at First Use	
Alcohol	15.0
Marijuana	18.0
Cocaine	18.0
Percentage Using in Last Month	
Alcohol	87.6%
Marijuana	35.1%
Cocaine	100.0%
Ever Injected Drugs	9.7%
Ever in Drug Treatment	4.4%

strongly related to HIV seropositivity. Condom use rates were extremely low, with approximately 81% of sexually active women reporting *unprotected* sex in the last 30 days. Those women who did indicate at least some condom use were significantly more likely than other women to be involved in sex for money exchanges.

DISCUSSION

With 8.5% of the women sampled in this study testing positive for HIV, it appears that cocaine-involved women in Rio de Janeiro are a highly vulnerable population. While only 9.7% (N = 33) of the respondents have histories of injection drug use (nineteen former and fourteen active injectors), it is clear that, among these women, the risk of HIV transmission associated with sharing drug paraphernalia is significant. Much more prevalent, however, are the risks associated with unprotected heterosexual contact. Although the services and intervention offered at PROVIVA provided the first HIV testing for 87.9% of the women in this study, virtually all were aware of AIDS and its consequences, and the great majority

TABLE 3. HIV Seropositivity by Selected Risk Factors Among 283 Cocaine Using Women in Rio de Janeiro, Brazil, 1997

	N (% Seropositive)		P-value
Total Sample	283	(8.5%)	
Injection Drug Use			
Yes	30	(26.7%)	.000
No	253	(6.3%)	
Exchange Sex for Drugs			
Yes	27	(18.5%)	.05
No	256	(7.4%)	
STD History			
Yes	44	(20.5%)	.001
No	239	(6.3%)	
Number of Sex Partners (previous month)			
None	60	(1.7%)	.006
One	175	(8.0%)	
Two or more	48	(18.8%)	

(76.7%) felt that they had little or no chance of becoming infected with HIV. Interestingly, even women at high risk shared this perception. For example, of the fourteen current injectors, 57% felt that they had little or no chance of getting AIDS; and of the 52 women who had multiple sex partners in the last 30 days, 46.2% believed that they had little or no chance of getting AIDS.

Apart from sexual abstinence and monogamous relationships between uninfected partners, the use of condoms is currently the only effective means available for preventing the sexual transmission of human immunodeficiency virus. Yet with women in general, and Brazilian women in particular, the opportunity to use condoms is not always viable or practical. In a recent study of sexual behavior and AIDS risks in 13 developing nations, including a sample of 1,130 men and women in Rio de Janeiro, it was clear that condom use was limited (Mehryar, 1995). Some 18% of the women in the Rio sample were not even aware of the existence of condoms, and only 9% of sexually experienced women had ever used one. Of those who had used a condom at least once, the overwhelming majority were under age 25, never married, and had at least a high school education. Further research in Brazil has also indicated that many low-income women have very limited knowledge about condoms. Many of these women expressed concern that condoms would become lost inside the vagina and travel to the throat, or if withdrawn, would remove their reproductive organs as well (Goldstein, 1993).

Brazilian cultural norms support notions of male dominance and control in sexual encounters (Gupta and Weiss, 1993), and as such, many women feel that discussing or negotiating safe sex with their partners is not permissible. Previous studies of sexual behavior in Brazil have confirmed that sexual negotiation is indeed unacceptable to many. An extremely large number of Brazilian women have reported choosing sterilization as their method of birth control in order to avoid discussions of contraception with their partners (Gupta and Weiss, 1993). For example, the proportion of married women of childbearing age in Brazil reporting the use of condoms was only 2% at the close of the 1980s (Goldberg et al., 1989). Similarly, in a study of Brazilian women of childbearing age, Goldstein (1994) reported that 71% used some method of birth control. However, of those who practiced birth control, 44% had been sterilized, 41% took oral contraceptives, and less than 2% used condoms. In subsequent focus groups with married females, none had broached the subject of condoms with their partners (Goldstein, 1994). Oftentimes, women who attempt to negotiate condom use are viewed as unfaithful or too "prepared" for sex (Carovano, 1991). Because of male resistance to using condoms, women appear more likely to rely on contraceptive strategies which do not require their partners' participation. Clearly, then, they remain at risk for exposure to HIV.

In this study, rates of condom use were higher than in the general Brazilian population, no doubt because of the targeting of drug users with information on AIDS and the risks of exposure to HIV. Nevertheless, their condom use was quite limited. Of the 255 women who engaged in vaginal sex during the past 30 days, 81% reported never using condoms and the remaining 18% reported using condoms only sporadically. The highest frequency of condom use appears to have occurred among those women who exchanged sex for money during the past 30 days, with 65.5% of these 29 women reporting "sometimes" use. However, the numerous occasions of sex among these women suggest that many contacts went *unprotected* as well, and this may explain why condom use was not related to HIV status in this sample. Importantly, however, high rates of HIV seropositivity among women reporting condom use may also speak to the poor quality of many of the condoms available in Brazil. A 1992 study conducted by International Consumer Research and Testing Limited of

Holland reported that 5 of the 7 major condom brands produced in Brazil did *not* prevent the transmission of HIV (Folha de São Paulo, 1992).

As a final point here, it is anticipated that reducing HIV risks within this population through the promotion of condom use will be especially difficult. Research has indicated that sexual inequality and limited opportunities for sexual negotiation are inversely related to socioeconomic status (Worth, 1989; Stein, 1990; Gupta and Weiss, 1993; Ulin, 1992). In this study, as indicated earlier in Table 1, the great majority of the women interviewed were of limited education, and almost all were indigent. In fact, most were residents of Manguiera and Maré, two of Rio de Janeiro's many hundreds of *favelas*.

The *favelas* have been a feature of urban Brazil for generations (Freyre, 1986). "Favela" in Brazilian Portuguese means "slum." Yet it is a particular type of slum that takes its name from the hill near Rio de Janeiro where the first one appeared. The *favelas* began to appear on the hillsides of Rio de Janeiro at the end of the nineteenth century, and spread rapidly after 1930 as shelters for newly-arriving migrants (Burns, 1980: 569). There has been a steady stream ever since, and at the close of the 1980s it was estimated that some 1,500 "favelados" were arriving each day (Archambault, 1989).

Brazil's Municipal Planning Institute has estimated Rio's *favelas* to number 545 and house more than 1 million persons (Loveman, 1991). Clustered on the hills and mountainsides that overlook Rio's fashionable beaches, the *favelas* are slums in which only a small portion of households have electricity, running water, or sewage facilities. In the absence of public medical facilities and unemployment benefits for the more than 50% of the out-of-work favelados, disease and social problems multiply. There is prostitution and drug use, and a key feature of most *favelas* is cocaine trafficking (Guillermoprieto, 1990). And not surprisingly, rates of sexually transmitted diseases and other infections and illnesses abound.

It is within the context of these social, cultural, and economic conditions that appropriate HIV/AIDS intervention programs for women at risk need to be structured and tested. For the women in Rio's *favela* communities, individual strategies for AIDS prevention appear to be confined to limiting the number and choice of sexual partners, and condom use. The first of these options may be the easier of the two. As for the second, until Brazilian women have the power to exercise protection independently, the use of condoms will require extremely persuasive tactics. This will be quite difficult for most of the women encountered at PROVIVA, given their economic dependency and expectations of a compliant female role.

REFERENCES

Archambault, C. (1989). Rio's Shaky Shantytowns. *IRDC Reports,* April, 18-19.

Berkley, S. (1993). AIDS in the Developing World: An Epidemiologic Overview. *Clinical Infectious Diseases,* 17(Sup 2), S329-336.

Brazilian Ministry of Health. (1996). *AIDS Epidemiologic Bulletin,* March-May.

Burns, E. B. (1980). *A History of Brazil.* New York: Columbia University Press.

Campbell, C. (1990). Women and AIDS. *Social Science and Medicine,* 30, 407-415.

Caraël, M., Cleland, J., Deheneffe, J., Ferry, B. and Ingham R. (1995). Sexual Behavior in Developing Countries: Implications for HIV Control. *AIDS,* 9, 1171-1175.

Carovano, K. (1991). More than Mothers and Whores: Redefining the AIDS Prevention Needs of Women. *International Journal of Health Services,* 21, 131-142.

De Bruyn, M. (1992). Women and AIDS in Developing Countries. *Social Science and Medicine,* 34, 249-262.

Folha de São Paulo. (1992). Brasil Revê Teste de Qualidade de Camisinha. February 12.

Freyre, G. (1986). *The Mansions and the Shanties.* Berkeley: University of California Press.

Goldberg, H.I., Lee, N.C., Oberle, M.W. and Peterson, H.B. (1989). Knowledge About Condoms and Their Use in Less Developed Countries During a Period of Rising AIDS Prevalence. *Bulletin of the World Health Organization,* 67, 85-91.

Goldstein, D. (1994). AIDS and Women in Brazil: The Emerging Problem. *Social Science and Medicine,* 39, 919-929.

Goldstein, D. (1993). The Culture, Class, and Gender Politics of a Modern Disease: Women and AIDS in Brazil. *Final Report, ICRW Women and AIDS Program.*

Guillermoprieto, Alma (1990). *Samba.* New York: Alfred A. Knopf.

Gupta, G.R. and Weiss E. (1993). Women's Lives and Sex: Implications for AIDS Prevention. *Culture, Medicine, and Psychiatry,* 17, 399-412.

Hankins, C.A. and Handley, M.A. (1992). HIV Disease and AIDS in Women: Current Knowledge and a Research Agenda. *Journal of Acquired Immune Deficiency,* 5, 957-971.

Heise, L. and Elias, C. (1995). Transforming AIDS Prevention to Meet Women's Needs: A Focus on Developing Countries. *Social Science and Medicine* 40, 931-943.

Loveman, B. (1991). Latin America Faces Public Enemy No. 1. *Institute of the Americas Hemisfile,* 2 (July), 6-8.

Mehryar, A. (1995). Condoms, Awareness, Attitudes and Use. In J. Cleland & B. Ferry (Eds.), *Sexual Behavior and AIDS in the Developing World* (pp. 124-156). London: Taylor & Francis.

Stein, Z. (1990). HIV Prevention: The Need for Methods Women Can Use. *American Journal of Public Health,* 80, 460-462.

Ulin, P.R. (1992). African Women and AIDS: Negotiating Behavioral Change. *Social Science and Medicine,* 34, 63-73.

World Health Organization Global Programme on AIDS. (1995). *Women and AIDS: Agenda for Action,* September 28.

Worth, D. (1989). Sexual Decision-Making and AIDS: Why Condom Promotion Among Women Is Likely to Fail. *Studies in Family Planning,* 20, 297-307.

Temporal Trends in HIV Risk Behaviors Among Out-of-Treatment Women Crack Users: The Need for Drug Treatment

Salaam Semaan, DrPH
Lynne Kotranski, PhD
Karyn Collier, BA
Jennifer Lauby, PhD
Joan Halbert, MA
Kelly Feighan, BA

SUMMARY. This study examines the levels of and temporal trends in HIV-related characteristics among 169 women crack users re-

Salaam Semaan, Lynne Kotranski, Karyn Collier, Jennifer Lauby, Joan Halbert, and Kelly Feighan are all affiliated with the Philadelphia Health Management Corporation, 260 South Broad Street, Philadelphia, PA 19102. Dr. Semaan is currently at the Centers for Disease Control and Prevention, 1600 Clifton Road, E-37, Atlanta, GA 30333.

Address correspondence to: Lynne Kotranski, Research and Evaluation, 260 South Broad Street, Philadelphia, PA 19102.

The authors gratefully acknowledge the contributions of the field staff and the project programmers, JoAnna Turner and Abdullahi Beraima, PhD.

This research was supported by Cooperative Agreement grant # U01 DA06919 from the National Institute on Drug Abuse to Philadelphia Health Management Corporation. The views expressed here are the authors and do not necessarily represent the policies of the funding agency. All of the authors were with Philadelphia Health Management Corporation at the time the research was conducted.

An earlier version of this paper was presented at the Society for Prevention Research Conference, Puerto Rico, June 1996.

[Haworth co-indexing entry note]: "Temporal Trends in HIV Risk Behaviors Among Out-of-Treatment Women Crack Users: The Need for Drug Treatment." Semaan, Salaam et al. Co-published simultaneously in *Drugs & Society* (The Haworth Press, Inc.) Vol. 13, No. 1/2, 1998, pp. 13-33; and: *Women and Substance Abuse: Gender Transparency* (ed: Sally J. Stevens, and Harry K. Wexler) The Haworth Press, Inc., 1998, pp. 13-33. Single or multiple copies of this article are available for a fee from The Haworth Document Delivery Service [1-800-342-9678, 9:00 a.m. - 5:00 p.m. (EST). E-mail address: getinfo@haworthpressinc.com].

13

cruited from South Philadelphia, PA over a two and one-half year period (January 1992-June 1994). Baseline data were collected as part of a five year, multi-site HIV intervention research project funded by the National Institute on Drug Abuse. The majority of the women were African American, had less than a high school education and were receiving public assistance. A high proportion of women continued to engage in high risk behaviors with no significant change over time. A seroprevalence rate of 7% was observed among the women who elected to take the project's confidential HIV antibody test (73%). Implications for the need for drug treatment and HIV risk reduction interventions are discussed. *[Article copies available for a fee from The Haworth Document Delivery Service: 1-800-342-9678. E-mail address: getinfo@haworthpressinc.com]*

INTRODUCTION

Rates of HIV infection and AIDS diagnosis continue to increase very rapidly among women, with heterosexual transmission accounting for an increasing proportion of these cases. The proportion of AIDS cases among women has increased from approximately 7% throughout the latter half of the 1980s to 17% in 1994 (Centers for Disease Control and Prevention [CDC], 1994). HIV infection is now the third leading cause of death among women aged 25-45 years, accounting for 11% of deaths, and the leading cause of death among African American women aged 25-45 years, accounting for 22% of deaths (CDC, 1996). Heterosexual transmission continues to account for an increasingly greater proportion of cases among women every year, from 29% in 1989 to 37% in 1995 (CDC, 1989, 1995).

Existing evidence from cross-sectional and cohort studies indicates that women crack users are at an elevated risk for HIV infection because of high rates of sexual risk behaviors (Chiasson et al., 1991; Chirgwin, De-Hovitz, Dillon, & McCormack, 1991; Cohen, Navaline, & Metzger, 1994; Edlin et al., 1994; Forney, Inciardi, & Lockwood, 1992; Lindsay et al., 1992; McCoy & Inciardi, 1993; Siegal et al., 1992; Weatherby et al., 1992) and low rates of entry into drug treatment. Researchers have also noted that although drug treatment is an important means of HIV risk reduction, women crack users wishing to enter drug treatment face many barriers, including long waiting lists and fear of losing custody of their children (Forbes, 1993).

This study examined temporal trends in several HIV-related characteristics among 169 out-of-treatment women crack users recruited from South Philadelphia, PA over a two and one-half year period (January 1992 through June 1994). Examining temporal trends in HIV-related characteristics among women crack users is critical for assessing relevant drug treatment needs and for monitoring and curtailing the spread of the HIV epidemic in this subgroup of drug users. Baseline data used in this study were collected as part of the Philadelphia site of the Cooperative Agreement for Community-Based Monitoring and AIDS Prevention Research Project funded by the National Institute on Drug Abuse (NIDA). The project targeted drug users in South Philadelphia, a low income urban area where aggressive community level HIV risk reduction intervention projects had not previously been implemented.

Crack, a smokable form of cocaine that became immensely popular during the mid 1980s, has been associated with HIV infection (Chiasson et al., 1991; Chirgwin, DeHovitz, Dillon, & McCormack, 1991). Data from the NIDA multi-site Cooperative Agreement projects found an HIV seroprevalence rate of 6% among crack users who reported no history of injection drug use (Needle, 1994). A study of non-injection drug users entering drug treatment between 1989 and 1992 found a median national seroprevalence rate of 3.2%, with the highest median rate of 5.6% reported for the Northeast Region (Lehman, Allen, Green, & Onorato, 1994). The same study reported a median seroprevalence rate of 5.4% for Philadelphia.

The popularity of crack, especially among inner-city, minority women, and its strong addictive power contributes to the role it has in the transmission of HIV and other STDs. Crack is less expensive than heroin or powdered cocaine and is easier to administer than injection drugs. As crack use results in decreased inhibition, it is associated with frequent and high risk sexual behaviors (Larrat & Zieler, 1993; Weatherby et al., 1992). Crack users are more likely than non-crack users to engage in sex with multiple partners and with injection drug users, to trade sex for money or drugs, and to report infrequent use of condoms (Balshem, Oxman, Van Rooyen, & Girod, 1992; Booth, Watters, & Chitwood, 1993; Cohen, Navaline, & Metzger, 1994; Edlin et al., 1992). Crack users are also more likely than non-crack users to have had an STD (Edlin et al., 1992; Kim, Galanter, Casteneda, Lifshutz, & Franco, 1992). Because the effects of crack use are more short-lived than those of heroin, crack users develop an obsessive tendency to search immediately for their next dose. For crack users, prostitution is often the only means to acquire more crack as they may lack skills for other income-producing activities or feel apprehensive about becoming involved in other illegal activities (Carlson & Siegal, 1991; Cohen, Navaline, & Metzger, 1994). Crack addicted women tend to be more successful in using prostitution to obtain drugs than intravenous drug-using women because their skin is not disfigured with needle tracks and resulting sores (Forbes, 1993).

Because of their strong addiction, crack users may not discontinue high risk sexual behaviors even if they are aware that they are HIV positive (Diaz & Chu, 1993). It is thus not surprising that crack users are forming a bridge for heterosexual transmission of HIV through unprotected sex, especially with injection drug users who are HIV infected (Chiasson et al., 1991).

As injection drug use was the first to be associated with HIV infection and to receive priority intervention funding, the majority of HIV risk reduction interventions targeted injection drug users rather than crack users (Forbes, 1993). Consequently, several studies have examined temporal trends in HIV-related characteristics among injection drug users (Beardsley, Goldstein, Deren, & Tortu, 1995; Colon, Sahai, Robles, & Matos, 1995; Davoli et al., 1995; Des Jarlais et al., 1994; Iguchi et al., 1994; Moss et al., 1994; Rebagliato et al., 1995; Rezza et al., 1994; Van Ameijden, Van Den Hoek, & Coutinho, 1994; Vlahov, Anthony, Celentano, Solomon, & Chowdhury, 1991; Watters, 1994; Watters, Estilo, Clark, & Lorvick, 1994). In contrast, few studies have examined temporal trends in HIV-related characteristics among crack users (Anglin, Annon, & Longshore, 1995). Results of studies with injection drug users have indicated that while a sizeable proportion continued to participate in high risk behaviors, many have reduced their drug risk behaviors rather than their sexual risk behaviors over time (Brown & Beschner, 1993).

The popularity and prevalence of crack use, the associated high risk sexual behaviors and high STD rates, and the increase in heterosexual transmission of HIV present policy makers, treatment providers, and researchers with tremendous challenges and opportunities for intervention. Increased attention should thus be given to assessing the needs of women crack users, recommending appropriate drug treatment interventions, and implementing targeted HIV prevention projects. Existing evidence indicates that drug treatment programs that are specifically designed for women crack users are effective in helping women end their addiction (Boyd, 1993; Karan, 1989; Lanehart, Clark, Kratochvil, & Rollings, 1994; Wald, Harvey, & Hibbard, 1995; Wallace, 1991). The risks associated with crack use and HIV infection suggest that drug treatment for women crack users should be an important part of the AIDS prevention process (Diaz & Chu, 1993; Forbes, 1993; Sugarman & Herman, 1995).

This study aims to contribute to our knowledge about the levels of and temporal trends in HIV-related characteristics among out-of-treatment women crack users. Based on prior allocation of HIV prevention resources, the popularity of crack use, and results of several HIV risk reduction interventions among injection drug users, we expect that the present study sample did not improve their HIV-related characteristics over time. Results of this study will be important in assessing local drug treatment needs and in recommending targeted prevention efforts.

METHOD

Study Sample and Procedures

Self-report, baseline data were collected from 169 out-of-treatment women crack users over a two and one-half year period (January 1992-June 1994) by the research staff of Philadelphia Health Management Corporation (PHMC). To analyze the temporal trends in HIV-related characteristics, the study sample was grouped into five semi-annual intake periods based on the date of their baseline interview. The five semi-annual periods were: January-June 1992 (n = 19); July-December 1992 (n = 29); January-June 1993 (n = 41); July-December 1993 (n = 42); and January-June 1994 (n = 38).

Data used in this study were collected as part of a large multi-site HIV research intervention project funded by the National Institute on Drug Abuse (NIDA) (Kotranski et al., 1998). Prior to implementing the study in the field, PHMC's Internal Review Board reviewed and approved the project's protocol. Indigenous outreach workers recruited the study sample from specific drug using areas in South Philadelphia, PA using targeted sampling methodology (Watters & Biernacki, 1989). Eligible study participants for the analysis reported in this article were at least 18 years old and during the 30 days prior to recruitment, used only crack and did not participate in drug treatment. Study participants had a positive urinalysis for cocaine use in the prior 48 hours and could have used drugs other than crack prior to the 30-day period. In order to avoid any confounding associated with injection drug use (Booth, Watters, & Chitwood, 1993), we did not include women who reported both crack use and injection drug use in the past 30 days in this analysis.

The Risk Behavior Assessment Questionnaire, developed by grantees of the NIDA Cooperative Agreement Project, was used for baseline data collection (NIDA, 1991). Experienced indigenous interviewers, with special training in interviewing drug users, collected the data. All participants provided informed consent before the interview.

Study participants were encouraged to take the project HIV antibody test, and remained in the study regardless of their decision to take the test. Blood samples were tested for HIV antibodies by an independent laboratory using repeat ELISA tests with confirmation by Western Blot. Pre- and post-test counseling was provided by a health educator and persons with positive HIV test results were referred to appropriate medical and social support services. Referrals for drug treatment, medical and social services were also provided to all study participants as needed. Study participants received $10 upon completion of the interview.

Dependent Variables

Dependent variables included drug treatment history, drug risk behaviors, sexual risk behaviors, perception of AIDS susceptibility, prior exposure to HIV/AIDS interventions, and HIV testing and seroprevalence. Drug treatment history was measured by two variables. The first variable assessed whether the woman had ever been in a drug treatment program, defined to include detoxification, inpatient, outpatient, or residential drug treatment programs (yes, no). The second variable assessed whether the woman had tried but was unable to enter drug treatment during the past year (yes, no). Drug risk behaviors included years of crack use; years of cocaine, heroin, or speedball use; frequency of crack use in the last 30 days; and number of days of crack use in the last 30 days.

Sexual risk characteristics and behaviors included sexual preference (heterosexual vs. lesbian or bisexual); having had vaginal sex in the past 30 days (yes, no); having had unprotected vaginal sex in the last 30 days, defined as inconsistent or no condom use (yes, no); crack use immediately before or during sex (yes, no); sex with an injection drug user in the past 30 days (yes, no); number of sexual partners in the past 30 days; number of drug injecting sexual partners in the past 30 days; history of STDs, defined to include hepatitis B, gonorrhea, syphilis, genital warts, chlamydia or genital herpes (yes, no); history of giving sex for money; history of giving sex for drugs; frequency of giving sex for money in the past 30 days; and frequency of giving sex for drugs in the past 30 days.

Perception of AIDS susceptibility measured respondents' perception of their chance of getting AIDS (less than a 50% chance, at least a 50% chance). Prior exposure to HIV/AIDS interventions measured: (1) whether participants had ever received HIV/AIDS information or supplies, including bleach kits and condoms, from people in their community (yes, no), and (2) whether they had received HIV/AIDS information or supplies from people in their community in the past 30 days. Variables describing HIV testing and seroprevalence included: (1) whether respondents elected to take the project's HIV antibody test (yes, no), and (2) HIV seroprevalence rates as reflected by the results of the project's test.

Control Variables

Sociodemographic characteristics were used as control variables in assessing temporal trends in the dependent variables. The sociodemographic variables included: age (as a continuous variable); ethnicity (African American, other); education (less than a high school education, at least a high school education); income in the last 30 days (less than $500, $500 or more); receipt of public assistance in the last 30 days (yes, no); current living situation defined to include living in transitional housing, on the street, or in a shelter as opposed to living in a house or in an apartment; self-report of homelessness at the time of data collection (yes, no); and arrest history (yes, no).

Data Analysis

Subsequent to examining the sociodemographic characteristics of the study sample, temporal trends in these characteristics were assessed. One-way analysis of variance (ANOVA) with Scheffe's test for post-hoc multiple comparisons was used to assess the relationship at the bivariate level between intake period and the dependent variables measured as continuous variables. Tests for linear or quadratic trends allowed us to examine whether the differences over time reflected a linear increase or decrease or a curvilinear trend. Pearson's chi-square test for association and Mantel-Haenszel's chi-square test for trends were used to assess the relationship between intake period and the dependent variables measured as categorical variables.

Sampling selection bias could occur with changes in the sociodemographic characteristics of the population or if women crack users with characteristics related to the dependent variables had been differentially recruited into the study over time. To control for potential bias, sociodemographic characteristics that showed a significant temporal trend were included in the multivariate analyses.

Multiple linear regression (for continuous variables) and multiple logistic regression (for categorical variables) were used to examine changes over time in the dependent variables controlling for education; the only sociodemographic variable that showed a significant temporal trend over time. All quadratic terms significant at the bivariate level were also included in the multivariate analysis. The independent variable, intake period, was used as a continuous variable. The period beta, reported in the tables, is the regression coefficient reflecting the magnitude and significance of change in the dependent variable between semi-annual periods. Since few significant changes were observed over time, the results section describes both the level of and temporal trends in HIV-related characteristics.

RESULTS

Sociodemographic Characteristics

The mean age of the women was 33 years with a standard deviation of 7 years. The majority were African American (96%), had less than a high school education (57%), had a monthly income of less than $500 (75%), received public assistance (67%), and lived in transitional housing, on the street, or in a shelter (73%). Over one-quarter of the women considered themselves to be homeless (28%) and nearly one-half of the women had ever been arrested (48%). Except for education, there were no changes over time in the sociodemographic characteristics of the study sample (Table 1). A higher proportion among those who were recruited in the fifth semi-annual period had at least a high school education compared to those who were recruited in the first semi-annual period (47% vs. 37%).

Drug Treatment History

Slightly more than one-half of the women (54%) had ever been in drug treatment and less than one-quarter of the women had tried, but had been unable to enter drug treatment during the year prior to data collection (21%). There were no changes over time in these variables, although rates of ever being in drug treatment were significantly higher for the third intake period (Table 2).

Drug Risk Behaviors

The women had used crack for an average of eight years (Table 3). Although no woman had injected drugs in the 30 days prior to data collection, the majority of the women reported that they had used cocaine, heroin, or speedball in the past (65%) for an average of eight years. Drug risk behaviors remained at high levels throughout the two and one-half year period. While there was a significant curvilinear increase in the mean number of *days* the women used crack in the last 30 days (19, 22, 25, 23, &

TABLE 1. Sociodemographic Characteristics of Women Crack Users by Intake Period (n = 169), Philadelphia, 1992-1994

Characteristic	Intake Period						Statistical Results		
	1-6/92 (n = 19)	7-12/92 (n = 29)	1-6/93 (n = 41)	7-12/93 (n = 42)	1-6/94 (n = 38)	Total (n = 169)	X² Assoc. P-Value	X² Trend P-Value	ANOVA F-Statistic P-Value
Mean age (S.D.)	32.37 (4.82)	33.62 (8.73)	32.73 (6.84)	32.95 (6.13)	33.58 (6.56)	33.09 (6.72)	—	—	N.S.
African American (%)	100	97	98	93	97	96	N.S.	N.S.	—
< High school education (%)	63	76	58	45	53	57	N.S.	0.05	—
< $500 past month (%)	58	79	78	73	76	75	N.S.	N.S.	—
Receiving public assistance (%)	74	65	67	64	68	67	N.S.	N.S.	—
Live in transitional housing, on the street or in a shelter (%)	89	72	72	79	61	73	N.S.	N.S.	—
Currently homeless (%)	37	28	35	32	13	28	N.S.	N.S.	—
Ever arrested (%)	33	42	50	52	55	48	N.S.	N.S.	—

Note. N.S. indicates not statistically significant at p = 0.05. — indicates not applicable.

TABLE 2. Distribution of Drug Treatment History of Women Crack Users by Intake Period (n = 169), Philadelphia, 1992-1994

Characteristic	Intake Period						Statistical Results		
	1-6/92 (N = 19)	7-12/93 (N = 29)	1-6/93 (N = 41)	7-12/93 (N = 42)	1-6/94 (N = 38)	Total (N = 169)	X^2 Assoc. P-Value	X^2 Trend P-Value	Period Beta[a] P-Value
Ever in drug treatment (%)	42	42	72	40	63	54	0.01	N.S.	N.S.
Tried but was unable to enter drug treatment/ past year (%)	26	24	20	22	18	21	N.S.	N.S.	N.S.

Note. N.S. indicates not statistically significant at p = 0.05.
a   Regression analysis was used, controlling for education.

TABLE 3. Distribution of Drug Risk Characteristics of Women Crack Users by Intake Period (n= 169), Philadelphia, 1992-1994

Characteristic	Intake Period						Statistical Results			
	1-6/92 (N = 19)	7-12/93 (N = 29)	1-6/93 (N = 41)	7-12/93 (N = 42)	1-6/94 (N = 38)	Total (N = 169)	ANOVA F-Statistic P-Value	ANOVA Linear Trend	ANOVA Quadratic Trend	Period Beta[a] P-Value
Years of crack use (S.D.)	7.21 (4.22)	8.71 (6.53)	7.88 (4.73)	8.33 (3.66)	8.54 (5.60)	8.21 (4.96)	N.S.	N.S.	N.S.	N.S.
Years of cocalne, heroin, or speedball use (S.D.)	8.11 (7.72)	9.07 (9.94)	7.35 (7.31)	8.00 (8.68)	8.08 (7.80)	8.06 (8.23)	N.S.	N.S.	N.S.	N.S.
No. of days used crack/past 30 days	18.53 (10.42)	21.76 (10.04)	25.28 (8.31)	22.86 (8.03)	21.76 (10.77)	22.51 (9.49)	N.S.	N.S.	0.02	0.01 (l) 0.02 (q)
No. of times used crack/past 30 days	138.47 (149.77)	219.33 (165.59)	186.03 (148.89)	123.85 (133.55)	90.58 (76.35)	147.57 (140.49)	0.001	0.003	0.02	0.08 (l) 0.02 (q)

Note. N.S. indicates not statistically significant at p = 0.05. (l) = linear trend; (q) = quadratic trend.
a   Regression analysis was used, controlling for education and including a quadratic term for intake period whenever the quadratic term was significant at the bivariate level.

22 days for the five intake periods), there was a significant linear and curvilinear decline in the mean number of *times* they used crack in the last 30 days (138, 219, 186, 124, 91 times).

Sexual Risk Behaviors

The majority of the women reported that they were heterosexual (92%) and that they had engaged in vaginal sex during the 30 days prior to data collection (83%). Sexual risk behaviors remained at high levels (Table 4). Three out of five of the women did not use condoms or used condoms inconsistently during vaginal sex (60%) and two-thirds of the women used crack before or during sex (67%). It is unfortunate that the only significant change noted over time was an increase in the proportion of women who had ever had an STD (from 21% to 49%).

The women reported an average of three sexual partners in the last 30 days and almost one-quarter of the women (22%) reported that they had one drug injecting sexual partner during that time. Of the study participants, two-thirds reported ever exchanging sex for money (66%) and more than one-half reported ever exchanging sex for drugs (54%). On average, the study sample gave sex for drugs three times and sex for money four times during the past month.

Perception of AIDS Susceptibility, Prior Exposure to HIV/AIDS Interventions, and HIV Testing and Seroprevalence Rates

Almost four out of five of the women (81%) reported having less than a 50% chance of getting AIDS with no change noted over time (Table 5). Slightly less than one-half of the women reported ever receiving HIV/AIDS information, bleach or condoms from people in their community (43%), and more than one-quarter of the women reported receiving this information or these supplies from a similar source during the 30 days prior to data collection (28%). Neither measure changed over time.

There was a significant increase over time in the proportion of women who took the project's confidential and voluntary HIV test (from 11% to 92%). HIV testing was strongly encouraged in the last two years of the project as a means to collect data on biological markers. Among the 73% who took the project test, 7% had positive HIV results.

DISCUSSION

This study examined temporal trends between January 1992 and June 1994 in key HIV-related characteristics in a sample of women crack users

TABLE 4. Distribution of Sexual Risk Characteristics and Behaviors of Women Crack Users by Intake Period (n = 169), Philadelphia, PA 1992-1994

Characteristic	Intake Period						Statistical Results					
	1-6/92 (N = 19)	7-12/93 (N = 29)	1-6/93 (N = 41)	7-12/93 (N = 42)	1-6/94 (N = 38)	Total (N = 169)	X^2 Assoc. P-Value	X^2 Trend P-Value	ANOVA F-Statistic P-Value	ANOVA Linear Trend	ANOVA Quadratic Trend	Period Quadratic Beta[a] P-Value
Current heterosexual preference (%)	74	86	93	95	100	92	0.01	0.000	—	—	—	—
Had vaginal sex/past 30 days (%)	72	75	83	86	89	83	N.S.	0.05	—	—	—	N.S.
Inconsistent or no condom use with vaginal sex/past 30 days (%)	56	59	65	55	63	60	N.S.	N.S.	—	—	—	N.S.
Used crack during sex/past 30 days (%)	56	61	72	71	68	67	N.S.	N.S.	—	—	—	N.S.
IDU sex partner/past 30 days (%)	18	15	33	21	18	22	N.S.	N.S.	—	—	—	N.S.
No. of sex partners/past 30 days (S.D.)	3.17 (3.33)	2.04 (2.26)	4.28 (6.39)	3.19 (4.27)	2.62 (4.19)	3.13 (4.55)	—	—	N.S.	N.S.	N.S.	N.S.
Ever had STDs (%)	21	48	60	57	49	50	N.S.	N.S.	—	—	—	0.03
Ever gave sex for money (%)	68	59	61	74	66	66	N.S.	N.S.	—	—	—	N.S.
Ever gave sex for drugs (%)	37	55	59	53	61	54	N.S.	N.S.	—	—	—	N.S.
No. of times gave sex for drugs/past 30 days	2.58 (4.51)	1.59 (3.80)	3.93 (7.29)	2.62 (5.98)	2.95 (6.60)	2.84 (6.02)	—	—	N.S.	N.S.	N.S.	N.S.
No. of times gave sex for money/past 30 days	3.76 (7.04)	2.74 (5.01)	6.00 (9.94)	3.49 (5.75)	3.39 (7.51)	3.99 (7.43)	—	—	N.S.	N.S.	N.S.	N.S.

Note. N.S. indicates not statistically significant at p = 0.05. — indicates not applicable.
a Regression analysis was used, controlling for education and including a quadratic term for intake period whenever the quadratic term was significant at the bivariate level.

25

TABLE 5. Perception of AIDS Susceptibility, Prior Exposure to HIV/AIDS Interventions, and HIV Testing and Seroprevalence Results of Women Crack Users by Intake Period (n = 169), Philadelphia, 1992-1994

Characteristic	Intake Period						Statistical Results		
	1-6/92 (n = 19)	7-12/92 (n = 29)	1-6/93 (n = 41)	7-12/93 (n = 42)	1-6/94 (n = 38)	Total (n = 169)	X^2 Assoc. P-Value	X^2 Trend P-Value	Period Beta[a] P-Value
Perception of AIDS Susceptibility									
< 50% chance of getting AIDS (%)	78	74	82	78	92	81	N.S.	N.S.	N.S.
Prior Exposure to HIV/AIDS Intervention									
Ever got HIV/AIDS info, bleach or condoms (%)	58	31	39	43	49	43	N.S.	N.S.	N.S.
Received HIV/AIDS info, bleach or condoms past 30 days (%)	28	10	20	33	35	28	N.S.	N.S.	N.S.
HIV Testing & Seroprevalence									
Took project HIV test (%)	11	52	80	93	92	73	0.000	0.000	0.000
HIV positive among testers (%)	0	7	3	8	11	7	N.S.	N.S.	N.S.

Note. N.S. indicates not statistically significant at p = 0.05.
a Regression analysis was used, controlling for education.

recruited from South Philadelphia, PA. Results of this study have indicated that a high proportion of the women crack users continued to engage in high risk drug and sexual behaviors with few significant changes noted over time. The moderate seroprevalence rate and the low levels of perception of AIDS susceptibility did not change over time. Variables measuring drug treatment history and prior exposure to AIDS interventions also remained stable over time. There were not any substantial changes in the sociodemographic characteristics of the study sample that could have affected the interpretation of the results. The only sociodemographic variable that showed significant change over time was education. To control for its potential effect on the results, we included education in the multivariate analysis.

The magnitude of the HIV-related characteristics observed in this study are similar to those reported in other studies of women crack users and indicate the alarming potential for sexual transmission of HIV infection. Key HIV-related characteristics of this study sample included a moderate prevalence of HIV infection, considerable sexual contact with the general population, consistent sexual contact with injection drug users by a substantial minority of the women crack users, and a low level of condom use. Despite these high risk behaviors, a majority of the women crack users perceived themselves to have less than a 50% chance of getting AIDS. It is possible that many women crack users consider themselves to have a low risk for HIV infection because they do not inject drugs. Accordingly, AIDS education and prevention activities in drug treatment and other settings must emphasize the sexual as well as the drug use risks associated with crack use.

It may be argued that HIV education, prevention, and risk reduction programs may have limited impact in changing the sexual behaviors of women who are addicted to crack. Teaching safer sex techniques to women who actively abuse crack without devoting necessary resources for their drug abuse treatment may not be enough to curtail the spread of the HIV epidemic (Sugarman & Herman, 1995). However, locating and successfully engaging crack addicted women who are at risk for HIV infection in drug treatment is often difficult. Fortunately, HIV outreach programs have been effective in accomplishing this activity. A major contribution of HIV outreach programs may be to locate drug using women and to help facilitate their entry into drug treatment especially when the women indicate a desire for recovery. Only one-half of the women in this study had ever had drug treatment. Moreover, a quarter of the women wanted drug treatment but could not obtain treatment services.

Providing drug treatment, may in turn, help to reduce the rate of sexual transmission of HIV among women crack users (Diaz & Chu, 1993).

Existing evidence indicates that there is a substantial interest in access to treatment among women crack users (Forbes, 1993). Barriers to drug treatment, such as long waiting lists and fear of losing custody of one's children, hinder access to drug treatment. A review of treatment funding history in the last decade, from 1980 to 1991, revealed that current federal spending for drug treatment per capita has decreased by 40% (Forbes, 1993). Sufficient funds must be provided to make substance abuse treatment accessible and available to crack addicted women wishing to enter treatment (Forbes, 1993).

Drug treatment approaches that include attention to the variety of physiological factors (e.g., physiological effects of addiction), psychological factors (e.g., low self-esteem), and social factors (e.g., lack of vocational and financial resources) that affect women's ability to function and overcome addiction have been successful in engaging women and retaining them in treatment (Marsh, & Miller, 1985; De Leon & Jainchill, 1991; Goddard, Bennett, & Ribgy, 1990; Tims, Fletcher, & Hubbard, 1991). Residential drug treatment programs that accept children, along with aftercare and relapse prevention programs are particularly effective for women crack users (Chasnoff, 1989). It has been estimated that drug addiction treatment is a highly cost effective alternative when compared to the costs of incarceration and the medical expenses incurred by AIDS patients (Forbes, 1993). Drug treatment would reduce drug addiction and with it drug-related HIV transmission.

Results of studies examining temporal differences are important for estimating current levels of and trends in HIV-related characteristics, monitoring the HIV epidemic, assessing relevant drug treatment needs, developing targeted HIV prevention efforts, planning for future morbidity and other health care and social needs, and allocating appropriate monetary and human resources. By the same token, temporal trend studies cannot replace more rigorous intervention research studies that explore the process of behavioral change and identify the effectiveness of specific intervention components (Colon et al., 1995). Temporal trend studies, however, can be an important adjunct to cohort studies and back-calculation and extrapolation models in projecting the incidence of AIDS and can help to assess more realistically what can be expected of prevention and treatment programs (Schwarcz et al., 1995). Monitoring of trends in HIV-related risk behaviors is an important adjunct to HIV seroprevalence and incidence studies, because together these observations allow us to plan for and assess the effectiveness of preventive interventions.

There are several limitations to this study that should be considered. The sample was drawn exclusively from Philadelphia and the results may not be generalizable to other locations. Since respondents were not randomly selected, selection bias is likely to over-represent those who were more visible on the streets and those who were motivated by the modest reimbursement incentive. Results were based on self-reported data that may have been affected both by recall and social desirability. The relatively brief time reference for most of the questions, 30 days prior to data collection, should have minimized this error. To the extent that social desirability influenced the responses of the women, their risk for HIV infection is even greater than indicated by our results. Finally, a two and one-half year study of temporal trends may not be long enough to assess changes over time. Replication of this study over a longer period of time and with a larger sample is important for monitoring the dual epidemics of drug addiction and HIV infection.

In conclusion, results of this study indicate that a moderate proportion of women crack users are HIV infected and a high proportion continue to engage in high risk HIV-related behaviors with no significant change noted over time. The results suggest that the current generalized mass media educational campaigns are not enough by themselves to induce positive behavior change in this unique population of drug users. Targeted drug treatment programs and other HIV risk reduction interventions are needed to stem the HIV epidemic among women crack users.

REFERENCES

Anglin, D., Annon, K., & Longshore, D. (1995, June). *Behavior trends among crack smokers in Los Angeles.* Poster presented at the National Institute on Drug Abuse Satellite Conference on AIDS and Drug Abuse, Scottsdale, AZ.

Balshem, M., Oxman, G., Van Rooyen, D., & Girod, K. (1992). Syphilis, sex and crack cocaine: Images of risk and morality. *Social Science and Medicine, 35,* 147-160.

Beardsley, M., Goldstein, M., Deren, S., & Tortu, S. (1995, October). *Assessing temporal trends in AIDS risk behaviors.* Paper presented at the American Public Health Association Annual Scientific Meeting, San Diego, CA.

Booth, R.E., Watters, J.K., & Chitwood, D.D. (1993). HIV risk-related behaviors among injection drug users, crack smokers, and injection drug users who smoke crack. *American Journal of Public Health, 83,* 1144-1148.

Boyd, C.J. (1993). The antecedents of women's crack cocaine abuse: Family substance abuse, sexual abuse, depression and illicit drug use. *Journal of Substance Abuse Treatment, 10,* 433-438.

Brown, B.S., & Beschner, G.M. (Eds.) (1993). *Handbook on risk of AIDS: Injection drug users and their sexual partners.* Westport, CT: Greenwood Press.

Carlson, R.G., & Siegal, H.A. (1991). The crack life: An ethnographic overview of crack use and sexual behavior among African-Americans in a midwest metropolitan city. *Journal of Psychoactive Drugs, 23,* 11-20.

Centers for Disease Control and Prevention (1989, February). *HIV/AIDS Surveillance Report,* 3-14. Atlanta: Author.

Centers for Disease Control and Prevention (1994, June). *HIV/AIDS Surveillance Report,* 8-12, Atlanta: Author.

Centers for Disease Control and Prevention (1995, July). *HIV/AIDS Surveillance Report,* 2-39, Atlanta: Author.

Centers for Disease Control and Prevention (1996). Update: Mortality attributable to HIV infection among persons aged 25-44 years–United States, 1994. *Mortality and Morbidity Weekly Report, 45,* 121-125.

Chasnoff, I. (Ed.) (1989). Drugs, Alcohol, Pregnancy, and Parenting. Boston: Kluwer Academic Publisher.

Chiasson, M.A., Stoneburner, R.L., Hildebrandt, D.S., Ewing, W.E., Telzak, E.E., & Jaffe, H.W. (1991). Heterosexual transmission of HIV-1 associated with the use of smokable freebase cocaine (crack). *AIDS, 5,* 1121-1126.

Chirgwin, K., DeHovitz, J.A., Dillon, S., & McCormack, W.M. (1991). HIV infection, genital ulcer disease, and crack cocaine use among patients attending a clinic for sexually transmitted diseases. *American Journal of Public Health, 81,* 1576-1579.

Cohen, E., Navaline, H., & Metzger, D. (1994). High-risk behaviors for HIV: A comparison between crack-abusing and opiod-abusing African-American women. *Journal of Psychoactive Drugs, 26,* 233-241.

Colon, H.M., Sahai, H., Robles, R.R., & Matos, T.D. (1995). Effects of a community outreach program in HIV risk behaviors among injection drug users in San Juan, Puerto Rico: An analysis of trends. *AIDS Education and Prevention, 7,* 195-209.

Davoli, M., Perucci, C.A., Abeni, D.D., Arca, M., Brancato, G., Forastiere, F., Montiroli, P.M., & Zampieri, F. (1995). HIV risk-related behaviors among injection drug users in Rome: Differences between 1990 and 1992. *American Journal of Public Health, 85,* 829-832.

De Leon, G., & Jainchill, N. (1991). Residential therapeutic communities for female substance abusers. *Bulletin of the New York Academy of Medicine, 67,* 277-290.

Des Jarlais, D.C., Friedman, S.R., Sothern, J.L., Wenston, J., Marmor, M., Yancovitz, S.R., Frank, B., Beatrice, S., & Mildvan, D. (1994). Continuity and change within an HIV epidemic. *Journal of the American Medical Association, 271,* 121-127.

Diaz, T., & Chu, S.Y. (1993). Crack cocaine use and sexual behavior among people with AIDS. *Journal of the American Medical Association, 269,* 2845-2846.

Edlin, B., Irwin, K., Ludwing, D., McCoy, H., Serrano, Y., Word, C., Bowser, B., Faruque, S., McCoy, C., Schilling, R., Holmburg, S., & the Multicenter Crack Cocaine and HIV Infection Study Team (1992). High-risk sex behavior among young street-recruited crack cocaine smokers in three American cities: An interim report. *Journal of Psychoactive Drugs, 24,* 363-371.

Edlin, B.R., Irwin, K.L., Faruque, S., McCoy, C.B., Word, C., Serrano, Y., Inciardi, J.A., Bowser, B.P., Schilling, R.F., Holmberg, S.D., & the Multicenter Crack Cocaine and HIV Infection Study Team (1994). Intersecting epidemics– Crack cocaine use and HIV infection among inner-city young adults. *The New England Journal of Medicine, 331,* 1422-1427.

Forbes, A. (1993). Crack cocaine and HIV: How national drug-addiction-treatment deficits fan the pandemic's flames. *AIDS & Public Policy Journal, 8,* 44-52.

Forney, M.A., Inciardi, J.A., & Lockwood, D. (1992). Exchanging sex for crack-cocaine: A comparison of women from rural and urban communities. *Journal of Community Health, 17,* 73-85.

Goddard, S., Bennett, G., & Ribgy, K. (1990). Change during residence in a rehabilitation center for female drug misusers. *Drug and Alcohol Dependency, 27,* 159-165.

Iguchi, M.Y., Bux, D.A., Lidz, V., Kushner, H., French, J.F., & Platt, J.J. (1994). Interpreting HIV seroprevalence data from a street-based outreach program. *Journal of Acquired Immunodeficiency Syndromes, 7,* 491-499.

Karan, L.D. (1989). AIDS prevention and chemical dependence treatment needs of women and their children. *Journal of Psychoactive Drugs, 21,* 395-399.

Kim, A., Galanter, M., Casteneda, R., Lifshutz, H., & Franco, H. (1992). Crack cocaine use and sexual behavior among psychiatric inpatients. *American Journal of Drug and Alcohol Abuse, 18,* 235-246.

Kotranski, L., Semaan, S., Collier, K., Lauby, J., Halbert, J., & Feighan, K. (1998). Effectiveness of an HIV risk reduction counseling intervention for out-of-treatment drug users. *AIDS Education and Prevention,* 10, 19-33.

Lanehart, R.E., Clark, H.B., Kratochvil, D., & Rollings, J.P. (1994). Case management of pregnant and parenting female crack and polydrug abusers. *Journal of Substance Abuse, 6,* 441-448.

Larrat, E.P., & Zierler, S. (1993). Entangled epidemics: Cocaine use and HIV disease. *Journal of Psychoactive Drugs, 25,* 207-221.

Lehman, J.S., Allen, D.M., Green, T.A., Onorato, I.M., & the Field Services Branch. (1994). HIV infection among non-injecting drug users entering drug-treatment, United States, 1989-1992. *AIDS, 8,* 1465-1469.

Lindsay, M.K., Peterson, H.B., Boring, J., Gramling, J., Willis, S., & Klein, L. (1992). Crack cocaine: A risk factor for human immunodeficiency virus infection type 1 among inner-city parturients. *Obstetrics and Gynecology, 80,* 981-984.

Marsh, J.C., & Miller, N.A. (1985). Female clients in substance abuse treatment. *The International Journal of the Addictions, 20,* 955-1019.

McCoy, H.V., & Inciardi, J.A. (1993). Women and AIDS: Social determinants of sex-related activities. *Women and Health, 20,* 69-86.

Moss, A.R., Vranizan, K., Gorter, R., Bacchetti, P., Watters, J., & Osmond, D.

(1994). HIV seroconversion in intravenous drug users in San Francisco, 1985-1990. *AIDS, 8,* 223-231.

National Institute on Drug Abuse (1991). Risk behavior Assessment. Rockville, MD: Author (Community Research Branch).

Needle, R. (1994). HIV risk behaviors of heterosexual male drug users. In Battjes, R.J., Sloboda, Z., and Grace, W.C. (Eds.). *The Context of HIV Risk Among Drug Users and Their Sexual Partners* (pp. 5-8). Rockville, MD: National Institute on Drug Abuse.

Rebagliato, M., Avino, M.J., Hernandez-Aguado, I., Ruiz, I., Perez-Hoyos, S., Bolumar, F., & Ferrer, L. (1995). Trends in incidence and prevalence of HIV-1 infection in intravenous drug users in Valencia, Spain. *Journal of Acquired Immune Deficiency Syndromes and Human Retrovirology, 8,* 297-301.

Rezza, G., Nicolosi, A., Zaccarelli, M., Sagliocca, M., Nespoli, M., Gattari, P., Spizzichino, L., Ippolito, G., & Lazzarin, A. (1994). Understanding the dynamics of the HIV epidemic among Italian intravenous drug users: A cross-sectional versus a longitudinal approach. *AIDS, 7,* 500-503.

Schwarcz, S.K., Kellogg, T.A., Kohn, R.P., Katz, M.H., Lemp, G.F., & Bolan, G.A. (1995). Temporal trends in human immunodeficiency virus seroprevalence and sexual behavior at the San Francisco municipal transmitted disease clinic, 1989-1992. *American Journal of Epidemiology, 142,* 314-322.

Siegal, H.A., Carlson, R.G., Falck, R., Forney, M.A., Wang, J., & Li, L. (1992). High-risk behaviors for transmission of syphilis and human immunodeficiency virus among crack cocaine-using women: A case study from the Midwest. *Sexually Transmitted Diseases, 19,* 266-271.

Sugarman, K., & Herman, M. (1995). Crack cocaine and HIV in the inner city. *The New England Journal of Medicine, 332,* 1233.

Tims, F.M., Fletcher, B.W., & Hubbard, R.L. (1991). Treatment outcomes for drug abuse clients. *NIDA Research Monograph, 106,* 93-113.

Van Ameijden, E.J.C., Van Den Hoek, A.A.R., & Coutinho, R.A. (1994). Injecting risk behavior among drug users in Amsterdam, 1986-1992, and its relationship to AIDS prevention programs. *American Journal of Public Health, 84,* 275-281.

Vlahov, D., Anthony, J.C., Celentano, D., Solomon, L., & Chowdhury, N. (1991). Trends of HIV-1 risk reduction among initiates into intravenous drug use, 1982-1987. *American Journal of Drug and Alcohol Abuse, 17,* 39-48.

Wald, R., Harvey, S.M., & Hibbard, J. (1995). A treatment model for women substance abusers. *International Journal of the Addictions, 30,* 881-888.

Wallace, B.C. (1991). Chemical dependency treatment for the pregnant crack addict: Beyond the criminal-sanctions perspective. *Psychology of Addictive Behaviors, 5,* 23-25.

Watters, J.K., & Biernacki, P. (1989). Targeted sampling: Options for the study of hidden populations. *Social Problems, 36,* 416-430.

Watters, J.K. (1994). Trends in risk behavior and HIV seroprevalence in heterosexual injection drug users in San Francisco, 1986-1992. *Journal of Acquired Immune Deficiency Syndromes, 7,* 1276-1281.

Watters, J.K., Estilo, M.J., Clark, G.L., & Lorvick, J. (1994). Syringe and needle exchange as HIV/AIDS prevention for injection drug Users. *Journal of the American Medical Association, 271,* 115-120.

Weatherby, N.L., Schultz, J.M., Chitwood, D.D., McCoy, H.V., McCoy, C.B., Ludwig, D.D., & Edlin, B.R. (1992). Crack cocaine use and sexual activity in Miami, Florida. *Journal of Psychoactive Drugs, 24,* 373-380.

Drug Use Patterns of Substance Abusing Women: Gender and Ethnic Differences in an AIDS Prevention Program

Margaret R. Weeks, PhD
Merrill Singer, PhD
David A. Himmelgreen, PhD
Phil Richmond, MS
Maryland Grier
Kim Radda, MA, RN

SUMMARY. The social context of drug use defines women's experiences of addiction and their patterns of use. Gender relations and roles, ethnic identity, poverty, and local circumstances, including drug-related epidemics such as the human immunodeficiency virus (HIV) and sexually transmitted diseases (STDs), constitute powerful

Margaret R. Weeks is affiliated with the Institute for Community Research, 2 Hartford Square West, Suite 100, Hartford, CT 06106. Merrill Singer and David A. Himmelgreen are affiliated with the Hispanic Health Council, 175 Main Street, Hartford, CT 06106. Phil Richmond is associated with the Hartford Dispensary, 345 Main Street, Hartford, CT 06106. Maryland Grier and Kim Radda are also affiliated with the Institute for Community Research.

The authors greatly appreciate the contribution of Project COPE II participants to the information reported here, and particularly those who shared in-depth information about their lives. The authors also thank Karen Breda, Nancy Churchill, and Karen Goodkin for comments on an earlier draft of this article.

[Haworth co-indexing entry note]: "Drug Use Patterns of Substance Abusing Women: Gender and Ethnic Differences in an AIDS Prevention Program." Weeks, Margaret R. et al. Co-published simultaneously in *Drugs & Society* (The Haworth Press, Inc.) Vol. 13, No. 1/2, 1998, pp. 35-61; and: *Women and Substance Abuse: Gender Transparency* (ed: Sally J. Stevens, and Harry K. Wexler) The Haworth Press, Inc., 1998, pp. 35-61. Single or multiple copies of this article are available for a fee from The Haworth Document Delivery Service [1-800-342-9678, 9:00 a.m. - 5:00 p.m. (EST). E-mail address: getinfo@haworthpressinc.com].

35

social forces that create a unique set of risky conditions for women drug users. This paper presents findings from a community-based AIDS prevention research project for 1,022 out-of-treatment drug users recruited through street outreach and targeted sampling. Data from a baseline risk behavior assessment and in-depth interviews on contexts of women's drug use show different patterns of use when comparing women to men, and among women comparing African Americans, Puerto Ricans, and Whites. Related differences in prevalence of HIV, STDs, and other consequences of drug use and addiction also are presented. Implications of these findings are discussed in terms of the development of drug treatment and harm reduction programs that are appropriate for women of different ethnic backgrounds. *[Article copies available for a fee from The Haworth Document Delivery Service: 1-800-342-9678. E-mail address: getinfo@haworthpressinc.com]*

INTRODUCTION

Over the past two decades as the AIDS epidemic has spread, patterns of drug use among women have gained increased attention. It has come to be recognized that the social context of women's use of drugs significantly influences the potential for their injection and sexual activities to result in HIV infection or transmission. To curb the spread of this deadly disease requires developing a thorough understanding of women's specific patterns of drug use and of the forces that define and shape their addiction and related health risks. Likewise, improving the effectiveness of drug treatment as a preventive measure for both HIV and a set of other addiction-related illnesses depends upon gaining better knowledge of the factors affecting women's use of drugs and their unique gender-related experiences with addiction.

Our research in Hartford, Connecticut includes assessment of out-of-treatment drug users' reported consumption of drugs and sexual HIV risk behaviors in the context of influential social and environmental conditions. This article reviews findings from an AIDS prevention research program called Project COPE II. We analyze patterns of drug use and drug-related sexual practices as these affect risk of HIV and other diseases and are conditioned by poverty, gender relations, and ethnic community variations. We conclude by examining the implications of this research for HIV prevention, drug use policy, and treatment programs.

WOMEN'S HIV AND AIDS IN SOCIAL CONTEXT

The primary route of HIV transmission among women continues to be through injection drug use. Nationally, injection drug users (IDUs) constitute 41% of female AIDS cases (Connecticut Health Department, 1994; Centers for Disease Control and Prevention [CDC], 1995). Some studies suggest that women injectors may be at even greater risk than their male counterparts because of higher injection rates (Weeks, Singer, Schensul, Jia, & Grier, 1993) and more frequent use of previously-used needles (Barnard, 1993), including those previously used by their male partners (Freeman, Rodriguez, & French, 1994). Drug and sexual risks converge in the transmission of HIV among women whose sex partners are IDUs or who are trading sex for crack or heroin. Unprotected sexual contact with an infected partner, particularly an IDU, accounts for an increasing percentage of AIDS/HIV cases among women (38% nationally in 1994) (CDC, 1995). Additionally, many of the women sex partners of IDUs use non-injection drugs, including crack cocaine (Deren, Davis, Tortu, & Ahluwahlia, 1993; Tortu, Beardsley, Deren, & Davis, 1994). Prostitution and crack cocaine use, alone or in combination, have been associated with increased rates of sexually transmitted diseases (STDs), including HIV, among women (Turner, Miller, & Moses, 1989; Fullilove, Fullilove, & Bowser, 1990; Longshore & Anglin, 1995; Cohen, 1991; Rolfs, Goldberg, & Sharrar, 1990).

It is well recognized that women in poverty are far more likely to have sex partners who inject drugs, have high rates of STDs and HIV, and face discrimination in access to health care and other services (Nyamathi, Leake, Flaskerud, Lewis, & Bennet, 1993; Singer, 1994; Cohen, 1991; Sobo, 1993, 1995). Combined with addiction, poverty decreases options for women to sustain their families and meet their personal needs, and increases the possible necessity to exchange sex for money or drugs to support themselves, their families, and their drug habit (Shayne & Kaplan, 1991; Weeks, Grier, Romero-Daza, Puglisi-Vasquez, & Singer, 1997). Additionally, women's economic dependence on men, gender expectations that force women into submissive roles, and women's denial of risk with intimate partners (Fullilove, Fullilove, Haynes, & Gross, 1990; Kane, 1990; Kline, Kline, & Oken, 1992; Sobo, 1993, 1995; Worth, 1989; Amaro, 1995) influence some, particularly in poorer economic circumstances, to limit adoption of AIDS preventive measures. Thus, many social, physical, and economic consequences of substance abuse intersect to create a highly risky situation for women addicts in the time of AIDS.

Among women in the U.S., African Americans and Latinas have the greatest risk of HIV, both through injection drug use and heterosexual transmission (Fullilove, Fullilove, Haynes, & Gross, 1990; Singer, Flores et al., 1990). AIDS cases in 1994 among African American and Latina women were seventeen times and seven times higher, respectively, than for non-Hispanic White women (CDC, 1995). Additionally, risk is higher for African American and Latina women living in poverty, particularly in urban areas (Nyamathi et al., 1993). These elevated rates are not readily understood in terms of reported risk behaviors. For example, a study by Lewis and Watters (1989) indicated higher HIV seroprevalence in African American women, despite lower reported "sharing" of injection equipment relative to other injecting women, particularly Whites. The investigators attributed these differences in rates of HIV incidence to different contexts of risky behaviors, such as the already higher prevalence of HIV in the African American community which increases the likelihood of these women's exposure at each sharing encounter. Rates of other STDs among minorities also have been rising since 1986, and have been found to be associated with crack use and exchange of sex-for-drugs, as well as multiple sex partners and sex for money exchanges among addicts in impoverished urban communities (Fullilove, Fullilove, & Bowser, 1990; Rolfs et al., 1990).

HIV infection among women associated with drug injection or unprotected sex with an IDU is particularly high in northeast urban areas, highlighting the importance of local and regional contextual factors defining drug use and HIV risk (Singer, Jia, Schensul, Weeks, & Page, 1992). Hartford reflects this pattern as one northeastern city facing significant HIV prevalence primarily related to drug use. Local patterns of drug distribution, drug consumption, injection patterns and contexts, condom use and other drug users' sexual practices, combined with higher rates of HIV infection in the general and drug-using populations, comprise the HIV risk profile in Hartford (cf. Singer & Jia, 1993; Singer, Jia et al., 1992; Weeks, Singer, Schensul et al., 1993). Currently, 46% of Hartford AIDS cases are among African Americans, 37% are among Latinos, and 17% are among Whites (CT Health Department, AIDS Division, Surveillance Department, 1994), although the city's general population is 36% African American, 32% Latino, and 30% White (City of Hartford, 1995). By 1994, 68% of female AIDS cases in Hartford were IDUs (CT Health Department, 1994). Given the dramatic increase in the number of women becoming infected with HIV, the numerous factors that impact HIV risk taking behavior, and ethnic differences in rates of HIV and other STDs, it is important to understand how local drug use patterns, drug and sexual risk behaviors, and health status contribute to high rates of HIV and other STDs. The following outlines some of the parameters of women drug users' risk in Hartford, and the potential ways local patterns of drug use might result in high rates of STDs, HIV and AIDS.

STUDY DESIGN AND METHODS

Project COPE II was a five-year cooperative agreement AIDS prevention research project funded by the National Institute on Drug Abuse (NIDA) and run by a community-based consortium.[1] The project was designed to reach active, out-of-treatment IDUs and crack users in Hartford's inner city. Eligibility criteria for participating in Project COPE II included being 18 years of age, self-reported active injection drug use or non-injection crack use within the thirty days prior to intake, and no participation in drug treatment of any kind during that same period. Street and community outreach and recruitment from October, 1992 through December, 1995 brought a targeted sample (Watters & Biernacki, 1989; Singer & Weeks, 1992) of 1,022 eligible participants into the study for assessment and intervention. Targeted sampling used epidemiological (e.g., STD and HIV) indicators, incidence indicators (e.g., drug or prostitution arrest data) and ethnographic description (e.g., of high risk injection or crack use settings) to map locations, such as shooting galleries, likely to contain a high percent of "hidden" individuals at drug-related HIV risk. This method of mapping allows targeted recruitment in key areas to insure over-representation of people at highest risk. Targeted sampling and street-based recruitment of this nature have been shown to be very successful in reaching representative samples among hidden populations of high-risk drug users who are not well served by drug treatment or other social service programs (Watters & Biernacki, 1989).

The study was designed to accomplish two primary tasks. The first was to track reported drug use and sexual practices of out-of-treatment IDUs and crack users over the project period to monitor patterns and changes in drug use activities, HIV-related risk behaviors, and health indicators. The second was to compare the outcomes of the NIDA Standard Intervention, an established HIV prevention educational/counseling model (Coyle, 1993), with two culturally targeted models enhanced to increase HIV risk reduction self-efficacy (Weeks, 1991). One of the culturally targeted programs was specifically designed for African Americans and one for Puerto Ricans, the two primary ethnic groups in Hartford's inner city (Singer, 1992; Weeks, Singer, Grier, Hunte-Marrow, & Haughton, 1993; Weeks, Schensul, Williams, Singer, & Grier, 1995).

The baseline standard survey instrument used in this project to monitor drug use and measure pre-intervention HIV risks was the Cooperative Agreement Risk Behavior Assessment (RBA) that was developed by a group of cooperative agreement principal investigators (NIDA, 1994). This instrument measures reported rates of drug use (injection and non-injection), needle use practices, and sexual activities in the thirty days prior to the interview. In addition, through supplemental studies on special issues, we conducted in-depth, semi-structured interviews with a subsample of men and women on selected topics, including interviewing women regarding their drug use practices in various contexts, their history of drug use, and, with a small number of women, risks related to exchanging sex for money. The following presents findings from the RBA and the in-depth interviews on women's drug using patterns and associated health risks. We compare women with men in the project, and among women, compare African Americans, Puerto Ricans, and Whites regarding these reported behavioral patterns and risks.

PROJECT COPE II STUDY PARTICIPANTS

The 1,022 study participants recruited during the first three years of intake (October 1992 to December 1995) included 791 men (77%) and 231 women (23%). Of these, 54% were IDUs, 26% were non-injecting crack smokers, and 20% reported both. Drug use classifications were based on reported behavior and were verified by evidence of fresh needle tracks and/or urine toxicological screens at intake. The study sample recruited through street outreach showed significant differences by sex in these drug-use categories ($p < 0.001$), with fewer men than women reporting crack use. Socioeconomic status of men and women in the project was comparable, with the majority of both (75%) reporting unemployment and nearly two-thirds (60%) earning incomes of less than $500 in the thirty days prior to entering COPE. Further, approximately one-third of both men and women reported being homeless.

The women in Project COPE II included 40% African Americans (N = 100), 49% Puerto Ricans (N = 105), 9% non-Hispanic Whites (N = 22), and 2% other ethnic groups (N = 4). Ninety percent were between the ages of 18 and 45. Over half (58%) of all the women reported less than a high school education. Ethnic differences in level of education among women were statistically significant ($p < 0.001$), with 54% of African American women having completed high school or the equivalent, compared to 62% of White women and 29% of Puerto Rican women. At the time of intake, almost half (43%) were living with a spouse or sex partner, 47% with other adult family members or friends, and 55% with children under 18 years of age.

Poverty was considerable among women in the project. Income levels of less than $500 in the month prior to entering COPE characterized 53% of the women, and 34% reported receiving between $500-$1,000 in that period. Two-thirds were unemployed, and three-quarters relied on Aid to Families with Dependent Children (AFDC) or other welfare as their key source of financial support. Only 3% of the women reported receiving child support. Differences by ethnicity in reported income in the month prior to intake showed lower incomes among Puerto Rican women than African American and White women, though these differences were not significant. More Puerto Rican women (38%) than African American or White women (29% of both groups) reported being homeless, though this difference, too, was not statistically significant. In general, baseline socio-economic indicators for all women in Project COPE II suggested that poverty circumscribed these women's lives. The constancy of their economic impoverishment provided an impetus for escape through drugs, yet exacerbated the potential for and limited options to protect against the myriad of health risks resulting from drug use in this context.

DRUG USE PATTERNS OF WOMEN COMPARED TO MEN IN PROJECT COPE II

Most women in the project used multiple drugs, and reported high rates of injection, crack use, or both, often in combination with other drugs or alcohol. Nearly half of both the women and men (41%) reported use of marijuana in the thirty days prior to the interview, though men reported alcohol use during that period more so than women ($p = 0.04$) (see Table 1). Women, however, were significantly more likely than men to use crack cocaine ($p < 0.001$). Moreover, among those who reported using crack, women reported higher rates of use than men.

Injection rates were extremely high among both women and men in Project COPE II. Over half of the IDU women reported injecting either heroin, cocaine, speedball (heroin and cocaine mixed), or some combination of these more than 120 times in the thirty days prior to the intake interview, that is, more than four times per day on average. Another one-third reported injecting 1-4 times daily (31-120 times per month).[2] Men were more likely to report lower frequencies of injection than women, though these differences did not achieve statistical significance. Nevertheless, the pattern of women's higher injection rates held for both overall monthly injections, and in the percent we identified and classified as injection "outliers" (i.e., those who injected more than 570 times per month; cf. Weeks, Himmelgreen et al., 1996, for further discussion of injection outliers in Project COPE II). This parallels reported patterns of use by participants in our earlier study of street recruited, out-of-treatment drug users in Hartford (Project COPE I) (Singer, Jia, Schensul et al., 1992; Weeks, Singer et al., 1993).

Women IDUs also reported higher rates of injection-related HIV risk

TABLE 1. Men and Women in Project COPE II: Sample Characteristics and Drug-Related HIV Risk Behaviors (Percentages)

Sample Characteristics:	Men (N = 791)	Women (N = 231)
Ethnicity:		
African American	37	40
Latino	55	49
White	6	9
Homeless	36	33
Mean age***	38.4 yrs.	36.5 yrs.
Drug Use Practices:		
Drug use (last 30 days):		
Alcohol*	75	69
Marijuana	41	41
IDU***	56	40
Crack***	22	39
Both IDU & crack	20	22
Crack use rates (last 30 days):*	(N = 335)	(N = 139)
low (1-15 times/mo)	46	37
moderate (16-60 times/mo)	32	28
high (61+ times/mo)	23	35
IDUs' HIV Risk Practices:	**Men (N = 583)**	**Women (N = 135)**
Injection rates (all drugs totaled):		
low (1-30 inj./mo)	17	13
moderate (31-120 inj./mo)	35	32
high (121+ inj./mo)	48	56
Average injections/month	146.3/mo	154.7/mo
(outliers removed)		
Injection outliers (570+ inj./mo)	2.9 (N = 18)	3.5 (N = 5)
Used a previously used needle	27	35
Used previously used cookers/cotton	41	37
Also used crack*	26	35
Has an IDU sex partner***	32	56

* $p < 0.05$.
*** $p < 0.001$.

behaviors compared to male IDUs in the project (Table 1). For example, women were more likely than men to have used a previously used needle. Though a higher percent of men than women reported having shared a cooker (e.g., a spoon or bottle cap used to mix/heat drugs) or cotton (used to filter the drug mixture as it is drawn up into the syringe prior to injecting), women who shared these ancillary equipment did so at a higher rate than men (24% of injections compared to 19%, respectively), although this difference was not statistically significant. This suggests different patterns of injection among men and women, or differences in context of use, such as a greater likelihood that women in the sample rely on partners for their needles and other injection equipment and use that equipment after their partner has injected (cf. Freeman, Rodriguez, & French, 1994). Also, as with the overall study population, IDU women were significantly more likely than IDU men to use crack in addition to injection drugs (p = 0.03). Finally, women IDUs were significantly more likely to have a sex partner who also was an IDU, a situation that amplifies HIV risks through both injection and sexual activities.

DRUG USE PATTERNS OF PROJECT COPE II WOMEN BY ETHNICITY

Differences in drug use patterns among women by ethnicity also were notable (Table 2). Significantly more African American women compared to either of the other two groups reported having used alcohol and marijuana in the prior thirty days. Additionally, over half of the African American women reported being non-injecting crack cocaine users, compared to one-third of Puerto Rican women and one-fifth of the White women. (The last group was small in size, and statistical comparisons between White women and African American or Puerto Rican women are thus limited.) However, significantly fewer African American women reported injection drug use. Among those who did, African Americans reported overall lower rates of injection than Puerto Rican or white women. High rates of injection among Puerto Rican women compared to African American women parallel the general trends in drug injection patterns among these two ethnic groups in the city overall (Himmelgreen, 1995; Singer, 1996; Singer, Himmelgreen, Radda & Weeks, 1995; Weeks, Himmelgreen et al., 1996).[3]

Of the IDU women, almost all reported injecting heroin, while 62% injected cocaine and 70% injected speedball in the thirty days prior to the interview. The primary injection drug of choice among African American women was speedball, and among Puerto Rican women, heroin. Differences in injection rates of these three drugs also varied among women by ethnicity, though only differences in heroin injection rates were statistically significant (p = .03). Puerto Rican women reported the highest rates of injecting each of the three primary drugs, and particularly heroin. The small number of women injection outliers (N = 5) all were Puerto Rican.

Again, these ethnic differences are consistent with patterns in Hartford overall (Himmelgreen, 1995; Weeks, Singer, Schensul et al., 1993; Weeks, Himmelgreen et al., 1996). The city's generally segregated neighbor-

TABLE 2. Drug-Related HIV Risk Behaviors Among Project COPE II Women by Ethnicity (Percentages)

Drug-Related HIV Risks:	African Am. (N = 100)	Puerto Rican (N = 105)	White (N = 22)
Drug use (last 30 days):			
Alcohol**	81	59	67
Marijuana**	53	31	42
IDU**	28	48	55
Crack**	52	31	18
Both IDU & crack	20	22	27
Crack use rates (last 30 days):	(N = 66)	(N = 51)	(N = 10)
low (1-15 times/mo)	27	45	60
moderate (16-60 times/mo)	33	22	20
high (61+ times/mo)	39	33	20
Injection rates (all drugs totaled):	(N = 47)	(N = 67)	(N = 18)
low (1-30/mo)	19	9	11
moderate (31-120/mo)	32	33	22
high (121+/mo)	49	58	67
Total average injections (outliers removed)	142.3/mo	162.5/mo	168.3/mo
Injection outliers (570+/mo)	(N = 0)	7 (N = 5)	(N = 0)
Used a previously used needle*	19	44	44
Used previously used cookers/cotton	30	40	47
Cocaine injection rates:	(N = 37)	(N = 37)	(N = 12)
low (1-15 times/mo)	38	38	42
moderate (16-60 times/mo)	38	16	42
high (61+ times/mo)	24	46	17
Heroin injection rates:*	(N = 39)	(N = 66)	(N = 16)
low (1-15 times/mo)	28	12	25
moderate (16-60 times/mo)	31	17	13
high (61+ times/mo)	41	71	63
Speedball injection rates:	(N = 40)	(N = 44)	(N = 12)
low (1-15 times/mo)	35	43	33
moderate (16-60 times/mo)	30	14	25
high (61+ times/mo)	35	43	42

* $p < 0.05$.
** $p < 0.01$.

hoods, circumscribed by ethnic boundaries and gang-defined turf lines, show differences in predominant drug of choice. Different patterns of use appear to result in part from drug availability in those neighborhoods, especially related to control of the drug market (often by ethnic-specific gangs), and from socialization of pockets of drug users into use of particular drugs (Singer, Valentin, Baer, & Jia, 1992). Thus, Blacks (including both African American and Caribbean American) and Black dominated gangs control the cocaine trade in Hartford, while Puerto Ricans and Puerto Rican dominated gangs control the heroin trade. Ethnic tension, racial and ethnic segregation, and turf-related violence result in each of these groups marketing and selling to people in their respective ethnic enclaves.

GENDER ROLES AND EXPECTATIONS
IN DRUG ACQUISITION, CONSUMPTION, AND ADDICTION

Many difficulties of drug acquisition, consumption, and addiction among impoverished drug users cross gender and ethnic lines. Women, however, experience these difficulties in particular ways related to gender roles and expectations. We conducted open-ended life history interviews with a sample of 20 IDU women in the project who agreed to participate in this substudy. Many described difficulties of dealing with their addiction, and issues of isolation, mistrust, and danger. Echoing the sentiments of other women in the project, one twenty-nine year old Puerto Rican woman described her feelings about being on the streets and acquiring drugs to support her addiction in the following words:

> You can't trust nobody nowadays. It's dangerous because too many people play too many tricks out there. If you give [your] money to somebody to go get something, you probably won't see him again. I buy for myself. I don't trust nobody. If I give somebody the money to go buy, he could switch bags on me. It'll be poison what he giving me, that's why I'd rather get it myself.

A thirty-nine year old African American woman described similar isolation and wariness while acquiring and using drugs on the streets. She also recounted her preference to buy her own drugs and use them alone:

> Sometimes I get down with somebody [buy drugs together], but usually I use alone. I just like to because then I'm in control of it. If you do it with somebody then it's more like they call the shots. . . . When you shoot up with someone else, [whoever buys it] goes first—who spent the money. You might have somebody else help you dump it in the cooker, you know, and they'll ask you how much water you want to put on it, but when it comes to drawing up the shots, it's mostly the person who bought it. Some people just want to be in control. Like me. I don't like nobody fixing up my stuff. I just feel like everybody does it different. . . . It's like making oatmeal. Some people make their oatmeal one way—that's the way I look at it.

Her inclination to control her preparation and use of drugs reflects her desire to control her own addiction, to the degree possible, as well as her drug-related risks. It also reflects her recognition of her own vulnerability in the context of being addicted and needing to get and use drugs in a highly dangerous environment.

While the desire is strong to use alone in order to avoid situations in which someone could take advantage of or harm a drug user desperate for the drug or money to buy it, women are particularly concerned about trying to avoid putting themselves at risk of being taken advantage of by other drug users on the streets. As a result, they are less evident in street drug use settings. The African American woman quoted above noted the following:

> [When I buy drugs with someone else], it's mostly with . . . men. There's not many women out there that I like to get high with. All last week only one woman I got high with. I don't think there's any difference [getting high with a woman or a man], I just think there's more men out there to get high with than women. I think a lot of women tend to be like me; they tend to just want to do it by themselves. . . . [They] tend to . . . hide more. More women get high in houses at home than in the streets like men. . . . I'm always in the minority in the streets getting high.

Her assessment that women are less visible by virtue of hiding their injection drug use in homes is consistent with reports of other women in the project and outreach workers seeking to track study participants. This preference to remain hidden reflects possible differences in levels of social stigma attached to male and female drug injectors as a result of gender-related role expectations of women as mothers and carriers of social morality. It also suggests differences in degree of danger on the streets for male and female IDUs and the considerable vulnerability of women addicts.

In addition to observing smaller numbers of women, which reflects both the general predominance of men in the injection drug using population (our studies suggest no more than 30-40% of IDUs in Hartford are women) and their greater numbers on the streets and in high-risk areas, this same woman noted gender differences in women's and men's experience of street drug use:

> With women, it's like if you're out there you're more on your own. The men clique together more. [They] look out for each other more. They depend on each other. A woman is on her own when she's out there.

Differences in supportive relationships among street drug users suggest different social networks between men and women in the drug use context. The increased isolation of women drug users limits their opportunities for mutual protection and reciprocal support (both financial and protective) with other male and female drug users in buying and using drugs on the streets.

We unfortunately did not ask specific questions regarding possible ways racial or ethnic identity and ethnic-specific gender roles might affect women's street drug using experiences and the women we interviewed in-depth volunteered none. Also, the lack of variation on the basis of ethnicity in their descriptions of street drug use or acquisition and addiction is notable. This suggests that at least on the surface these women did not recognize their color or ethnic background as directly affecting their personal drug use practices. Nevertheless, as mentioned earlier, neighborhood ethnic segregation and ethnic-identified gang control of neighborhood drug markets, combined with social factors influencing poverty and health for people of color and other factors in the availability, use, and consequences of drug use are directly impacted by racism and ethnic distinctions. Further research is warranted to elicit more specific dialogue on the ways race and ethnicity shape personal experiences of women drug users.

DRUG USE AND SEXUAL HIV RISK PATTERNS

The women in Project COPE II also reported significant sexual HIV risk associated with their use of illicit drugs (Table 3). A quarter of the women and 37% of the men reported no sexual activity in the thirty days prior to the intake interview. Nearly half of the rest said they had only one sex partner during that period, and another one-fifth reported between two and five partners, with virtually no difference between men and women in these two categories. However, 11% of the women, compared to only 3% of the men, said they had more than five partners in that thirty day period, a difference that was statistically significant ($p < 0.001$). Consistent with this, 26% of the women reported having exchanged sex for money, and 17% had exchanged sex for drugs during that period, compared to 3% of men reporting both practices, accounting for the difference between men and women in the percent reporting multiple sex partners.

Men and women's reported rates of condom use were nearly identical. Of those who were sexually active in the thirty days prior to intake, slightly over half of both men and women reported never using condoms during that period, and another one-quarter of each reported infrequent or

TABLE 3. Sexual HIV Risks of Project COPE II Men and Women (Percentages)

Sexual HIV Risk Practices:	Men (N = 791)	Women (N = 231)
Number of sex partners (last 30 days):***		
none	37	25
1	44	46
2-5	17	18
6 or more	3	11
Condom use (last 30 days):	(N = 511)	(N = 180)
never	55	54
less than half time	11	11
half the time or more (not always)	13	14
always	22	21
Has an IDU sex partner**	28	40
Exchanged sex for money in last 30 days***	3	26
Exchanged sex for drugs in last 30 days***	3	17

** $p < 0.01$.
*** $p < 0.001$.

inconsistent condom use. Only about 20% of both men and women reported using condoms all the time. However, women in COPE were significantly more likely than men in the project to have an IDU sex partner, which profoundly changes the context of risk associated with the intermittent or inconsistent condom use reported by both sexes. Additionally, women's higher reported rates of exchanging sex for money or drugs, a context that appears to be one in which condoms are more likely to be used (Weeks, Grier et al., 1997; Weissman, Brown et al., 1991; Worth, 1990), suggests that women's use of condoms at other times, namely, with intimate partners, is even lower than that of men.

Ethnic differences among women regarding sexual HIV risks associated with drug use were notable (Table 4). Fewer Puerto Rican women than African American or White women were sexually active. Nearly half of the African American and Puerto Rican women had only one sex partner, while white women reported the highest rate of multiple sex partners. Reported condom use also varied significantly by ethnicity ($p = 0.04$), with Whites reporting the highest rates of use, followed by African American and Puerto Rican women. Additionally, Puerto Rican women drug users in the project were more likely to have an IDU sex partner than African American women, though white women reported this at the highest rate. Whites also reported the highest rates of exchanging sex for money or drugs in the prior thirty days, followed by African

TABLE 4. Sexual Risk Among Project COPE II Women by Ethnicity (Percentages)

Sexual HIV-Risk Practices:	African Am. (N = 100)	Puerto Rican (N = 105)	White (N = 22)
Number of sex partners (last 30 days):*			
none	23	29	17
1	48	45	38
2-5	20	17	13
6 or more	10	9	33
Condom use:*	(N = 76)	(N = 82)	(N = 18)
never	54	60	28
less than half time	9	11	22
half time or more (not always)	9	17	28
always	28	12	22
IDU Sex Partner**	31	41	65
Exchanged sex/$ in last 30 days**	33	18	44
Exchanged sex/drugs in last 30 days*	22	12	26

* $p < 0.05$.
** $p < 0.01$.

American women, accounting in part for the higher reported rates of condom use by both groups compared to Puerto Rican women.

The degree to which women can maintain economic independence, rely on resources other than from sex partners (whether intimate, casual, or customers), and find means to support themselves, their children, other family members, and their addiction directly impacts their options for decisions regarding HIV risk reduction in sexual practice and drug use. One African American woman, for example, discussed her efforts to support a $300-$500/day cocaine and heroin addiction through prostitution, the context of which, along with her interaction with an intimate partner, were generally defined by the degree to which she was sick from drug withdrawal. She is now HIV-positive, a condition that affects her control over her drug use and sexual practices. The following interview excerpts portray the complex relationship between addiction, HIV, and her sexual relationships and activities:

[As a teenager,] I was a runaway from home and prostitution was my form of getting money that I knew. . . . [I started at] age 15. [Now] I found that in the progression of my disease [i.e., HIV] that [my prostitution work] is an exchange for some things other than money. *That* at one point I wouldn't compromise; it was just sex for money. But I see now that I've compromised myself to the point where I have exchanged sex for drugs. . . . I was involved [in a relationship] with somebody up until three weeks ago and at which time my disease, oh man, escalated. . . . At first it was just me, him, and getting high, but then it reached a point where I needed more drugs and at that point I had to do more things to get money, and then I had to let him go. It just wasn't right. . . . There's nothing that conditions whether or not I use, it's mandatory that I use because I have a drug habit.

Her comments on the changes in her commercial sex work suggest that she perceives exchanging sex for drugs to be significantly more degrading than exchanging sex for money (cf. Fullilove, Lown, & Fullilove, 1992). The former implies less control over the exchange situation and greater desperation to relieve the pain of HIV illness or drug withdrawal. Her ability to support her habit financially is counterbalanced by her level of addiction, producing a willingness to accept greater risks to meet the financial demands of that addiction, a situation that is exacerbated by the physical effects of HIV. Her ability to maintain a desired intimate relationship likewise is circumscribed by her addiction and the difficulties of supporting it financially. Yet her comments also imply that gender-related roles and expectations in the context of that relationship led her to feel uncomfortable maintaining intimacy with a partner while her addiction and HIV illness forced her to increase her sexual exchanges for money and drugs, and to commit more of her efforts to supporting her addiction.

Gender differences impact many aspects of drug addiction, sexual practice, and the procurement of drugs or money to support a habit. The social environment created by poverty, the war on drugs, gang turfism, and male dominance create multiple opportunities for life-threatening dangers for all drug users, with particular risks for women in vulnerable circumstances. A 35-year-old African American woman described the role of violence in the lives of women drug users:

[Women addicts have different worries] . . . because a man doesn't have to feel threatened of rape and violent crimes. When a woman is out there, first of all, there's not much self-respect on her part or on the other part, the guys that are out there. You know, they seem to think because you're out there it's open field day on you, that they could just do what they want with you because first of all you're not living like a lady is supposed to. So, there's a lot of threats of violence for a woman out there.

Much of the violence places men and women in equal physical danger. Yet, even in the context of similar life threats and comparable need resulting from addiction, which men and women alike face on the streets, gender definitions differentiate the context for women in relation to the difficulties, options, and dangers associated with financing and using the drug. This gender context complicates women's already risky and isolating experience in dealing with poverty and addiction on the streets.

HEALTH STATUS AND TREATMENT HISTORY

The combined drug-related and sexual HIV risks of Project COPE II participants contributed to high rates of HIV infection. A total of 475 men and 128 women opted to receive the HIV antibody test at intake into the project, of whom a total of 109 (18%) tested HIV-positive. An additional 147 COPE II participants chose not to test because they reported already knowing they were HIV-positive through an earlier test (though our project could not confirm these tests results). When project tests were combined with self-reported seropositivity, a total of 34% of both men and women in Project COPE II were HIV infected (Table 5). Seropositivity rates among women varied significantly by ethnicity, with the highest rates of HIV among African American women.

Among IDUs in the project, though differences in HIV rates between men and women were not statistically significant ($p = .3$), they were notable, with 43% of the IDU men compared to 49% of the IDU women reporting or testing seropositive. Higher HIV rates among injecting women compared to IDU men reflect the greater potential risk women face, given their reported higher rates of injection, more frequent use of previously used injection equipment, greater likelihood of participation in sex-for-money/drugs exchanges, and other conditions of their drug use described above. Even more notable is the significant difference among ethnic groups of IDU women in HIV seropositivity. Though the numbers in these groups for whom we have HIV information are quite small in some cases, the extreme rates of infection among African American IDU women, despite their having the lowest rates of injection and reported sharing of injection equipment, reflects the clear difference in risk resulting from current HIV prevalence within their social environment and social networks.

In addition to HIV, Project COPE II participants reported histories of a variety of illnesses related to drug use and drug-related sexual risks (Table 5). For example, 20% of the participants, undifferentiated by sex, reported having had a hepatitis B diagnosis at some time in the past. Many also reported a history of STDs, including gonorrhea and syphilis (differences by sex in prior diagnosis of these two STDs were not statistically signifi-

TABLE 5. HIV Seropositivity and History of Hepatitis B and STDs Among Project COPE II Participants (Percentages)

| | | | | WOMEN | |
Disease:	Men (N = 791)	Women (N = 231)	African Am. (N = 100)	Puerto Rican (N = 105)	White (N = 22)
HIV-positive[1] (project tested plus self-report)	34 (n = 200/585)	34 (n = 56/165)	47 (n = 26/55)	27 (n = 26/95)	23 (n = 3/13)
HIV-positive IDUs[2] (project tested plus self-report)	43 (n = 175/408)	49 (n = 43/88)	73 (n = 19/26)	40 (n = 21/53)	25 (n = 2/8)
Hepatitis B	20	19	17	20	30
Gonorrhea[2]	35	27	41	18	29
Syphilis	10	15	19	13	4
Genital warts	3	3	4	3	4
Chlamydia[3]	3	13	15	11	22
Genital herpes[4]	2	4	7	2	4

Note 1. Differences by ethnicity among women were statistically significant ($p < 0.05$).
Note 2. Differences by ethnicity among women were statistically significant ($p < 0.01$).
Note 3. Differences by sex were statistically significant ($p < 0.0001$).
Note 4. Differences by sex were statistically significant ($p = 0.02$).

cant). Less than 5% of both women and men reported a history of genital warts or genital herpes, although 13% of the women reported having had chlamydia compared to 3% of the men ($p < 0.0001$).

Few differences were statistically significant among women by ethnicity regarding history of hepatitis B or STDs. The exception is gonorrhea, which 41% of African American women reported, compared to 29% of White women and 18% of Puerto Rican women. Other differences were evident, however. White women reported the highest rates of hepatitis B and chlamydia, and the lowest rates of syphilis. By contrast, African American women reported the highest rates of gonorrhea, syphilis and genital herpes, and the lowest rates of hepatitis B. Puerto Rican women reported the lowest rates of most STDs, though their syphilis rates were closer to the high rates reported among African Americans than the low rates reported by White women.

Ethnic differences in reported hepatitis B show a direct relationship between infection rates and average injection frequency (reportedly highest among White and Puerto Rican women). Variation by ethnicity among women in prevalence of STDs suggests the possibility of differences related to frequency of exchanging sex for money or drugs, resulting in greater opportunity for infection (e.g., African American women in the study reported the practice more so than Puerto Rican women). This explanation, however, does not hold for the small group of white women, whose rates of all STDs except chlamydia were lower than African American women's. We have not yet tested individual patterns of drug use and sexual practice for these statistical associations in history of hepatitis and STDs that appear across ethnic groups in our study. Such associations indicate the need for further inquiry at both the individual level and within socially defined groups, such as those delimited by ethnic identity or separated by color.

Targeted sampling and street outreach resulted in recruiting a large population of high-risk drug users who had limited drug treatment histories (Table 6). Over a third of all participants reported never having been in any kind of drug treatment or detoxification program prior to entering Project COPE II. As would be expected, reported history of treatment increased with age. Forty percent of younger participants in COPE II (18-35 years old) had never been in treatment, compared to 32% of participants over 35 years of age ($p = 0.006$). More women than men reported use of nearly all types of drug treatment, though the differences in treatment history by sex were significant only for methadone maintenance. Further, over one-third of both men and women had tried unsuccessfully to enter drug treatment in the prior twelve months, undifferentiated by sex.

Among women in the project, no significant differences appeared by ethnic group in history of drug treatment, though variation is evident in types of treatment used. White women appear to make the greatest use of nearly all treatment programs, particularly methadone (both detoxification and maintenance) and residential, possibly the result of a greater sense of cultural appropriateness and acceptability of treatment programs, or otherwise greater access for these women, such as financial support. Differences in drug of choice affect variation in use of specific types of treatment by women of different ethnic groups. For example, limited use of heroin but higher rates of cocaine and crack use among African American women presumably contributes to their lesser history of methadone treatment and greater use of outpatient drug free programs, likewise with heroin use among Puerto Rican and White women and their use of methadone. From these figures, it is not possible to determine whether cultural differences in beliefs about effective treatment have an impact on history of use. Nevertheless, White women's apparently greater access and/or motivation to enter drug treatment suggests by counterposition possible

TABLE 6. History of Drug Treatment Among Project COPE II Participants (Percentages)

Treatment History (ever)	Men (N = 791)	Women (N = 231)	African Am. (N = 100)	WOMEN Puerto Rican (N = 105)	White (N = 22)
Never in treatment:	35	35	30	41	25
Under 36 yrs. old	40	38	42	34	56
Over 35 yrs. old[1]	32	31	23	49	7
Methadone detox[2]	41	45	35	48	67
Methadone maint.[3]	22	32	23	35	56
Outpat. drug free[4]	23	24	42	11	11
Residential	67	63	65	59	78
Prison/jail treatment	12	14	11	13	28
Other treatment	9	7	13	4	0
Tried but unable to enter treatment (in last 12 months)	36	36	31	39	42

Note 1. Differences among women by ethnicity were significant ($p < 0.001$).
Note 2. Differences among women by ethnicity were significant ($p < 0.04$).
Note 3. Differences by sex were significant ($p < 0.01$) as were differences among women by ethnicity ($p = 0.02$).
Note 4. Differences among women by ethnicity were significant ($p < 0.0001$).

barriers for African American and Puerto Rican women that warrant further inquiry and response.

IMPLICATIONS FOR PREVENTION AND TREATMENT FOR WOMEN

The interplay of poverty, ethnicity, and gender relations affects drug use patterns of women addicts and creates a context within which their drug using behavior is defined and shaped. For example, the economic context of drug use, social relationships with other users, and the significance of drug use for those relationships are likely to define the situations in which women use drugs or become addicted. These factors also condition the interactions of drug using women with others regarding issues not directly related to the use of drugs, such as economic activity, social support, kinship ties, relations of intimacy, and sexual behavior.

Understanding women's patterns of addiction requires assessing the implications of their gender-defined roles as mothers, lovers, and wives, and the relationships between men and women, including intimacy and harmoniousness as well as hierarchy and struggles for power. The words of women participating in our project underscore their special sense of vulnerability suggested by their preference to hide while using drugs, particularly when injecting. This desire to hide also highlights the unique stigma attached to women drug users given the contradiction their addiction creates with social expectations of women's roles, including their responsibility for children. Hierarchical relations with men can also result in special "risks" for women, for example if this hierarchy defines injection order, placing women second, or circumscribes negotiation of condom use. Finally, exchanging sex for money or drugs is a practice to which women yield more readily than men in order to provide the funds necessary to support their addiction and to meet their own and their family's basic financial needs. Despite the greater acceptability of condom use in this context, the resulting higher number of sex partners combined with the potential for occasions in which condoms are not used during the sex-for-money/drugs exchanges as a result of drug sickness, financial need, or disempowerment by the male client (cf. Weeks, Grier et al., 1997) create a special context of risk for women drug users that is uncommon for men.

Ethnic identity as well as racial and ethnic divisions also create particular contexts within which women use drugs, become addicted, and seek (or avoid) treatment. Ethnic boundaries defining sources and available types of drugs as well as learned consumption patterns affect drug use practices for both men and women, and must be taken into account when designing appropriate treatment. Combined gender and racial/ethnic social subordination and disempowerment and the resulting reduction in self-esteem also shape women's experiences with addiction and their patterns of use. These factors are focal areas to address in order to change the context of drug use and to reduce social conditions that reinforce addiction among women.

Drug-related diseases, such as hepatitis, STDs, endocarditis, and HIV also are tied to gender and ethnic social relations. For example, as the data above suggest, reported differences by ethnicity in prior STD diagnosis as well as in HIV infection are directly linked to a set of social conditions that can promote or impede the spread of infection. Socially created segregation on the basis of race, color, and ethnic identity construct *de facto* boundaries around groups of individuals. Such boundaries often define preferred choice or availability of sex partners, particularly intimate partners with whom condoms are less likely to be used. When combined with prevalence of a disease that has increased to epidemic proportions in these ethnically and racially segregated populations, as is the case with syphilis, gonorrhea, and HIV in the African American community, the likelihood of encountering a partner who is infected increases dramatically.

Separate epidemics also intersect to increase the virulence of each other. Because lesions and local inflammation caused by an STD facilitate entry of HIV into the bloodstream during intercourse, STD infection acts as a cofactor to HIV transmission (Nelson et al., 1991). This partially explains the higher rates of HIV among African American women compared to other women in the project, despite their reported greater frequency of condom use. Additionally, as with the Lewis and Watters (1989) study noted above, already high HIV seroprevalence in Hartford's African American community increases the likelihood that African American women's intimate partners (either sexual or drug using) will already be infected. Socially constructed population boundaries thus can result in the explosive spread of an STDs or HIV in one ethnic community while prevalence remains limited in another within the same city. This creates a set of relatively discrete and uniquely constructed epidemics in each ethnic community requiring a separate set of approaches to prevention of further infection.

In addition to gender and ethnicity, conditions of poverty, as well as other local contextual factors, directly shape women's experiences with drug use, addiction, and drug treatment, as well as addiction-related diseases. Lack of financial resources reduce options for women to access appropriate and effective drug treatment programs and other health services. Women addicts living in poverty who seek income through prostitution face an additional set of social and health risks and consequences. Chronic poverty not only provides the impetus to initiate drug use (as a means of medicating personal distress), it increases the likelihood of relapse after treatment when a woman's economic and social circumstances provide the same crippling stress and relentless denigration she experienced before entering treatment. Furthermore, when drug use prevails in these circumstances, environmental factors, such as treatment availability, access to clean needles, prevention messages in the community, HIV load in the population, and opportunities to link hidden drug users to prevention and treatment services all have an impact on the consequences of addiction and the course of related epidemics such as syphilis, gonorrhea, and HIV.

Studies like Project COPE II and the other NIDA cooperative agreement studies have demonstrated targeted outreach to increase effective identification and engagement of individuals that have never received drug treatment of any kind, as well as those who have cycled into and out of programs and returned to street drug use. In particular, COPE II has been able to reach economically impoverished women and minority ethnic groups whose access to treatment programs and other health and social services has been particularly limited. Utilizing these recruitment methods increases the potential for reaching individuals whose drug use and sexual behavior, within specific environmental and social contexts of high disease prevalence and limited mechanisms for prevention, places them at greatest risk for addiction-related illnesses.

Women's higher rates of injection compared to men's, and among women, various rates and patterns of use within different ethnic groups, demonstrate the need to provide treatment and after-care designed to address specific local practices and populations, and that focus on women's particular needs and issues of addiction. Yet, efforts towards this end have not been overly successful. The 1989 federal government mandated 10% "carve out" of money directed towards women's services (Department of Health and Human Services) has since been repealed. Now the only special consideration for women's drug treatment needs is for pregnant women. Even when the mandate was in force, however, treatment programs were not required to address specifically the local practices or ethnic differences within their service area. In Connecticut, the Department of Mental Health and Addiction Services instituted six Regional Action Councils (RACs) in 1992 to try to address these particular concerns. These state funded entities were to bring together individuals for planning purposes, identify gaps in the treatment system for that particular region, prioritize needs, and try to develop appropriate services by presenting priorities to the state for inclusion in the drug treatment planning process. Though this may appear to be a local solution to the lack of public input into the planning process, in practice the RACs have been marginally effective at changing the practice of most substance abuse programs or developing new services. For example, through their own planning council, Connecticut identified the need for residential treatment for poly-drug users in the Hartford area who are not appropriate for outpatient treatment, and submitted that recommendation to the governor. The local RAC, however, could not successfully advocate to the state legislature for funding for such a program. Consequently, funds for new treatment ventures were cut from the state budget and never restored, leaving a critical gap in needed services.

At the national level, the federal Center for Substance Abuse Treatment (CSAT) and Center for Substance Abuse Prevention (CSAP) have funded demonstration projects specifically designed to increase the participation of women in drug treatment and to evaluate which types of programs are most effective at retaining and successfully treating women. Unfortunately many of these programs are now ending as a result of the cutbacks within the federal government and the congressional defunding of drug treatment demonstration projects by CSAT and CSAP. As a result, important evaluation findings on treatment effectiveness will never be shared nor successful programs and program elements replicated.

In addition to the need to increase availability and acceptability of drug treatment programs for women, particularly women of color, the HIV and STD epidemics require renewed focus on the conditions leading to high risk among these drug users. Many, but certainly not all, drug treatment programs have adopted AIDS prevention education as part of their treatment protocol. Health education programs that focus on other drug-use and addiction related health problems, such as hepatitis B and STDs, also are critical, as are other aspects of health promotion. Harm reduction education is necessary given the recurrent nature of addiction and the intertwined STD, hepatitis, and HIV epidemics, limitations to the availability and effectiveness of drug treatment, and the continuing initiation of young people into use of and addiction to illicit injection and non-injection drugs.

Given the complexity of social processes affecting risk and behavior for women drug users, and particularly women of color who use drugs, further research is warranted on the intersection of poverty, gender relations, racial and ethnic identity and divisions, disease-prevalent social environments, and social contexts that mitigate against control of risks. Particularly needed is further analysis of the ways ethnic culture and divisions on the basis of ethnicity or race, as well as gender roles and expectations, define particular contexts that increase the potential for ill effects on individuals beyond the direct physical, mental, and emotional consequences of addiction. Because individually oriented, behaviorally focused prevention programs are limited in effectiveness, despite documented positive outcomes, modification of social and environmental conditions as well as increasing harm-reduction opportunities, such as sterile syringe exchange programs, are key next steps to reducing the negative health and social effects of drugs, including the rising deadly HIV epidemic.

NOTES

1. The Community Outreach Prevention Effort, or Project COPE II, was part of the National Institute on Drug Abuse (NIDA) Cooperative Agreement for Community Outreach/Intervention for AIDS Prevention Programs. The authors greatly appreciate NIDA's financial support for this study (grant #U01 DA07284, April 1992-March 1997). The Hartford community-based organizations that participated in this project included the Hispanic Health Council, the Institute for Community Research, the Hartford Dispensary, the Urban League of Greater Hartford, Latinos/as Contra SIDA, and the Hartford Health Department.

2. We created three categories each (low, moderate, and high) for total injections in the prior thirty days, injections of each individual drug, and crack use incidents. We determined these categories using normal and detrended probability plots and interviewed former drug users to verify natural divisions between levels of use. The final categories represent approximate monthly, weekly, and daily measures.

3. It is notable that, although the number of White women in Project COPE II is small, they reported the highest injection rates of any ethnic group in the study sample. They also reported the highest rates of sexual HIV risks related to drug use and addiction, including having an IDU sex partner and exchanging sex for money or drugs. Yet, they appear to have the lowest rates of HIV infection and of most other STDs. This apparent contradiction suggests the need for further study into the context and patterns of HIV risk for white drug using women in Hartford.

REFERENCES

Amaro, H. (1995). Love, sex, and power: Considering women's realities in HIV prevention. *American Psychologist, 50*, 437-447.

Barnard, M. (1993). Needle sharing in context: Patterns of sharing among men and women injectors and HIV risks. *Addiction, 88*, 837-840.

Centers for Disease Control and Prevention. (1995). Update: AIDS among women–United States, 1994. *MMWR, 44*, 81-84.

City of Hartford. (1995). The State of the City, 1995. Hartford, CT: Department of Planning and Economic Development.

Cohen, J.B. (1991). Why women partners of drug users will continue to be at high risk for HIV infection. In L.K. Morgan, & J.E. Taper (Eds.), *Cocaine, AIDS, and Intravenous Drug Use* (pp. 99-110). CA: The Haworth Press, Inc.

Connecticut Health Department, AIDS Section. (1994). AIDS in Connecticut. AIDS Surveillance Report, December 31.

Coyle, S.L. (1993). The NIDA Standard Intervention Model for Injection Drug Users Not-In-Treatment. Rockville, MD: National Institute on Drug Abuse.

Deren, S., Davis, W.R., Tortu, S., & Ahluwahlia, I. (1993). Characteristics of female sexual partners. In: B. Brown & B. Beschner, (Eds.). *At Risk for AIDS: Drug Injection Users and Their Sexual Partners.* Westport, CT: Greenwood Press.

Freeman, R. C., Rodriguez, G. M., & French, J. F. (1994). A comparison of male and female intravenous drug users' risk behaviors for HIV infection. *American Journal of Alcohol Abuse, 20*, 129-157.

Fullilove, M. T., Fullilove, R. E., Haynes, K., & Gross, S. (1990). Black women and AIDS prevention: A view towards understanding the gender rules. *The Journal of Sex Research, 27*, 47-64.

Fullilove, M. T., Lown, E. A., & Fullilove, R. E. (1992). Crack ho's and skeezers: Traumatic experiences of women crack users. *The Journal of Sex Research, 29*, 275-287.

Fullilove, R.E., Fullilove, M.T., & Bowser, B. (1990). Crack users: The new AIDS risk group? *Cancer Detection and Prevention, 14*, 363-368.

Himmelgreen, D. (1995). *Changes in needle access legislation and HIV risk among female injection drug users in Hartford, CT.* Presented at the Society for Applied Anthropology Annual Meeting, Albuquerque, NM, March.

Kane, S. (1990). AIDS, addiction, and condom use: Sources of sexual risk for heterosexual women. *The Journal of Sex Research, 27,* 427-444.

Kline, A., Kline, E., & Oken, E. (1992). Minority women and sexual choice in the age of AIDS. *Social Science and Medicine, 34,* 447-457.

Lewis, D.K., & Watters, J.K. (1989). Human immunodeficiency virus seroprevalence in female intravenous drug users: The puzzle of black women's risk. *Social Science Medicine, 29,* 1071-1076.

Longshore, D., & Anglin, M.D. (1995). Number of sex partners and crack cocaine use: Is crack an independent marker for HIV risk behavior? *Journal of Drug Issues, 25,* 1-10.

National Institute on Drug Abuse. (1994). Risk Behavior Assessment Questionnaire. Community Research Branch, Bethesda, MD.

Nelson, K.E., Vlahov, D., Cohn, S., Odunmbaku, M., Lindsay, A., Anthony, J.C., & Hook, III, E.W. (1991). Sexually transmitted diseases in a population of intravenous drug users: Association with seropositivity to the human immunodeficiency virus (HIV). *The Journal of Infectious Diseases, 164,* 457-463.

Nyamathi, A. M., Leake, B., Flaskerud, J., Lewis, C., & Bennett, C. (1993). Outcomes of specialized and traditional AIDS counseling programs for impoverished women of color, *Research in Nursing & Health, 16,* 11-21.

Rolfs, R. Goldberg, M., & Sharrar, R. (1990). Risk factors for syphilis: Cocaine use and prostitution. *American Journal of Public Health, 80,* 853-857.

Shayne, V.T., & Kaplan, B.J. (1991). Double victims: Poor women and AIDS. *Women & Health, 17,* 21-37.

Singer, M. (1992). AIDS and U.S. ethnic minorities: The crisis and alternative anthropological responses. *Human Organizations, 51,* 89-95.

Singer, M. (1994). AIDS and the health crisis of the U.S. urban poor: The perspective of critical medical anthropology. *Social Science & Medicine, 39,* 931-948.

Singer, M. (1996). Providing substance abuse treatment to Puerto Rican clients living in the continental United States. In: O. Amulezu-Marshall (Ed.), *Substance Abuse Treatment in the Era of AIDS* (pp. 93-114). Rockville, MD: Center for Substance Abuse Prevention.

Singer, M., Flores, C., Davison, L., Burke, G., Castillo, Z., Scanlon, K., & Rivera, M. (1990). SIDA: The economic, social, and cultural context of AIDS among Latinos. *Medical Anthropology Quarterly, 4,* 72-114.

Singer, M., Himmelgreen, D.A., Radda, K., & Weeks, M.R. (1995). *Structural changes in AIDS risk: Findings on the impact of needle access legislation in Hartford, CT.* Presented at the 3rd Science Symposium on HIV Prevention Research, Flagstaff, Arizona, August.

Singer, M., & Jia, Z. (1993). AIDS and Puerto Rican injection drug users in the United States. In: B.S. Brown & G.M. Beschner (Eds.), *Handbook of risk of AIDS: Injection drug users and sexual partners* (pp. 227-255). Westport, CT: Greenwood Press.

Singer, M., Jia, Z., Schensul, J.J., Weeks, M.R., & Page, J.B. (1992). AIDS and the IV drug user: The local context in prevention efforts. *Medical Anthropology, 14,* 285-306.

Singer, M., Valentin, F., Baer, H., & Jia, Z. (1992). Why does Juan Garcia have a drinking problem? *Medical Anthropology, 14,* 77-108.

Singer, M., & Weeks, M.R. (1992). *Hartford targeted sampling plan.* Community Alliance for AIDS Programs (unpublished document).

Sobo, E.J. (1993). Inner-city women and AIDS: The psycho-social benefits of unsafe sex. *Culture, Medicine & Psychiatry, 17,* 455-485.

Sobo, E.J. (1995). *Choosing Unsafe Sex: AIDS-Risk Denial Among Disadvantaged Women.* Philadelphia: University of Pennsylvania Press.

Tortu, S., Beardsley, M., Deren, S., & Davis, W.R. (1994). The risk of HIV infection in a national sample of women with injection drug-using partners. *American Journal of Public Health, 84,* 1243-1249.

Turner, C. Miller, H., & Moses, L. (1989). *AIDS: Sexual behavior and intravenous drug use.* Washington, D.C.: National Academy.

Watters, J.K., & Biernacki, P. (1989). Targeted sampling: Options for the study of hidden populations. *Social Problems, 36,* 416-430.

Weeks, M.R. (Ed.). (1991). Community Outreach Prevention Effort: Designs in Culturally Appropriate AIDS Intervention. (Unpublished manual prepared for the National Institute on Drug Abuse.)

Weeks, M.R., Singer, M., Grier, M., Hunte-Marrow, J., and Haughton, C. (1993). AIDS prevention and the African American injection drug user. *Transforming Anthropology, 4,* 39-51.

Weeks, M.R., Singer, M., Schensul, J., Jia, Z., & Grier, M. (1993). Project COPE: Preventing AIDS among injection drug users and their sex partners: Descriptive Data Report. Hartford, CT: Institute for Community Research.

Weeks, M.R., Grier, M., Romero-Daza, N., Puglisi-Vasquez, M.J., & Singer, M. (1997). Streets, drugs, and the economy of sex in the age of AIDS. *Women and Health, 25* (2) (forthcoming).

Weeks, M.R., Himmelgreen, D.A., Singer, M., Woolley, S., Romero-Daza, N., & Grier, M. (1996). Community-based AIDS prevention: Preliminary outcomes of a program for African American and Latino injection drug users. *Journal of Drug Issues 26,* 561-590.

Weeks, M.R., Schensul, J.J., Williams, S.S., Singer, M., & Grier, M. (1995). AIDS prevention for African American and Latina women: Building culturally and gender appropriate intervention. *AIDS Education and Prevention, 7,* 251-263.

Weissman, G., Brown, V., & the National AIDS Research Consortium. (1991). Drug use and sexual behavior among sex partners of injecting-drug users— United States, 1980-1990. *MMWR, 40,* 855-860.

Worth, D. (1989). Sexual decision-making and AIDS: Why condom promotion among vulnerable women is likely to fail. *Studies in Family Planning, 20,* 297-307.

Worth, D. (1990). Women at high risk of HIV infection: Behavioral, prevention, and intervention aspects. In D.G. Ostrow (Ed.). *Behavioral aspects of AIDS,* NY: Plenum, pp. 101-119.

II. DIFFERENCES BETWEEN DRUG USING WOMEN WHO ARE IN AND OUT OF TREATMENT

Differences Found Between Women Injectors In and Out of Treatment: Implications for Interventions

Wendee M. Wechsberg, PhD
Elizabeth R. Cavanaugh, BA

SUMMARY. Women substance abusers, particularly those who are injecting drug users, are at high risk for HIV infection. It has been

Wendee M. Wechsberg and Elizabeth R. Cavanaugh are affiliated with the Research Triangle Institute, Research Triangle Park, NC 27709-2194.

The authors wish to thank Bruce MacDonald for his tireless efforts.

This work was supported by the National Institute on Drug Abuse (NIDA) Grant No. DA 09001-01. The interpretations and conclusions do not represent the position of NIDA or the Department of Health and Human Services.

[Haworth co-indexing entry note]: "Differences Found Between Women Injectors In and Out of Treatment: Implications for Interventions." Wechsberg, Wendee M., and Elizabeth R. Cavanaugh. Co-published simultaneously in *Drugs & Society* (The Haworth Press, Inc.) Vol. 13, No. 1/2, 1998, pp. 63-79; and: *Women and Substance Abuse: Gender Transparency* (ed: Sally J. Stevens, and Harry K. Wexler) The Haworth Press, Inc., 1998, pp. 63-79. Single or multiple copies of this article are available for a fee from The Haworth Document Delivery Service [1-800-342-9678, 9:00 a.m. - 5:00 p.m. (EST). E-mail address: getinfo@haworthpressinc.com].

demonstrated that injecting drug users found out of drug treatment settings show different patterns of drug use and HIV risk than those who enter treatment. Previous studies, however, have not indicated the extent to which women injectors in and out of treatment exhibit these same differences. This study examines data from two studies sponsored by the National Institute on Drug Abuse to determine similarities and differences between women encountered by outreach efforts in four cities and those entering methadone treatment programs in the same cities.

The results indicate significant differences in race, drugs used (both injecting and non-injecting), injecting risk behavior, and treatment history. However, the two groups of women shared similar histories of first injecting use and sexual risk. Women who entered methadone treatment reported higher frequencies of injecting drug use and HIV risk behaviors, both direct (sharing needles) and indirect (sharing cookers, cotton, and water); yet they were also more likely to clean needles and to use new needles than the women encountered through outreach. The outreach women were more likely to be African American, to inject less than daily, and to use alcohol, crack, and non-injecting cocaine daily.

The results suggest that women injectors entering treatment and those encountered in outreach are very different in their injecting intensity and HIV risk behaviors. However, both groups are still at risk for HIV infection, particularly as a result of multiple sexual partners and little reported condom use. The need to identify the risk, reinforce risk reduction maintenance, and further develop HIV prevention strategies that successfully address both the needs of these women and the differences that exist between them will be essential to stopping the spread of HIV. *[Article copies available for a fee from The Haworth Document Delivery Service: 1-800-342-9678. E-mail address: getinfo@haworthpressinc.com]*

INTRODUCTION

In 1981-1982, women comprised 4% of AIDS cases reported in the U.S. By December 1995, they comprised 14% of all AIDS cases ever reported in the U.S. (Amaro, 1995), and 19% of the cases diagnosed in 1995 (Centers for Disease Control and Prevention [CDC] Surveillance, 1995). Women are the fastest growing group with AIDS, and women substance abusers have dominated this group.

Anyone can get AIDS, but everyone does not have an equal opportunity to become infected. Women who are injecting drug users (IDUs), who are the sex partners of bisexuals and injecting drug users, who are African American or Hispanic, who are poor, or who are members of other groups in which the prevalence of infection is high are far more likely to be exposed to HIV than other women in the U.S. Forty-seven percent of the women who have ever contracted HIV were infected by injecting drugs; 37% were infected by heterosexual contact. AIDS rates also vary widely by race and socioeconomic category. In 1993, AIDS was the fifth leading cause of death for white American women between the ages of 25 and 44, but AIDS was the most likely cause of death for black women in that age group (CDC Facts, 1995). An Hispanic woman is 7 times more likely than a white woman to get AIDS. A black woman is 16 times more likely.

Public education programs, hotlines, and clearinghouses have been established to disseminate information to mass audiences about how HIV is transmitted, what behaviors place one at risk for infection, and how infection can be prevented. More specific audiences, such as injecting drug users and women who have a high probability of having sexual partners who are HIV positive, have been an important focus of prevention activities such as outreach, risk-reduction programs, HIV antibody testing, and counseling programs (CDC Surveillance, 1995).

Women IDUs in methadone treatment comprise one of the most obvious targets for prevention efforts. Drug treatment programs have been a main focus of HIV prevention campaigns since confirmation in the mid-1980s that HIV is transmitted through blood by sharing needles. Treatment programs and in-house HIV prevention messages are an important vehicle for changing drug-using behaviors associated with the transmission of HIV (Liebman, Knezek, Coughey, & Hua, 1993). Yet treatment programs do not reach large numbers of substance abusers. In addition, programs have traditionally geared treatment for the white male substance abusers, leaving women and minorities less likely to fit the "model" (Mondanaro, 1989; Reed, 1985; Wallen, 1992). Innovations to reach hidden populations of IDUs and their sexual partners were developed as a response to the dramatic increases in the AIDS epidemic in these populations (Brown & Beschner, 1993). Street outreach became an important way to engage "hard-to-reach" populations such as the many substance abusers who were not in treatment (Wechsberg, Smith, & Harris-Adeeyo, 1992).

Large scale national programs to reach IDUs through outreach for HIV prevention have been successful in reducing HIV risk among these populations for many years now (Wiebel, Biernacki, Mulia, & Levin, 1993; Gross & Brown, 1993). Yet some studies have demonstrated that there are differences among IDUs who enter treatment and those who do not. For example, many IDUs contacted through outreach do not report chronic daily injecting patterns, yet they do report an extended history of injecting use with never seeking treatment (Wechsberg, Dennis, Cavanaugh, & Rachal, 1993). Preliminary studies involving women injectors have also demonstrated important differences in injecting practices and HIV risk behaviors between those in and out of treatment (Wechsberg, 1994; Wechsberg, Dennis, & Ying, 1995).

These studies suggest the need to further identify specific differences among women injectors so that future intervention efforts may target women more effectively. To that end, this study examines two samples of women IDUs, one consisting of women who have entered methadone treatment and the other consisting of women encountered in outreach. We compare the two samples on the basis of drug injecting practices, sexual behavior, and HIV risk behaviors.

METHODS

We examined data on women IDUs encountered in outreach during the National AIDS Demonstration Research (NADR) in four cities as well as data from the Methadone Enhanced Treatment (MET) study in the same four cities. Respondents were interviewed when they were first encountered in outreach or as they entered the methadone program. To minimize the effect of any differences caused by the initial interviews being conducted at different times, only data from the time periods when both the outreach and treatment programs in a site were conducting interviews were compared. The data collection period varied slightly by site, but the overall time period was from November 1989 to December 1991.

Respondents in both the outreach and treatment programs were interviewed using the AIDS Initial Assessment (AIA) instrument (National Institute on Drug Abuse [NIDA], 1988). These structured interviews were designed to assess the patterns, frequency, and route of drug use as well as risk for contracting or spreading HIV through drug use and sexual behavior. Assessment of these variables allows for identification of differences between out-of-treatment women injectors (NADR) and those enrolled in methadone treatment (MET).

For purposes of ongoing analysis, the sample consists of respondents for whom both intake and follow-up data is available; however, this study is cross-sectional only. The methadone treatment sample consists of 204 women IDUs drawn from four methadone treatment programs, one in each of four cities. Similarly, the outreach sample consists of 394 women IDUs drawn from four outreach programs, one in each of the same four cities. The data from the AIA are largely categorical with discrete variables such as drug patterns, frequency of use, and descriptive data presented in proportions. Therefore analysis was typically performed with chi-squares for testing differences between the two groups of women.

RESULTS

Sociodemographic Comparison

Although the pattern of age distribution was similar for both groups, significant differences were found with regard to race/ethnicity, employment status, and legal status (Table 1). African American women comprised a much larger percentage of the outreach group than of the methadone group. The methadone women were more likely than the outreach women to classify themselves as homemakers, disabled, or not in the labor force for other reasons. Both groups had similarly low formal educational levels, and a large majority of women in both groups were on welfare. The methadone women were also more likely to have been involved in illegal activities in the past 6 months.

Years Since First Injection and Treatment History

Both groups of women reported a long history of injecting drug use after their first injection of any drug (Table 2). Over 50% in both groups reported first injecting 11 years ago or more, although individuals had not necessarily used continuously since their first injection. Despite the long history of use for both groups, large differences were found in their use of drug treatment services. The methadone women reported multiple episodes of treatment; more than half reported being admitted to some type of drug treatment program three or more times. In contrast, more than half of the outreach women (54%) reported never having been in treatment.

Non-Injecting Drug Use in the Past 6 Months

As shown in Table 3, these two groups of women IDUs demonstrated many more differences than similarities in their daily use of drugs in the previous 6 months; similarities, however, are more evident in their less-than-daily use. The outreach women who drank alcohol were significantly more likely to be daily drinkers (24%) than were the methadone women (16%), but similar proportions (58% methadone, 53% outreach) reported less-than-daily alcohol use. More than twice as many outreach women reported daily use of non-injecting cocaine by itself (10% outreach, 4% methadone), but similar proportions reported less-than-daily use (29% outreach, 28% methadone). Small proportions reported any non-injecting heroin use, but the methadone women reported slightly more daily (6%) and less-than-daily (8%) use than the outreach women (3% in both categories). More outreach women also reported smoking crack daily (12%) and

TABLE 1. Demographic Comparison of Women IDUs

	Methadone (N = 204)	Outreach (N = 394)
Age		
Under 30 years old	25%	27%
30-35 years old	37%	37%
36 years old and over	38%	36%
Race/Ethnicity***		
White (non-Hispanic)	56%	16%
African-American	35%	83%
Hispanic	9%	1%
Employment Status ***		
Working 35+ hours a week	13%	12%
Unemployed	49%	68%
On welfare	70%	73%
Education		
Less than high school graduate	58%	53%
Legal Status***		
Involved in illegal activities	41%	13%

***$p < .001$

less than daily (27%) than did women in methadone treatment (4% and 21% respectively).

Injecting Drug Use in the Past 6 Months

As shown in Table 4, the methadone women were far more likely than the outreach women to have injected any drugs (including heroin) daily (94% vs. 24%) in the past 6 months. On the other hand, the outreach women were more likely to report less-than-daily injecting (76% vs. 6%). As expected, the methadone women reported a greater daily use of injecting heroin (89% vs. only 10% for the outreach women), and the outreach women again reported more less-than-daily use (25%) than the methadone women (9%). For other opiates, the methadone women consistently reported both greater daily use (12% vs. 1%) and less-than-daily use (25%

TABLE 2. Years Since First Injection and Treatment History by Women IDUs

	Methadone (N = 204)	Outreach (N = 394)
Years of Injecting[1]		
1-5	19%	23%
6-10	20%	19%
11-15	24%	19%
16-20	23%	22%
21+	14%	18%
Treatment Admissions[2]***		
None	12%	54%
Ever	88%	46%
Three episodes or greater	61%	21%

[1]Years of injecting was derived from age of any first injecting use of heroin, cocaine, or heroin and cocaine together; it does not account for periods of abstinence.
[2]Includes drug detoxification, residential or therapeutic community, methadone, outpatient drug free, or prison program.
***$p < .001$

TABLE 3. Non-Injecting Drug Use in the Last 6 Months by Women IDUs

Drug Use	Methadone (N = 204)	Outreach (N = 394)
Alcohol		
Less than Daily	58%	53%
Daily	16%	24%
Non-injecting Cocaine		
Less than Daily	28%	29%
Daily	4%	10%
Non-injecting Heroin**		
Less than Daily	8%	3%
Daily	6%	3%
Crack use***		
Less than Daily	21%	27%
Daily	4%	12%

**$p < .01$
***$p < .001$

TABLE 4. Injecting Drug Use in the Last 6 Months by Women IDUs

Injecting Drug Use	Methadone (N = 204)	Outreach (N = 394)
Any injecting drug use*** Less than Daily Daily	6% 94%	76% 24%
Heroin*** Less than Daily Daily	9% 89%	25% 10%
Other Opiates*** Less than Daily Daily	25% 12%	10% 1%
Speedball*** Less than Daily Daily	36% 40%	16% 5%
Cocaine*** Less than Daily Daily	50% 23%	29% 18%

***p < .001

vs. 10%) than the outreach women. The percentages were larger for both groups for speedball (injecting of heroin and cocaine), but the methadone women reported greater use, both daily (40%) and less than daily (36%), than the outreach women (5% and 16%, respectively). For cocaine, on the other hand, the proportions reporting daily use were more nearly equal (23% methadone, 18% outreach), while there were greater differences in less-than-daily use (50% methadone, 29% outreach).

Injecting Practices with Others

The behaviors associated with injecting drugs with others are the main cause of the escalation of HIV infection among IDUs. Understanding variations in specific injecting risk behaviors among the women is important for designing appropriate interventions. Table 5 reports behavior in the previous 6 months, including who the women shared needles with, how often they shared (never, sometimes, always), and how often they injected alone. Because the risk of becoming infected with HIV is less for the initial injector (the person who injects first and then passes the needle on), the table also indicates the percentage of women who reported that they always passed the needle on to their partners after injecting.

A large majority (72%) of the outreach women reported that they never shared needles with their sexual partners, 20% reported doing so some-times, while only 8% said they always shared. In contrast, among the methadone women, only 38% reported never sharing, while a substantial 28% said they always shared. In both groups, the percentage of women injecting first was relatively low: 13% for the methadone group and an even smaller 4% for the outreach group.

Similarly, a large majority of the outreach women (79%) reported that they never shared needles with their running partners; only 3% reported they always shared, while less than 1% reported always injecting first. In contrast, only slightly more than half of the methadone women (51%) reported never sharing needles with running partners, while 10% reported doing so always. Only 7% reported always being the initial user. For both groups, the percentages for sharing with friends are similar to those for running partners. Only relatively small percentages of women in each group reported ever shooting with strangers (16% methadone, 7% outreach).

Although women in both groups reported injecting alone, 60% of the outreach women reported they never injected alone, compared to only 17% of the methadone women. The percentages of those who always injected alone were similar for both groups (16% methadone, 14% out-reach), but 67% of the methadone women reported sometimes injecting alone, compared to only 26% of the outreach women.

In general, then, the women in treatment report much more sharing of needles than do the outreach women. While the outreach women do share needles, a relatively large percentage in each category report never shar-ing. Only very small percentages of women in both groups report always being the first injector.

Sharing Behaviors

Empirical evidence as to what sharing behaviors place one at greater risk is still being investigated. For the purposes of this study, however, any sharing of injecting equipment is considered risk behavior. Table 6 shows important differences between the two groups. While 81% of the outreach women reported that they never borrowed used needles, only half of the methadone women (50%) reported never borrowing. An even larger pro-portion of the outreach women (87%) reported never renting needles, compared to 66% of the methadone women.

The differences between the two groups are even greater with respect to sharing cookers and cotton. Among the outreach women, 67% reported never sharing while only 15% of the methadone women said they never shared. In addition, nearly a quarter of the methadone women (23%) re-ported that they always shared cookers and cotton, as compared to only 8%

TABLE 5. Injecting Practices with Others in Last 6 Months by Women IDUs

Needles Shared With	Methadone (N = 204)	Outreach (N = 394)
Sexual Partner***		
Never	38%	72%
Sometimes	35%	20%
Always	28%	8%
Initial Injector[1]***	13%	4%
Running Partner***		
Never	51%	79%
Sometimes	40%	18%
Always	10%	3%
Initial Injector[1]***	7%	.5%
Friends***		
Never	48%	76%
Sometimes	49%	22%
Always	3%	3%
Initial Injector[1]***	1.5%	.5%
Injecting Alone***		
Never	17%	60%
Sometimes	67%	26%
Always	16%	14%

[1]Reported always passing needle on after injecting.
***$p < .001$

of the outreach group. The percentages for sharing rinse water are similar: 25% of the methadone women reported never sharing rinse water, as compared to 71% of the outreach women. Nearly a fifth of the methadone women (19%) and 8% of the outreach women reported always sharing rinse water.

Although both groups are engaging in injecting behaviors that put them at risk for HIV, the methadone group is clearly at much higher risk. More-

TABLE 6. Sharing Behaviors in Last 6 Months by Women IDUs

	Methadone (N = 204)	Outreach (N = 394)
Borrowing Used Needles***		
Never	50%	81%
Sometimes	48%	18%
Always	1%	1%
Renting Used needles***		
Never	66%	87%
Sometimes	32%	13%
Always	1%	0%
Sharing Cooker and Cotton***		
Never	15%	67%
Sometimes	63%	24%
Always	23%	8%
Sharing Rinse Water***		
Never	25%	71%
Sometimes	56%	22%
Always	19%	8%

***$p < .001$

over, the percentage of women who reported never engaging in these behaviors is significantly higher in all categories for the outreach women.

Drug Risk Reduction Practices

Because the data reported here are based on initial interviews, they do not reflect the effects of intervention efforts. However, as Table 7 shows, some of the women were already engaging in behaviors to reduce their risk for HIV. Only 5% of the methadone women reported never using sterile needles, and almost 40% reported they use sterile needles all the time. Among these same women, however, only 8% reported throwing the sterile needle away after its initial use. By contrast, 59% of the outreach

TABLE 7. Drug Risk Reduction Practices in Last 6 Months by Women IDUs

Needle Practices	Methadone (N = 204)	Outreach (N = 394)
Using Sterile Needles***		
Never	5%	59%
Sometimes	56%	22%
Always	40%	19%
Getting Needles Legally		
Never	84%	82%
Sometimes	7%	8%
Always	9%	10%
Cleaned with Bleach and Water***		
Never	36%	78%
Sometimes	48%	15%
Always	16%	7%

***p < .001

women reported never using sterile needles, and only 19% said they always used them. As with the methadone group, however, only a small percentage (9%) reported throwing the sterile needle away after its initial use. There were no significant differences between the two groups with respect to obtaining needles legally: a large majority (over 80%) of both groups reported that they never did so.

The methadone women reported significantly greater cleaning behavior than the outreach women. While 78% of the outreach women reported never cleaning needles with bleach and water, only 36% of the methadone women said they never cleaned. However, only small percentages of both groups (16% for methadone and 7% for outreach) reported always cleaning.

In general, the methadone women reported more overall risk reduction practices than the outreach women, but the relatively low percentages of women reporting that they always engaged in these behaviors indicates continued risk for both groups.

Sexual Partners and Condom Use

Although women IDUs are primarily at risk for HIV through their injecting drug use, the lack of risk reduction in sexual behavior continues to be an area of concern. Many women IDUs are unmarried and sexually active with multiple partners. In a single year, about 15% of women in their thirties in the general U.S. population have two or more sex partners (Michael, Gagnon, Laumann, & Kolata, 1994), but 38% of the methadone women and 43% of the outreach women had two or more sexual partners in the past 6 months.

As Table 8 shows, there was very little difference between the two groups in their reported condom use. In both groups, the women with more than one sex partner were more likely to use condoms than women who reported monogamous relationships. However, more than half of the women with multiple partners in each group reported never using condoms. For both groups, only about one in ten women with multiple partners reported always using condoms.

DISCUSSION

Women IDUs are at high risk for HIV infection. Not only is HIV more prevalent in their drug use and sexual networks than in the general population but individuals within these networks tend to engage in behavior that puts others at risk for HIV. While women IDUs share some basic similarities, the results of this study point to important differences between those women who enter methadone treatment and those who are contacted through street outreach.

The study does have some limitations. Our two groups are not probability samples within each of the four metropolitan areas; nevertheless, they

TABLE 8. Condom Use in Last 6 Months by Women IDUs with Single and Multiple Partners

	Methadone	Outreach
Single Partner	**(N = 113)**	**(N = 207)**
Never	85%	82%
Sometimes	34%	34%
Always	4%	11%
Multiple partners	**(N = 70)**	**(N = 158)**
Never	56%	54%
Sometimes	11%	7%
Always	10%	11%

are probably representative of the large differences between outreach and methadone clients in large cities. Furthermore, the analyses are based on self-reported behaviors so that some unknown biases could be present. However, we are mainly concerned with comparing women found in outreach to women methadone clients, and if the self-reporting bias is similar across the two groups, then the large differences between the two groups are less biased since the similar within-group biases cancel out when the groups are compared.

Previous studies on reliability and validity with current drug users further explain some of the limitations of this study (Harrison, 1995). Nevertheless, the data clearly suggest substantial similarities and differences between these two groups of women. The two groups are essentially similar with respect to age, education, employment status (most are on welfare), and the age at which they first injected. The outreach group, however, is comprised of a large majority of African Americans, suggesting the need for more culturally relevant interventions for this group.

The methadone women, in general, have extensive treatment histories, while many of the outreach women have never been in treatment. It is probable, therefore, that the outreach women are less aware of HIV risk than the methadone women, suggesting that outreach women may benefit from a much more basic pretreatment intervention than would be appropriate for the methadone women.

Overall, the methadone women tend to inject more frequently and share needles more often, particularly with their sexual partners. The data on injecting frequency, drug use, injecting practices, and sharing practices all suggest that the outreach women do not inject as much or share as much as the methadone women. On the other hand, the outreach women do tend to use more alcohol, non-injecting cocaine, and crack, behaviors which may put them at greater sexual risk. Moreover, although the outreach women do not tend to be chronic daily injectors, even occasional injecting puts them at risk, particularly when they report injecting with others more often than alone. The data suggest the possibility that the outreach women who inject infrequently may do so recreationally and with a variety of partners. Although the methadone women also reported injecting with others, they report significantly more injecting alone, possibly out of need to maintain their addiction and ward off sickness. It may be that interventions need to be tailored more precisely to their social patterns of drug use and to the relative HIV risk that still exists.

The data indicate that the methadone women are much more careful in using sterile needles and cleaning needles before use than the outreach women. This suggests that the outreach women are in particular need of basic education on the importance and correct methods of cleaning their injection equipment. However, methadone women still report substantial sharing of cookers, cotton, and rinse water, suggesting the need for continuing education on the risk posed by these items. Moreover, with their greater frequency of injection, it is not surprising that the methadone women tend to borrow used needles more than the outreach women. This suggests the need for careful consideration of the policy question of providing legal access to needles for IDUs. Studies in needle exchange (Normand, Vlahov, & Moses, 1995) have addressed the importance of accessibility to needles without increasing drug use.

The fact that only small percentages in both groups of women reported always passing their used needles on to their partners suggests the possibility that a power dynamic between men and women may be involved not only in who cops the drugs but also in who gets the first injection. If so, then interventions addressing this issue need to be tailored to both women and men IDUs, and education strategies need to be devised to help them negotiate risk reduction without making the women more vulnerable.

Despite the elevated HIV risk for women in both groups due to having multiple sexual partners, and with the high probability that these sexual partners also come from high risk groups, the women reported lower rates of condom use than respondents in a study of the general U.S. population (Michael et al., 1994, p. 197). Women in both groups had far more sexual partners than women in their age brackets in the general population. Nevertheless, women in neither group consistently used condoms to protect themselves and their partners against sexually transmitted diseases. All women IDUs, no matter what setting, may need educational programs and easily accessible gynecological services to protect themselves against pregnancy and disease. Many may also need culturally sensitive women's programs to teach them how to assert themselves against forces that threaten their well-being.

Although this is a cross-sectional study, it suggests the possibility that women IDUs reached by methadone treatment programs and outreach services may be so different that positively influencing their risk behaviors may require strategies specifically tailored to each group. Our findings suggest, for example, that new prevention goals should consider culturally appealing and appropriate materials for use in outreach where more African American women are contacted. Many of these outreach women may be poorly matched for existing treatment programs because they are less involved in drug injecting than the methadone women. However, recent studies stress that women encountered in outreach and reporting substantial crack use are at the greatest sexual risk for HIV infection (McCoy & Inciardi, 1993; Wechsberg, Dennis, & Stevens, 1996).

New HIV-prevention and drug-treatment strategies need to be devised which take into account the differences between these at-risk women. In structuring interventions that will have the greatest positive impact, we need to be particularly aware of the various types of risk to which these women are exposed, and we need to realize that the risk is not the same for all of them. While it is important to continue HIV prevention efforts among women found both in street outreach and in drug treatment programs, the patterns of risk found in this study suggest that HIV prevention strategies may be most effective when they address specific drug risk; moreover, the continuing sexual risk evident among these women suggests the need to explore new and evolving sexual risk reduction methods.

REFERENCES

Amaro, H. (1995). Love, sex, and power. Considering women's realities in HIV prevention. *American Psychologist, 50*(6), 437-447.

Brown, B.S., & Beschner, G.M. (Eds.). (1993). *Handbook on risk for AIDS: Injection drug users and their sexual partners.* Westport, CT: Greenwood Press.

Centers for Disease Control and Prevention (CDC). (1995, February 13). *Facts about women and HIV/AIDS.* Rockville, MD: CDC National AIDS Clearing-house.

Centers for Disease Control and Prevention (CDC). (1995). *HIV/AIDS Surveillance Report.* Vol. 7, No. 2. Atlanta, GA: Centers for Disease Control and Prevention.

Gross, M., & Brown, V. (1993). Outreach to injection drug-using women. In B.S. Brown, G.M. Beschner (Eds.), *Handbook on risk for AIDS: Injection drug users and their sexual partners.* Westport, CT: Greenwood Press.

Harrison, L.D. (1995). The validity of self-reported data on drug use. *Journal of Drug Issues, 25,* 91-111.

Liebman, J., Knezek, L., Coughey, K., & Hua, S. (1993). Injection drug users, drug treatment, and HIV risk behavior. In B.S. Brown & G.M. Beschner (Eds.), *Handbook on risk for AIDS: Injection drug users and their sexual partners.* Westport, CT: Greenwood Press.

McCoy, H.V., & Inciardi, J.A. (1993). Women and AIDS: Social determinants of sex-related activities. *Women & Health, 20*(1), 69-86.

Michael, R.T., Gagnon, J.H., Laumann, E.O., & Kolata, G. (1994). *Sex in America.* New York: Little Brown and Company.

Mondanaro, J. (1989). *Chemically dependent women: Assessment and treatment.* Lexington, MA: Lexington Books.

National Institute on Drug Abuse (NIDA). (1988). *AIDS Initial Assessment Questionnaire.* Rockville, MD: NIDA Community Research Branch.

Normand, J., Vlahov, D., & Moses, L.E. (1995). *Preventing HIV transmission: The role of sterile needles and bleach.* Washington, DC: National Academy Press.

Reed, B.G. (1985). Drug misuse and dependency in women: The meaning and implications of being considered a special population or minority group. *International Journal of Addictions, 13,* 863-885.

Wallen, J. (1992). A comparison of male and female clients in substance abuse treatment. *Journal of Substance Abuse Treatment, 9,* 243-248.

Wechsberg, W.M. (1994, September). *Lessons from the past with future implications: HIV risk differences found among samples of women IDUs in and out of treatment and those lost to follow-up.* Poster presented at the 2nd Science Symposium on Drug Abuse, Sexual Risk, & AIDS: Prevention Research 1995-2000, Flagstaff, AZ.

Wechsberg, W.M., Dennis, M.L., & Stevens S.J. (1996, July). *AIDS outreach/intervention for risk reduction among women substance abusers: Trends, outcomes, and future implications.* Presentation at the International AIDS Conference, Vancouver, BC, Canada.

Wechsberg, W.M., Dennis, M.L., & Ying, Z. (1995, November). *Women and men injectors: Differences and trends in their drug use patterns and HIV risk.* Presentation at the meeting of the American Public Health Association, San Diego.

Wechsberg, W.M., Dennis, M.L., Cavanaugh, E.R., & Rachal, J.V. (1993). A comparison of injecting drug users reached through outreach and methadone treatment. *Journal of Drug Issues, 23,* 667-687.

Wechsberg, W.M., Smith, F.J., & Harris-Adeeyo, T. (1992). AIDS education and outreach to I.V. drug users and the community: Strategies and results. *Psychology of Addictive Behaviors, 6*(2), 107-113.

Wiebel, W.W., Biernacki, P., Mulia, N., & Levin, L. (1993). Outreach to IDUs not in treatment. In B.S. Brown, G.M. Beschner (Eds.), *Handbook on risk for AIDS: Injection drug users and their sexual partners.* Westport, CT: Greenwood Press.

Ethnic and Cultural Differences in Drug-Using Women Who Are In and Out of Treatment

Sally J. Stevens, PhD
Antonio L. Estrada, PhD
Peggy J. Glider, PhD
Robin A. McGrath, CSAC

SUMMARY. In recent years, increasing emphasis has been placed on race, ethnicity and culture as they relate to recruitment into and retention in substance abuse treatment as well as treatment effectiveness. Racial/ethnic and cultural differences were studied among women participating in two programs located within a large southwestern city. One of these programs was residential treatment for drug-using women and the other program provided street outreach for HIV prevention/education to drug-using women. Significant differences were found among racial/ethnic groups within each program and between the two programs. Differences were explored for the following factors: marital status; education; age at entry into the program; drug use history; drug treatment history; current use pat-

---

Sally J. Stevens, Antonio L. Estrada, and Peggy J. Glider are affiliated with the University of Arizona. Robin A. McGrath is affiliated with the National Development and Research Institutes.

Address correspondence to: Sally J. Stevens, PhD, 3912 South 6th Avenue, Tucson, AZ 85714.

This work was supported by the National Institute on Drug Abuse, Grant # 1 U01 DA0 7470 and Center for Substance Abuse Treatment, Grant # 1 H86 SF0 5696.

[Haworth co-indexing entry note]: "Ethnic and Cultural Differences in Drug-Using Women Who Are In and Out of Treatment." Stevens, Sally J. et al. Co-published simultaneously in *Drugs & Society* (The Haworth Press, Inc.) Vol. 13, No. 1/2, 1998, pp. 81-95; and: *Women and Substance Abuse: Gender Transparency* (ed: Sally J. Stevens, and Harry K. Wexler) The Haworth Press, Inc., 1998, pp. 81-95. Single or multiple copies of this article are available for a fee from The Haworth Document Delivery Service [1-800-342-9678, 9:00 a.m. - 5:00 p.m. (EST). E-mail address: getinfo@haworthpressinc.com].

terns; injection rates; history of arrests and exchange of sex for drugs. The authors conclude with a discussion of these differences and their potential ramifications for conducting future research and in developing/implementing effective prevention and treatment programs. *[Article copies available for a fee from The Haworth Document Delivery Service: 1-800-342-9678. E-mail address: getinfo@haworthpressinc.com]*

In recent years, increasing emphasis has been placed on race, ethnicity and culture as they relate to recruitment into and retention in substance abuse treatment as well as treatment effectiveness. Ethnicity, race and culture often are used interchangeably. Race has been defined as a group that is *socially* defined on the basis of *physical* criteria (Van den Berghe, 1967). Ethnic groups are groups of individuals who share some culture or are descendants of such people who identify themselves and/or are identified by others as belonging to the same involuntary group (Isajiw, 1974). Webster's dictionary defines culture as the totality of socially-transmitted behavior patterns, arts, beliefs, institutions and all other products of human work and thought typical of a population or a community at a given point in time. In examining this definition, race/ethnicity does not appear as a defining characteristic nor is culture tied to this type of grouping. Culture is an evolving, dynamic phenomenon which is shaped by social, psychological and historical processes (Szapocnik, 1995).

Cheung (1990-91) stated that ethnicity is one of the most popular independent variables in the study of alcohol and other drug use. Many findings have indicated differential use among ethnic groups. This relationship has not, however, been thoroughly examined. There have been two major limitations: (1) methodological problems facing studies of other correlates of alcohol and other drug use and (2) the failure to adequately deal with the complexity of ethnicity and culture. This has led to inadequate conceptualization and operational treatment of ethnicity and culture within the substance abuse literature (Cheung, 1990-91).

Most studies have been descriptive and have offered no theoretical explanation for racial/ethnic differences (Johnson & Nishi, 1976). Cheung stated that ethnicity/culture was still a relevant issue as little progress had been made in moving beyond the descriptive level (Cheung, 1990-91). This lack of depth in looking at the phenomena of ethnicity and culture has a direct bearing on the development of quality programs to serve diversified participants. For programming to be effective, an understanding of the values and norms regrading alcohol and other drug use embedded in different racial/ethnic groups and cultures is critical.

Unfortunately, relatively little is known about the meaning that substances hold in the everyday lives of users, and even less is known about the ways in which their use is related to the social and economic institutions of communities (Clatts, 1993). In order to adequately understand the motivations which underpin the use of substances and the relationship of substance use to other risk behaviors such as unprotected sex, research must examine the experiential functions which the use of these drugs accomplish (discrimination, poverty–necessitating participation in particular sexual roles which are demeaning and exploitive). Effective therapeutic approaches to drug dependency among women is likely to be contingent upon alternative modalities in which to explore such motivations.

In some cases, racial/ethnic comparisons provide useful descriptive information on patterns of drug use. In other cases, basic comparisons by race/ethnicity can be misleading because they do not account for differences in the social environment experienced by community residents or for other determinants of illicit drug use. Sometimes, these comparisons result in reinforcing racial prejudices and drawing public attention away from community characteristics or other factors that may serve better to explain patterns of drug use (Lillie-Blanton, Anthony & Schuster, 1993).

Lillie-Blanton and colleagues (1993) looked at the data from the 1988 National Household Survey on Drug Abuse (NIDA, 1990) which reported lifetime crack cocaine use was twice as high for African-American and Hispanic respondents than for Caucasians. The authors suggest that these reported differences in drug use patterns between African-American, Hispanic and Caucasian crack cocaine users might be an artifact of macrosocial environmental risk factors (social forces that operate at the societal rather than the individual level, have their origin in constructs such as what is valued by people, the strength of the belief and the extent that the individual experiences his/herself as part of the larger social organism). Community level variables include such factors as the availability of drugs in the neighborhood while macrosocial variables include employment rates, premature death rates, community contact with the criminal justice system, distribution of wealth and access to social resources. The authors re-analyzed the 1988 data, controlling for these variables statistically and found no significant differences among the three racial/ethnic groups. Those neighborhoods with at least one crack user, when compared to neighborhoods with no crack users, had a larger share of racial/ethnic minorities, more young and middle-aged adults (12-39 years of age) and were concentrated in large metropolitan areas or in the western United States.

The authors suggested that researchers need to give greater attention to analysis and the presentation of data. Ignoring other contributing factors may lead to ineffective prevention/intervention strategies.

Romero, Argulles and Rivero (1993) discussed how generally-used categories such as Latina and Hispanic cover groups with diverse history, ethnic mix, gender socialization and immigration status. Understanding this diversity is critical to developing and providing effective education and treatment services, for these differences influence an individual's perceived personal power and her ability to effect changes in her life. This categorization has been called "ethnic gloss" by Trimble (1990-91) who believes that this gives little sense of the richness and cultural variation within groups. He claims that these are not meaningful units in a sociocultural sense.

Sylvia Orlarte, chair of the National Committee of Hispanic Psychiatrists, discussed the importance of developing a cross-cultural understanding (Cody, 1995). Cultural competence is especially important because by the year 2000, Caucasians will make up less than half of the United States' population (20 percent will be Latino and 12 percent will be African-American). She further states that therapists must be aware of their client's heritage and perceptions.

A study of the life histories of African-American substance-abusing women (Lewis, 1993) found several common themes which were considered pertinent to effective treatment (i.e., recruitment into and dynamics of drug use, the role of fellow addicts and family members in patterns of addiction and risk-taking, and the women's attitudes toward health and risk). All women in the study (regardless of socio-economic status) grew up in primarily African-American neighborhoods with pervasive drug use and the use of drugs was one dimension of their relationship with family, schoolmates and boyfriends. These women were generally drawn into drug use by people they trusted and initially viewed the drug use as an exciting and "in" thing to do. All of the women in this study said that family was important and they felt that they had at least one family member they could count on if they needed help.

Application of this understanding to effective programming was also studied by Kalichman and colleagues (1993). These authors demonstrated that minority women had a stronger tendency to underestimate their risk for HIV/AIDS and had greater levels of misinformation. These differences may be due to the lack of cultural and personal relevance in the AIDs prevention messages. It was hypothesized that knowledge acquisition and threat sensitization would be increased through culturally and personally-relevant programming and this would lead participants to contemplate behavior change. The results of this study supported the hypotheses (those in the cultural condition were more likely to identify AIDS as a personal threat and two weeks later reported changed behaviors consistent with this belief of personal threat (18% sought HIV testing vs. none in non-cultural group). The authors concluded that cultural values related to ethnicity, family and community influenced the women's perceptions of their risk and the behaviors they engaged in to protect themselves. Therefore, HIV prevention efforts and antibody testing campaigns may benefit from both using presenters matched for ethnicity with the target populations and linking behavior change recommendations to values that are important and culturally-relevant to the target populations.

Aguilar, DiNitto, Franklin and Lopez-Dilkinton (1991) found that Hispanic women who drank were stigmatized because this behavior conflicts with the ideal role of mother and wife. This stigmatization may lead to lack of recognition of the problem and delayed/nonexistent seeking of help. Within this ethnic culture, there is high family cohesion and women with substance abuse problems may either seek a solution within the family or totally external from the family network (due to shame). These women tended to use naturally supportive treatment methods/techniques which respected (not violated) family norms and protected their ethnic integrity. They were also more likely to ask for/respond to help for their child than for themselves.

To further explore questions of racial/ethnic and cultural differences among substance-abusing women, the participants in two programs located within a large southwestern city were studied: (1) women in a residential treatment program and (2) women identified through a street outreach program for HIV prevention/education. The following is a description of the women as they entered these programs. A number of variables were examined, looking for differences among the four racial/ethnic groups present. These variables may be of importance when designing programs for substance-abusing women from various ethnic/cultural backgrounds.

For the women recruited through the street outreach program, the racial/ethnic breakdown for the sample of 397 women was as follows: 36% Hispanic; 33% Caucasian; 18% African-American and 13% Native American. For the 150 women in residential treatment, the racial/ethnic breakdown was as follows: 61% Caucasian; 18% African-American; 14% Hispanic and 7% Native American.

Marital status showed significant differences among the racial/ethnic groups in the street outreach program ($p < .00005$) but not for the residential treatment program. Combining women into three categories (single, married, other), 46% of Hispanic women, 43% of African-American women and 42% of Native American women were single compared to 17% of Caucasian women in the street outreach program. There were greater differences among racial/ethnic groups for those who were married: 24% of African-American women; 29% of Hispanic women; 32% of Native American women and 41% of Caucasian women reporting. For those in residential treatment, the largest percentage for each racial/ethnic group was single (42% Caucasian, 62% Hispanic, 67% African-American and 82% Native American. For all groups except Caucasians, the next most frequent status category was married (29% Hispanic, 19% African-American and 18% Native American). Caucasians reported a higher rate of the other category (divorced/separated/widowed) at 32%.

Differences in educational attainment were statistically significant for both programs (p < .000 for street program; p < .038 for residential treatment). Responses were broken into two categories for analysis: less than high school and high school/GED or beyond. In both programs, the majority of Caucasians (73%) had a high school education or beyond. This pattern was reversed for Native Americans who had a majority (72%) in the less than high school group in both programs. While about half of African-American women in the street program fell into each group, almost three quarters (74%) of the African-American women in the residential program had a high school education or beyond. This pattern was reversed for Hispanic women with about two-thirds (62%) of the women in the street outreach program having less than a high school education and about half of the women in residential treatment falling in each group.

Age at entry showed considerable differences between the two programs, with participants of the street outreach program being older (average age ranged from 32 years for Hispanic women and 33 years for Native American women to 35 years for both African-American women and Caucasian women). Women in the residential program ranged from an average of 27 years for Hispanic and Native American women to 30 years for both African-American and Caucasian women.

In addition to demographics, variables related to substance use, treatment history, involvement with the criminal justice system and the exchange of sex for drugs were also investigated. Each of these is described below.

Age of first use is generally expected to vary between types of substances with alcohol being first (entry level drug since it is legal, easily available and relatively inexpensive), leading to marijuana (gateway substance) and then to the "harder" substances such as cocaine or heroin (Wambach et al., 1992). This pattern was found for all racial/ethnic groups in the street outreach program with alcohol and marijuana use beginning much earlier than other substances. Average age of first alcohol and marijuana use was the same for Caucasians, Hispanics and Native Americans.

Alcohol use began around 15 years of age with marijuana use beginning about six months later. For African-Americans in the street outreach program, the average ages of first alcohol and first marijuana use were both around 17 years. These differences between the African-Americans and the other racial/ethnic groups were significant (p < .000 and p < .028 respectively). More variance was found among the groups in the street outreach program when looking at average age of first use of crack/cocaine which ranged from 24 years for Hispanics to 26 years for Native Americans and 27 years for both Caucasians and African-Americans) (p < .05) and heroin which ranged from 22 years for Hispanics, 23 years for Native Americans and Caucasians to 27 years for African-Americans (p < .05).

For all substances and for all racial/ethnic groups, the average age of first use was younger for women in residential treatment. As with the women in the outreach program, the African-American women in residential treatment began use of each substance at a later age. Use of alcohol began around 14 years (16 years for African-Americans). Unlike the pattern usually reported in the literature, marijuana use began earlier than alcohol use for Hispanics and Native Americans (13 years), at the same age for Caucasians (14 years) and a year later (17 years) for African-American women in the residential program (p < .002). The largest discrepancies between the two samples were found in the average age of first cocaine/crack use with the ages for residential women ranging from 17 years for Native Americans, 19 years for Hispanics, 21 years for Caucasians to 22 years for African-Americans (compared to a range of 24-27 for street outreach participants). First heroin use was, in general, at least one year earlier for residential women (18 years for Native Americans, 23 years for Caucasians and Hispanics and 25 years for African-Americans).

Amount of substance use is also of interest when one is attempting to engage participants in a change process, i.e., the heavier the use, the more psychological or physical dependency may be present and, therefore, use behaviors may be harder to change. For women in the street outreach program, statistically significant differences were found in average use rates within the last 30 days for all substances except alcohol which ranged from 11 days for Caucasians, 12 days for Hispanics, 13 days for African-Americans to 14 days for Native Americans. Marijuana use was much lighter for African-American women (5 days) than Native Americans/Hispanics (9 days) and Caucasians (11 days) (p < .004). Crack and cocaine use (separated for this analysis) showed similar use rates for Hispanics (8 days). Heavier cocaine than crack use was found for both Caucasians (10 and 6 days respectively) and Native Americans (10 and 7 days respectively). The opposite pattern was found for African-American women who reported using cocaine an average of 3 days as compared to an average of 17 days for crack (p < .000). Average heroin use was also statistically less for African-American women (11 days) than for Caucasian women (17 days), Native American women (18 days) and Hispanic women (19 days) (p < .05).

Rates of use in the last 30 days were also analyzed for the women in the residential program; however, only two items focused on this issue: days used any drug other than alcohol and days used two or more drugs including alcohol. Statistically significant differences were found between groups on both items (p < .05 and p < .01 respectively). The average number of days for which women reported using any drug other than alcohol ranged from 10 for African-Americans, 15 for Native Americans, 18 for Caucasians to 20 for Hispanic women. Caucasian women reported the highest average number of days using two or more substances including alcohol (11 days) with Hispanic and African-American women both reporting 9 days and Native American women reporting 7 days.

Injection of drugs is an extremely important question given the risk for HIV infection, especially among women of racial/ethnic minorities who have over the past decade continued to show the greatest increase in HIV/AIDS cases among all groups. More drug injection data was available from the street outreach project due to the nature of the project as HIV prevention/education. Injection rates varied by type of drug and by racial/ethnic groups. African-American women had lower injection rates than all other groups for cocaine (2 days vs. 7 days for Hispanics, 9 days for Caucasians and 10 days for Native Americans) (p < .000) and heroin (11 days vs. 17 days for Caucasians, 18 days for Native Americans and 19 days for Hispanics) (p < .041). While there were differences for injection rates of speedballs (5 days for African-Americans, 8 days for Caucasians and Native Americans and 10 days for Hispanics), these did not reach statistical significance. Injection rates of all other substances were extremely low for all groups (1 day or less) with the exception of amphetamines for Caucasians (average of 4 days).

Injection of drugs was asked in the residential program for only the substance which was their biggest problem (yes/no for injection as route of administration). No statistically significant differences were found between racial/ethnic groups for injection of any substance; however, rate of injection did vary by substance. Although crack/cocaine was reported as the primary problem substance for most women in each group, only 5% (n = 1) of African-American women and 17% (n = 5) of Caucasian women reported injecting. Injection of heroin was high for Caucasians (88%, n = 15) and for Hispanics (100%, n = 5) with no African-Americans or Native Americans reporting this substance as their biggest problem. For women who reported amphetamines as their biggest problem, fifty percent (n = 1) of Native American women and 62% (n = 13) of Caucasians reported injecting. Overall, Caucasian women reported the highest rates of injecting drugs (49% total).

Treatment history varied by type of treatment among the four groups. Among the various modalities, African-American women from the street outreach program reported an average of 5 weeks for residential treatment, 3 weeks for methadone maintenance, 2 weeks for prison/jail treatment and 1 week for both drug-free outpatient and methadone detox. Caucasian women in street outreach reported an average of 19 weeks in methadone maintenance, 6 weeks in both methadone detox and residential treatment, 3 weeks in drug-free outpatient and .2 weeks in prison/jail treatment. Average rates for Hispanics and Native Americans in the street outreach program were fairly similar for methadone maintenance and prison/jail treatment (1 and 0 weeks respectively) but varied for other modalities. Hispanic women reported 1 week for residential treatment, .5 weeks for methadone detox and .2 weeks for drug-free outpatient while Native American women reported 1 week for residential treatment and metha-done detox and .2 weeks for drug-free outpatient.

Data for the women in residential treatment provides information on number of times in their lifetime that women were in residential treatment for alcohol or drugs, detox for alcohol or drugs and any other type of alcohol or drug treatment. No significant differences were found among the racial/ethnic groups for any of these items. Average times in residential treatment for alcohol ranged from 2 times for African-Americans, Hispanics and Native Americans to 3 times for Caucasians. Average number of treatment episodes for drugs was 2 for all groups except Native Americans who reported an average of 1 treatment episode. For alcohol and drug detox, rates were higher for Caucasians (3 and 5 times in treatment respectively), with African-American women reporting an average of 2 times for each type, Hispanics an average of 1 time for each type and Native Americans reporting an average of 1 time for alcohol detox and 0 for drug detox. Average rates were also higher for Caucasians for times in other alcohol or drug treatment (5 and 4 times respectively). African-American women reported an average of 3 times in other alcohol treatment and 2 times in other drug treatment. Hispanic women reported the same rate for both types of treatment (3 times) as did Native American women (2 times).

Due to the close connection between substance use/abuse and involve-ment with the criminal justice system, data related to criminal justice involvement was analyzed. Average number of arrests was higher for most groups in residential treatment than for the street outreach program (16 and 5 respectively for African-American women, 10 and 3 respectively for Caucasians and 14 and 4 respectively for Hispanics). The pattern was reversed for Native American women with higher rates for street outreach (7) than for women in residential treatment (6). Age of first arrest was not available for women in the street outreach program. For those in residential treatment, the average age of first arrest was 19 for Caucasian and Hispanic women, 18 for African-American women and 17 for Native American women.

The final variable for which comparisons were made was the exchange of sex for drugs. Women were asked if they had ever exchanged sex for drugs (yes/no). The following percentages were found for women responding "yes" in the street outreach and residential treatment programs respectively: 37% vs. 67% for Hispanic women; 37% vs. 0% for African-Americans; 35% vs. 48% for Caucasian women and 29% vs. 50% for Native Americans.

The above data bring several interesting points to the surface. First, the marital status data indicate a potential lack of consistent relationships for all racial/ethnic groups in both programs as percentages of those married ranged from 24% for African American women to 41% for Caucasian women in the street outreach program and from 18% for Native American women to 26% for Caucasian women in the residential program. These low percentages of married women in the residential program are particularly striking given that this program was for pregnant and post-partum women and their children. The lack of a supportive partner may impact the level of participation/length of stay in treatment for these women. Programs need to assist women to explore family dynamics and to identify sources of support which are culturally-appropriate.

The educational attainment data suggest that substance-abusing women, especially women from racial/ethnic minority groups, may have academic deficits which could affect the degree to which these women participate in program activities and how effective these activities are for them. Regardless of the type of program, the percentages of women who had less than a high school education ranged from 27% for Caucasian women to 72% for Native American women. These figures suggest that potentially one fourth of all participants may lack vocabulary, reading, communication or problem solving skills. Consequently, residential, street outreach and other programs that work with drug using women need to design their program curriculum to match the education level while also offering or encouraging women's advancement in this area.

The data on the age at entry into the program and age of first use of a variety of substances suggest that women in the residential treatment program had a more severe drug use history as they started use of each substance at an earlier age and entered treatment at a younger age, regardless of race/ethnicity. In both programs, use of alcohol and marijuana began early for all groups, ranging from age 14 to 17 for alcohol and age 13 to 18 for marijuana. It is interesting to note that African-American women consistently reported a later initiation into use of each type of drug, generally a 2 year lag. It is possible that something within the culture of these women may provide a protective factor through much of the teen years and an exploration of these protective factors might provide insight into prevention programming. In addition, it is important to note that not all women began use in their teens. This was especially true for first use of cocaine and heroin, both of which had several groups in each program with an average age of first use in the mid-twenties. This data supports the idea that prevention/education should not stop with young children but should be focused on multiple age groups. The days of use for each substance also showed variations with no one racial/ethnic group consistently reporting the highest use across substances and across programs. Again, there may be cultural factors which encourage or inhibit the use of certain substances. A clearer understanding of these factors would assist in the development of prevention and treatment programming that is culturally-appropriate.

Although differences were found among the four racial/ethnic groups of participants in both programs, it is difficult to determine how much of the differences reported by the groups is due to the cultures of the various ethnic groups vs. social opportunities, social biases, etc. For example, Caucasian women in the street outreach program had considerably higher numbers of past treatment episodes than did any of the other racial/ethnic groups. Additionally, the percentage of Caucasians enrolled in the residential treatment program was 61% compared to 38% in the street outreach program. The data on number of arrests and age of first arrest also shows differences with Caucasian women in both programs reporting fewer arrests than all other racial/ethnic groups, except for Native American women in the residential treatment program. Caucasian women were also older at the time of their first arrest (age 19 vs. age 17 for Native Americans and age 18 for African-Americans). Why these differences were found can not be determined from the data, however, questions do arise as to whether these data are due to: (1) bias in who is referred to treatment or arrested; (2) bias in who is accepted into treatment; (3) whether social barriers impact minorities' willingness to enter treatment, or (4) if there is a lack of culturally-appropriate treatment modalities for minority populations.

It is clear that culture goes beyond race/ethnicity (e.g., culture of women, streets, prostitution, prison, drug users, poverty, etc.). The field needs to begin looking at culture from a broader perspective. Women on the street may be more similar to each other (regardless of race/ethnicity) than women of the same race/ethnicity who have never shared this common street culture. This has been supported by the first and fourth authors, evaluator and director of the residential treatment program, who have observed that women within the program often congregate and build friendships on the basis of common experiences (i.e., prostitution, prison time) rather than racial/ethnic similarities.

Racial/ethnic lines may also be blurring within the substance-abusing culture. This is evidenced by the number of bi-racial children living with their mothers in the residential treatment program. Twenty-seven percent of the 116 children enrolled in the project between 1992 and 1996 were bi-racial with the largest number having a Caucasian mother and Hispanic father, closely followed by children with an African-American mother and Caucasian father. Moreover, this trend has been increasing. Of those enrolled in 1997, 39% of the 28 children were bi-racial. This further supports the importance of looking at the experiences of culture (in this case the culture of substance abuse brings together men and women of different racial/ethnic backgrounds) vs. limiting cultural discussions to issues of race/ethnicity.

The National Institutes on Drug Abuse (1994) focused on the culture of women, stating that women of all races and socioeconomic status suffer from the serious illness of drug addiction. Women of all races, income groups, levels of education and types of communities need treatment. Many women who use drugs have faced serious challenges to their well-being during their lives. For example, research indicates that about 70% of women who reported using drugs also reported having been abused sexually before the age of 16; and more than 80% had at least one parent addicted to alcohol or one or more illicit drugs. Often, women who use drugs have low self-esteem and little self-confidence and may feel powerless. They often feel lonely, isolated from positive support networks and less worthy of help than men in similar situations. In addition, ethnic/racial minority women may face additional cultural and language barriers that can affect or hinder their treatment and recovery. Many do not seek treatment because they fear not being able to take care of or to keep their children. They may also fear reprisal from their spouses or boyfriends, and fear punishment from authorities in the community. Many women report that their drug-using male sex partners initiated them into drug abuse and then sabotaged their efforts to quit using drugs.

The viewpoint of many researchers and service providers is that the treatment needs as well as HIV prevention needs of substance-abusing females have not been adequately met (Stevens & Glider, 1994; Stevens & Bogart, in press), and research has particularly ignored women who are injection drug users (Cohen, Hauer & Wofsy, 1989). Even though there are important differences between males and females in terms of life experiences, attitudes and self-perceptions, few programs have been designed to meet the gender specific needs of these women.

There is also a need to target factors other than the substance abuse problem among women users such as housing, employment and child care (McCoy & Inciardi, 1995; Reback & Melchior, 1992; Stevens & Bogart, in press). It is important to meet the client where she is, making an attempt to understand her perceived needs, offering genuine support and understanding, and systematically empowering her with skills and perceptions necessary for her to change and control her life (Wechsberg, 1995).

Perez-Arce, Carr and Sorensen (1993) focused on the types of interventions which were appropriate for various racial/ethnic and cultural groups. These authors stated that while confrontation therapy appeared to be useful for males regardless of race/ethnicity for Caucasians, African-Americans and Hispanics, this may be an inappropriate approach to use with females unless the confrontation style is varied to fit the communication and relational patterns of women. Regardless of gender, Native Americans place importance on inter-dependence of family or clan and respect for elders. They are generally non-assertive, non-spontaneous and soft spoken, with limited eye contact and self-disclosure. Native Americans, therefore, may not be well suited to group dynamics, especially confrontation (Perez-Arce, Carr & Sorensen, 1993).

In conclusion, the data from the two programs reviewed demonstrate variations in substance use patterns (age of first use, amount of use, injection and treatment history), demographics (education and marital status), involvement in the criminal justice system and involvement in the exchange of sex for drugs on the basis of race/ethnicity. What the data do not reflect are the underlying cultural factors which may have contributed to these differences, including the potential for a variety of cultures to be combined into the general racial/ethnic categories of Hispanic and Native-American. In addition, considerations such as the culture of women in general, women on the streets, women who have served time in prison and so on have been raised as important for programming and research but not addressed by the available data. It is suggested by these authors that such broader issues of culture must be considered when designing research studies to insure the appropriateness of the questions asked and the data collected. Such data would then assist in illuminating underlying cultural issues that are broader than race/ethnicity but not exclusive of it. Such data would provide enlightening information that can be used to development of more culturally-relevant and, therefore, more effective intervention/ treatment programs for substance-abusing women.

REFERENCES

Aguilar, M., DiNitto, D., Franklin, C. & Lopez-Dilkinton, B. (1991). Mexican-American families: A psycho-educational approach for addressing chemical dependency and co-dependency. *Child and Adolescent Social Work*, 8(4), 309-326.

Cheung, Y. W. (1990-91). Ethnicity and alcohol/drug use revisited: A framework for future research. *The International Journal of the Addictions*, 25 (5A & 6A), 581-605.

Clatts, M. (1993). Poverty, drug use, and AIDS: Converging issues in the life stories of women in Harlem. In B. Bair and S. Cayleff (Eds.), *Wings of Gauze: Women of Color and the Experience of Health and Illness*, Detroit, MI: Wayne State University Press, 328-339.

Cody, P. (Ed.) (1995). Women's and cultural issues. Key to treatment in the "90's". *Mental Health Report*, 19(21), 191-192.

Cohen, J., Hauer, L., & Wofsy, C. (1989). Women and IV drugs: Parental and heterosexual transmission of Human Immunodeficiency Virus. *The Journal of Drug Issues*, 19, 39-56.

Isajiw, W.W. (1974). Definitions of ethnicity. *Ethnicity*, 1, 11-124.

Johnson, B. D., & Nishi, S. M. (1976). Myths and realities of drug use by minorities. In P. Iiyama, S. M. Nishi & B.D. Johnson (Eds.), *Drug Use and Abuse Among U.S. Minorities: An Annotated Bibliography*, New York: Praeger.

Kalichman, S., Kelly, J., Hunter, T., Murphy, D., & Tyler, R. (1993). Culturally-tailored HIV-AIDS risk-reduction messages targeted to African-American urban women: Impact on risk sensitization and risk reduction. *Journal of Counseling and Clinical Psychology*, 61(1), 291-295.

Lewis, D. (1993). Living with the threat of AIDS: Perceptions of health and risk among African-American women IV drug users. In B. Bair and S. Cayleff (Eds.), *Wings of Gauze: Women of Color and the Experience of Health and Illness*, Detroit, MI: Wayne State University Press, 312-327.

Lillie-Blanton, M., Anthony, J., & Schuster, C. (1993). Probing the meaning of racial/ethnic group comparisons in crack cocaine smoking. *JAMA*, 269(8), 993-997.

McCoy, H.V., & Inciardi, J.A. (1993). Women and AIDS: Social determinants of sex-related activities. *Women & Health*, 20(1), 69-86.

National Institute on Drug Abuse (1990). National Household Survey on Drug

Abuse: Main Findings of 1988. Washington, D.C.: NIDA, US Department of Health and Human Services, Publication number ADM 90-1692.

National Institute on Drug Abuse (1994). *NIDA Capsules: Women and Drug Abuse*, Rockville, MD: NIDA Press Office.

Perez-Arce, P., Carr, K., & Sorensen, J. (1993). Cultural issues in an outpatient program for stimulant abusers. *Journal of Psychoactive Drugs*, 25(1), 35-44.

Reback, C.J., & Melchior, L.A. (1992, August). *Women at risk: Drug use, outreach and HIV intervention.* Paper presented at the American Sociological Association Meeting, Pittsburgh, PA.

Romero, G., Argulles, L., & Rivero, A. (1993). Latinas and HIV infection/AIDS: Reflections on impacts, dilemmas and struggles. In B. Bair and S. Cayleff (Eds.), *Wings of Gauze: Women of Color and the Experience of Health and Illness*, Detroit, MI: Wayne State University Press, 340-352.

Szapocznik, J. (1995). Research on disclosure of HIV status: Cultural evolution finds an ally in science. *Health Psychology*, 14(1), 4-5.

Stevens, S.J., & Bogart, J.G. (In press). Reducing HIV risk behaviors of drug involved women: Social, economic, medical and legal constraints. In W.N. Elwood (Ed.) *Power in the Blood: AIDS, Politics and Communication*, Praeger Publishers.

Stevens, S.J., & Glider, P. (1994). Therapeutic communities: Substance abuse treatment for women. In F. Tims, G. DeLeon and N. Jainchill (Eds.), *National Institute on Drug Abuse Research Monograph Series; Therapeutic Community: Advances in Research and Application. Technical Review on Therapeutic Communities*, NIDA Research Monograph 144, U.S.DHHS.

Trimble, J. (1990-91). Ethnic specification, validation prospects, and the future of drug use research. *International Journal of the Addictions*, 25(2A), 149-170.

Van den Berghe, P.L. (1976). *Race and Racism*, New York: Wiley.

Wambach, K., Byers, J., Harrison, D., Levine, P., Imershein, A., Quadagno, D., & Maddox, K. (1992). Substance use among women at risk for HIV infection. *Journal of Drug Education*, 22(2), 131-146.

Wechsberg, W. (1995). Strategies for working with women substance abusers. In B. Brown (Ed.), *Substance Abuse Treatment in the Era of AIDS*, Rockville, MD: Center for Substance Abuse Treatment, 119-152.

How Are Women Who Enter Substance Abuse Treatment Different Than Men?: A Gender Comparison from the Drug Abuse Treatment Outcome Study (DATOS)

Wendee M. Wechsberg, PhD
S. Gail Craddock, MS
Robert L. Hubbard, PhD

SUMMARY. Literature on gender differences among those entering substance abuse treatment is limited. Using data from intake interviews in a large multisite prospective clinical epidemiological study, this study provides the opportunity to explore gender differences with implications for treatment response. Comparisons are made not only between women and men but also between four different treatment modalities.

Traditional gender differences were found with regard to age,

Wendee M. Wechsberg is affiliated with the Research Triangle Institute, Research Triangle Park, NC 27709. S. Gail Craddock and Robert L. Hubbard are associated with the National Development and Research Institutes.

The authors wish to thank Bruce MacDonald for his tireless efforts.

This work was supported by the National Institute on Drug Abuse (NIDA) Grant Nos. 271-89-8233 and 1-P50-DA06990-01A. The interpretations and conclusions do not represent the position of NIDA or the Department of Health and Human Services.

[Haworth co-indexing entry note]: "How Are Women Who Enter Substance Abuse Treatment Different Than Men?: A Gender Comparison from the Drug Abuse Treatment Outcome Study (DATOS)." Wechsberg, Wendee M., S. Gail Craddock, and Robert L. Hubbard. Co-published simultaneously in *Drugs & Society* (The Haworth Press, Inc.) Vol. 13, No. 1/2, 1998, pp. 97-115; and: *Women and Substance Abuse: Gender Transparency* (ed: Sally J. Stevens, and Harry K. Wexler) The Haworth Press, Inc., 1998, pp. 97-115. Single or multiple copies of this article are available for a fee from The Haworth Document Delivery Service [1-800-342-9678, 9:00 a.m. - 5:00 p.m. (EST). E-mail address: getinfo@haworthpressinc.com].

97

education and employment. Although some drug use patterns were similar, men reported more alcohol use while women reported more daily use of cocaine. Women reported more problems related to health and mental health. In addition, women reported much greater proportions of past and current physical and sexual abuse. Women also reported greater concerns about issues related to children, although both women and men reported concern about drug treatment affecting custody of children. *[Article copies available for a fee from The Haworth Document Delivery Service: 1-800-342-9678. E-mail address: getinfo@haworthpressinc.com]*

BACKGROUND

Literature on gender differences among those entering substance abuse treatment is limited. Moreover, concern has been voiced for some time that treatment programs have been structured to meet only the needs of male clients (Wallen, 1992). According to estimates by the National Institute on Drug Abuse, the majority of clients entering substance abuse treatment are men (Mondanaro, 1989), and most research studies have been dominated by male subjects (Peluso & Peluso, 1988). In fact, Harrison and Belille (1987) found in a review of literature that only 8% of subjects in published studies of alcoholism treatment were women. Because women are so poorly represented, many studies include them without gender differentiation (Annis & Liban, 1980).

In the literature that has differentiated between male and female clients, large differences in alcohol and drug use patterns have been found. In early studies, though samples were small, a greater proportion of women were found to abuse barbiturates, sedatives, tranquilizers and amphetamines (Burt, Glynn, & Sowder, 1979; Prather, 1981; Prather & Fidell, 1978). A number of older substance abuse studies reveal how patterns of drug use have changed over the years in different treatment settings (Bray, Schlenger, Craddock, Hubbard, & Rachal, 1982; Hubbard et al., 1986). In the past, very few males and females reported single substance abuse, but females reported using heroin only more than males (Craddock, Hubbard, Bray, & Ginzburg, 1981). Males reported more alcohol and marijuana use, whereas females more often reported use of other narcotics and mild tranquilizers. A large proportion of these women reported psychological problems (particularly depression), as well as family, financial and medical problems. Women also reported involvement in the criminal justice system, but at a lower level than men. In general, patterns of drug use in the past indicated more exclusive use of greater amounts of a single substance, most often alcohol or heroin, while more recent studies find more polydrug use, with cocaine use becoming much more prevalent (Hubbard et al., 1989).

An analysis of data from a study of women entering methadone treatment found that women were less likely to be daily drinkers than men but more likely to be daily cocaine users (Wechsberg, Craddock, & Hubbard, 1994). Another study found that women IDUs were more likely than men to report daily injection of heroin and speedball (Brown & Weissman, 1993). Further analysis of data from the same study suggested that crack cocaine had become a drug of choice for many women IDUs out of treatment (Weissman, Sowder, Young, and the National AIDS Research Consortium, 1990).

Other studies found that women entering treatment had poorer self-concepts and more emotional symptoms than men, including depression and anxiety (Blume, 1986; Beckman, 1978; De Leon & Jainchill, 1986; Griffin, Weiss, Mirin, & Lange, 1989; Wallen, 1992). Twice as many women in treatment as men reported having a major depressive episode (Wechsberg et al., 1994). Studies also indicate that women reported more physical problems (Anderson 1980; Brown, Garvey, Meyers, & Stark, 1971), and that they were more dependent on public financial assistance and had greater medical needs (Marsh & Simpson, 1986). In addition, women have reported more childhood sexual abuse (Boyd, Blow, & Orgain, 1993; Rohsenow, Corbett, & Devine, 1988; Wechsberg et al., 1994; Wallen, 1992) than men, more physical abuse (Ladwig & Anderson, 1989; Wechsberg et al., 1994), more psychosexual disorders and anorexia nervosa (Fornari, Kent, Kabo, & Goodman, 1994; Ross, Glaser, & Stiasny, 1988), and more post-traumatic stress disorder (Cottler, Compton, Mager, Spitznagel, & Janca, 1992).

A series of papers on gender and ethnic differences reported on a large sample of addicts entering methadone treatment programs in California, particularly stressing the need to separate out the analysis of women. Hser, Anglin, & McGlothin (1987) found traditional differences among the genders, depicting women in a more passive and more dependent role financially. Women were more dependent on welfare and/or disability payments, whereas men were more likely to work at skilled jobs. Women were more likely to be initiated into drug use by their male partners, but many also reported self-initiation into heroin use, multiple drug use and drug dealing. Women were also more likely to be involved in tranquilizer use, whereas men reported more regular marijuana and alcohol use.

Several other studies have found gender differences in economic areas and in the related area of child care. One study found that men reported higher incomes and higher status jobs than women, while many of the women were single parents with primary or sole responsibility for children (Brady, Grice, Dustan, & Randall, 1993). Another study found that women in treatment were more likely than men to lack employment skills and more likely to need job readiness skills (Karuntzos, Caddell, & Dennis, 1994). One study of women entering methadone treatment found that half as many men as women had children in their households and had child care problems (Wechsberg et al., 1994). Another smaller study, however, found men's child care issues to be similar to women's (Wallen, 1992).

Gender differences have also been noted in the area of criminal involvement (Hser, Anglin, & Booth, 1987). Anglo women were less likely than Anglo men to have been involved in the criminal justice system, yet more likely to report having engaged in prostitution. Both genders reported theft, yet more men reported burglary and robbery, and women reported more forgery. Though traditional roles were evident, they noted changing status with regard to women reporting a more active role in their behaviors to maintain drug use. Among a sample of substance abusers involved in the criminal justice system, a higher proportion of women than men reported health and mental health problems, few vocational skills, and child-rearing problems (Yang, 1990). Another study revealed that large percentages of both men and women who enter treatment report involvement in the criminal justice system, but men report their first arrest at an earlier age than women (Wechsberg et al., 1994). Another study of women IDUs (Brown & Weissman, 1993) found that out-of-treatment women worked fewer days in legitimate employment than men; these women had other means of support, including illegal activities.

In a small study of gender differences in alcoholics entering treatment, Thom (1987) found many similarities and some differences worth noting. Both men and women reported psychological and daily living problems. Yet, women were more likely to have experienced violence recently from their partners and to have received little support for getting help. Differences were also found in the reporting of current distress related to seeking treatment.

Although the majority of these studies focused on one treatment modality, Weisner (1993) compared a more representative sample of gender differences across both alcohol and drug treatment settings. Differences were found in alcohol use, drug use and criminal behavior. Contrary to previous studies, however, sedatives were not found to be used by more women than men.

Researchers and substance abuse professionals have become more sensitive to the differences that exist between women and men entering substance abuse treatment; however, larger gender studies that focus on identifying and understanding these differences across modalities of treatment are needed. Such studies are particularly important for structuring gender-specific treatment programs that will lead to more effective outcomes, but little research has yet been done in this area.

To that end, in this paper we explore gender differences in a very large sample of women and men entering four major substance abuse treatment modalities. We consider not only traditional demographic comparisons and issues surrounding employment, criminal justice involvement, health and mental health, and drug use patterns; we also examine issues that are often considered to be primarily of concern to women: child care and child custody. In addition, we look at patterns of physical and sexual abuse, past and current, for both men and women. Both the differences and the similarities that emerge from this comparison may point treatment providers toward a greater awareness of client differences and concerns and may lead ultimately to more effective treatment processes and outcomes.

METHODS

The data presented here are drawn from the Drug Abuse Treatment Outcome Study (DATOS), conducted by Research Triangle Institute (RTI) and funded by the National Institute on Drug Abuse (NIDA). DATOS is a multisite prospective clinical and epidemiological study of clients entering drug abuse treatment and of outcomes within and after treatment (Hubbard, 1995). DATOS used a longitudinal prospective cohort design in which clients were interviewed at intake to treatment and at several key points during treatment. Although the participating programs were purposively chosen, not randomly selected, they reflect typical, stable drug treatment programs in large and medium-sized U.S. cities (Craddock, Rounds-Bryant, Flynn, & Hubbard, in press).

Subjects in DATOS were 10,010 clients aged 18 or older recruited from 96 programs in 11 cities. The programs represented the four major treatment modalities that were common in the early 1990s: outpatient methadone (29 programs; n = 1,540), long-term residential (21 programs; n = 2,774), outpatient drug-free (32 programs; n = 2,574), and short-term inpatient (14 programs; n = 3,122).

The data were collected by personal interviews with clients enrolling in the program between 1991 and 1993 by independent professional interviewers trained and supervised by RTI staff. An initial 90-minute interview covering psychosocial issues was conducted as soon as possible after admission. A second 90-minute interview covering clinical and diagnostic issues was conducted approximately one week later.

The DATOS study offers a particularly rich opportunity to study clients entering both private and publicly-funded substance abuse treatment programs. It is susceptible to the usual limitations of large survey studies (quality control of data collection, instrumentation and measurement errors), and, in common with most studies of substance abusers, it relies heavily on self-report and individual item response. However, a previous study conducted through both intra-interview analyses and longitudinal analysis of measurement reliability indicated high level of internal consistency in the self-reports of DATOS clients (Adair, Craddock, Miller, & Turner, 1996).

The findings in this study indicate differences between women and men who enter substance abuse treatment. Because the sample was drawn from four different treatment modalities, it offers unusual opportunities to compare gender differences within and across program types, and an examination of these differences is particularly relevant for identifying treatment needs. Statistical tests were not used in these analyses since large numbers typically result in statistical significance. The clinical significance and utility of these findings is of greater concern. However, any difference of 10% between genders within the treatment modalities would be highly significant, and most gender differences greater than 5% would be significant.

RESULTS

Table 1 presents the percentages of selected demographics by gender within treatment modality. The racial/ethnic composition of clients in the sample varies across modalities, although for all modalities except methadone approximately half the clients are African American. The methadone modality has a much lower percentage of African American men and women and much higher percentages of Hispanic clients and non-Hispanic Caucasian women than the other modalities. The greatest difference between the genders is found in the residential setting, which has substantially more non-Hispanic Caucasian males than females and substantially more African American females than males.

In general, the women tend to be younger than the men in all modalities. A substantially greater percentage of men than women are over age 36 in all settings. Moreover, a greater percentage of women than men are age 35 or under in all settings except residential, where a slightly greater percentage of men are under age 25.

In all modalities, a greater percentage of men than women have never been married. However, the percentages for both genders are high in this

TABLE 1. Selected Demographics at Admission, by Treatment Modality and by Gender

	Short-term Inpatient		Outpatient Methadone		Outpatient		Long-term Residential	
	Female (1,042) %	Male (2,080) %	Female (600) %	Male (940) %	Female (844) %	Male (1,730) %	Female (921) %	Male (1,853) %
Race								
African-American	53.5	46.6	26.7	29.0	49.8	53.5	55.2	45.8
Hispanic	5.3	7.6	22.0	26.0	13.2	10.7	13.2	13.1
Non-Hispanic Caucasian	38.9	43.0	50.3	42.9	34.1	32.7	27.8	38.7
Other	2.4	2.7	1.0	2.1	3.0	3.1	3.8	2.4
Age								
≤ 25	17.3	15.5	8.0	5.0	21.3	19.1	23.3	24.1
26-35	55.8	49.1	49.0	32.4	56.5	49.0	59.0	52.0
36+	27.0	35.3	43.0	62.6	22.2	31.9	17.8	23.9
Marital status								
Married/Living as married	37.3	36.8	43.9	39.1	28.8	30.5	25.5	21.3
Sep/Div/Wid	24.0	20.9	28.0	28.6	25.5	20.5	23.1	20.4
never married	38.7	42.3	28.0	32.1	45.7	49.0	51.5	58.4
Education								
High school graduate	70.5	70.2	61.6	66.2	56.2	63.3	48.5	59.7
Employment								
Working	23.5	39.8	17.1	29.5	19.7	38.4	8.5	19.5
Homemaker	27.9	5.5	36.6	4.7	33.4	4.2	15.9	2.7
Prior drug treatment	46.2	45.5	74.7	74.1	54.5	41.7	62.9	57.8

category, ranging from a little less than one third of the clients in the methadone modality to over half in the residential modality. Higher percentages of women than men are married or living as married in all modalities, with the most substantial differences in the methadone and residential modalities.

With the exception of the short-term inpatient program (where the percentages are nearly equal), greater percentages of women than men have not graduated from high school. Note, too, that the percentages of those not graduating are large, ranging from approximately 30% of the men and women in the short-term modality up to more than half of the women in the residential modality.

In all modalities, much greater percentages of men than women reported that they were working, while much greater percentages of women than men reported that they were homemakers. Employment, however, is generally low, with between approximately 60-80% of the men, and a greater percentage of the women, not employed.

A large percentage of clients in all modalities reported that they had previously been in drug treatment. Percentages range from nearly half of the clients entering short-term programs to nearly three-quarters of those entering methadone treatment. In general, a higher percentage of women than men reported prior drug treatment, most notably among outpatient and long-term residential women.

Table 2 presents percentages of women and men reporting weekly or daily use of drugs in the year prior to treatment. Across all four treatment modalities, men consistently reported more use of alcohol than women in both the daily and weekly categories; however, both women and men reported substantial alcohol use, especially those in short-term and residential treatment. Only in daily use among those in residential treatment is women's use nearly equivalent to men's. Although marijuana use is not as prevalent as alcohol use, men are also more frequent users across all the treatment modalities, both daily and weekly.

Cocaine use, however, presents a different pattern. Men reported somewhat greater weekly cocaine use in all treatment modalities except outpatient, where men and women reported similar use. But women reported substantially more daily cocaine use than men in all modalities. Use was greatest in short-term and residential treatment, where African American women predominate.

As expected, the greatest heroin use by both genders is found in the methadone treatment modality, where nearly 80% of both men and women reported daily use. In the other modalities, where heroin use is much less, women's daily use was somewhat greater than men's, while the men reported somewhat greater weekly use in all modalities.

In the remaining three drug categories, the percentages reporting daily or weekly use are generally smaller than in the first four categories. For the most part, women reported more use of sedatives and barbiturates than men, although men in the outpatient and methadone treatment modalities reported slightly more weekly use than women. The pattern is similar for amphetamines: women's use is generally greater than men's, although men in methadone treatment report very slightly greater use than women. The greatest use was reported in the residential modality, where men and women reported about the same use. For other opioids, women again

TABLE 2. Weekly or Daily Reported Use of Specific Drugs in Year Before Admission, by Treatment Modality and by Gender

Weekly or Daily Use	Short-term Inpatient		Outpatient Methadone		Outpatient		Long-term Residential	
	Female (1,042) %	Male (2,080) %	Female (600) %	Male (940) %	Female (844) %	Male (1,730) %	Female (921) %	Male (1,853) %
Alcohol								
Weekly	36.1	41.1	14.1	19.1	25.7	32.4	29.3	34.3
Daily	20.6	28.4	8.5	13.9	13.8	18.2	22.5	23.5
Marijuana								
Weekly	14.9	16.9	8.7	12.5	10.5	14.5	11.6	14.4
Daily	11.9	15.7	5.2	8.3	11.7	13.7	10.8	17.0
Cocaine								
Weekly	29.4	35.4	16.8	22.0	23.2	22.8	21.3	27.3
Daily	36.5	29.9	25.7	19.1	24.5	16.6	53.7	35.8
Heroin								
Weekly	1.1	2.1	7.4	9.4	1.8	2.5	3.2	4.5
Daily	6.2	5.6	79.1	79.2	5.1	3.5	13.0	11.9
Sedatives/ Barbiturates								
Weekly	6.3	4.9	6.4	7.2	1.3	1.5	3.4	2.9
Daily	5.7	3.5	5.2	3.8	1.7	1.2	2.1	1.6
Amphetamine								
Weekly	3.0	2.6	1.0	1.2	3.1	2.3	2.7	2.6
Daily	2.4	1.8	1.3	1.4	3.5	2.1	4.1	4.2
Other Opioids								
Weekly	5.8	5.1	8.4	7.1	1.6	1.9	2.6	3.1
Daily	6.1	4.9	13.9	11.8	2.4	1.6	3.1	2.3

reported more use than men in all categories except in the outpatient and residential modalities, where men's weekly use was slightly greater.

Table 3 presents percentages of the most severe depressive symptoms reported in the past year and current concern over emotional or psychological problems, by gender and treatment modality. In general, more men than women reported no depressive symptoms in the year prior to admis-

TABLE 3. Depressive Symptoms, by Treatment Modality and by Gender

	Short-term Inpatient		Outpatient Methadone		Outpatient		Long-term Residential	
	Female (1,042) %	Male (2,080) %	Female (600) %	Male (940) %	Female (844) %	Male (1,730) %	Female (921) %	Male (1,853) %
Most Severe Depressive Symptom								
Suicidal attempts[1]	13.9	7.6	5.0	2.4	8.9	4.2	10.0	7.6
Suicidal thoughts[1]	25.1	19.5	14.2	13.5	17.4	12.8	15.0	15.7
Feeling depressed[1]	3.4	3.2	6.2	3.8	3.9	3.3	3.8	3.1
No symptoms[1]	57.6	69.7	74.5	80.4	69.8	79.7	71.1	73.6
Very troubled over current emotional/psychological problems	21.6	11.5	9.7	5.9	15.3	8.4	18.6	12.6

[1]In year before admission.

sion. The highest rates of depressive symptoms are found among the women in short-term programs: they have the highest rates of suicidal attempts and suicidal thoughts.

Across all modalities, women reported almost twice as much distress as men over current emotional and psychological issues at time of admission. The percentages were highest overall, and for both genders, in the short-term inpatient and long-term residential modalities.

Table 4 presents health-related issues by gender and modality. Medical conditions diagnosed by a physician display consistent differences between women and men, with women reporting greater proportions of most conditions. Respiratory problems are the most frequently diagnosed condition for both women and men, although women reported substantially higher rates. For women, gynecological problems appear as the next most frequent diagnosis, followed by STDs. For men, respiratory, heart, and digestive problems are the most frequent, but women have higher rates of all three.

As to current health issues, one-quarter to one-third of both women and men reported that their health impaired their ability to work or go to school. However, women's rates are higher in all modalities, which is consistent with their higher reported rates of medical conditions. The percentages of hospital stays also reflect the women's higher rates of medical conditions and reported poorer health. Note that both women and

TABLE 4. Health Issues, by Treatment Modality and by Gender

	Short-term Inpatient		Outpatient Methadone		Outpatient		Long-term Residential	
	Female (926) %	Male (1,860) %	Female (526) %	Male (814) %	Female (716) %	Male (1,456) %	Female (803) %	Male (1,654) %
Medical diagnosis[1]								
None	57.0	37.0	50.9	36.9	63.2	44.4	58.2	38.5
Respiratory system	21.7	13.1	31.1	16.7	25.5	12.3	24.9	14.3
Tuberculosis	1.7	0.8	1.7	2.7	1.5	2.2	1.6	1.6
Heart/circulatory	15.4	11.3	17.2	11.3	13.5	9.2	12.5	8.7
Digestive/stomach	17.6	10.6	16.6	15.2	15.5	8.1	12.5	9.9
Liver(hep/cirroh)	6.5	6.8	13.1	10.4	7.6	5.0	8.4	5.5
Bone or muscle	14.1	9.4	17.6	14.6	11.9	9.9	9.2	9.1
Nervous system	13.8	7.9	15.5	7.0	10.5	5.1	11.2	7.1
Gyn. (females)	21.4	0.0	18.0	0.0	15.8	0.0	19.1	0.0
Prostate (males)	0.0	2.3	0.0	2.1	0.0	1.0	0.0	1.5
STD or VD	13.9	5.2	5.2	5.4	8.5	4.4	18.3	6.1
Other diagnosis	8.5	8.7	9.5	9.8	8.0	7.0	11.0	8.2
Hospital stays[2]	26.2	18.6	21.8	16.6	24.9	8.8	24.5	12.3
Current health impaired work or school	34.4	32.2	40.3	35.8	31.2	23.6	28.5	23.5
Poor health at admission	20.0	17.7	16.2	13.8	9.7	8.3	11.0	10.1
Health insurance at admission								
None	24.5	37.3	25.5	30.5	39.7	62.8	60.4	76.8
Private	33.8	43.4	10.3	11.9	13.4	15.8	5.5	5.9
Public	41.7	19.3	64.1	57.5	46.8	21.4	34.0	17.4

[1] Health problems diagnosed by a physician in past year as self-reported by client. Multiple response: percentages do not add to 100%.

[2] Overnight hospitalizations in past year for physical health problems including pregnancy, drug overdoses, and alcohol-related d.t.'s but not formal drug or alcohol detox or treatment.

men in short-term inpatient programs reported the greatest proportion of hospital stays in the past year.

Across all modalities, a greater proportion of men than women reported having no health insurance, public or private. The highest uninsured rates are found in long-term residential programs, where a majority of both women and men do not have insurance. When insured, however, women in all modalities are more likely to have public insurance than private insurance.

Among other results related to health, the majority of clients across all treatment settings had had an HIV antibody test, although serostatus is not available in this study. Only a small percentage of women reported being pregnant at the time of admission, with the highest percentages found in the methadone and long-term residential programs.

Table 5 presents percentages reporting criminal justice involvement by treatment modality and gender. More men than women reported criminal justice involvement (defined as serving a sentence, awaiting trial, awaiting sentencing, on probation or parole, or having a case pending) at intake. The difference between men and women is greatest in the outpatient modality, while the largest percentages of judicially involved clients are in the residential modality.

For previous arrests, in all four treatment modalities, the men reported being arrested before age 18 at about twice the rate of the women. The difference between genders narrows for those reporting arrests after age 18, but the men still have the larger percentages. The percentages in this category are substantial (i.e., large numbers of the clients, both men and women, in all treatment modalities, have been arrested).

In general, however, women reported more weekly and daily illegal activity in the past year than men. The percentages are similar for the short-term modality (with men reporting slightly higher illegal daily activity), but the women reported substantially more weekly activity in the other three modalities and substantially more illegal daily activity in the outpatient modality. Moreover, a larger percentage of women than men reported committing any serious illegal acts in the past year in two of the treatment modalities: methadone and outpatient.

Table 6 presents data on physical and sexual abuse. The gender differences here, as expected, are substantial. Across the four modalities, approximately two-thirds to three-quarters of the men reported no history of physical or sexual abuse; a much smaller percentage of women in all modalities reported no abuse.

In the year before treatment, the incidence of abuse, both physical and sexual, for women is markedly greater than for men in all modalities, and

TABLE 5. Criminal Justice Involvement and Illegal Activities Reported, by Treatment Modality and by Gender

	Short-term Inpatient		Outpatient Methadone		Outpatient		Long-term Residential	
	Female (1,042) %	Male (2,080) %	Female (600) %	Male (940) %	Female (844) %	Male (1,730) %	Female (921) %	Male (1,853) %
Criminal justice involvement at admission[1]	20.3	27.8	23.4	29.1	44.9	62.3	55.2	68.2
Arrested before age 18	13.7	31.7	22.3	44.0	20.8	41.4	25.9	50.6
Arrested after age 18	47.1	65.7	63.9	80.4	70.5	80.7	72.6	86.1
Frequency of illegal activity in past year Weekly Daily	10.4 10.9	10.0 11.5	12.1 27.3	11.8 24.9	8.0 10.0	6.3 7.8	14.7 28.2	14.6 24.1
Any serious illegal acts in past year[2]	24.1	26.7	30.1	26.7	22.9	21.5	33.9	43.2

[1] Currently serving a sentence, awaiting trial, awaiting sentencing, on probation, parole, or having a case pending.
[2] Includes theft, aggravated assault, burglary, forgery or embezzlement, or dealing in stolen property.

the percentages of sexual abuse or physical combined with sexual abuse for men is very low in all modalities. The picture changes, however, for reported abuse that took place prior to the year before treatment. For that time period, the percentages of physical abuse reported by men and women are more nearly equal, with men in the short-term and residential modalities reporting more abuse than the women. Women, however, reported a greater incidence of sexual abuse than men in all four modalities— approximately twice as much. Furthermore, when physical and sexual abuse are taken together, the women in all modalities reported substantially more than the men, ranging from about 3 times as much for the short-term modality to more than 6 times as much for the methadone modality.

Table 7 reports current issues related to children by treatment modality and by gender for those clients who had children. Significant differences

TABLE 6. Reported Current and Past Physical and Sexual Abuse, by Treatment Modality and by Gender

Reported Abuse	Short-term Inpatient		Outpatient Methadone		Outpatient		Long-term Residential	
	Female (1,042) %	Male (2,080) %	Female (600) %	Male (940) %	Female (844) %	Male (1,730) %	Female (921) %	Male (1,853) %
No history of abuse	39.5	71.9	41.1	75.6	33.6	73.8	28.4	68.1
Year before treatment								
Physical	14.8	2.7	9.9	1.5	11.1	2.3	13.4	2.2
Sexual	5.0	0.5	1.3	0.2	2.5	0.5	5.0	1.3
Physical & sexual	5.3	0.1	1.7	0.0	4.9	0.1	7.3	0.2
More than year before treatment[1]								
Physical	11.2	14.8	16.3	16.0	15.3	14.8	12.9	18.4
Sexual	9.0	5.2	7.8	3.3	9.8	4.3	11.0	4.2
Physical & sexual	15.0	4.9	21.9	3.3	22.6	4.1	22.0	5.5

[1] But not in the year before treatment.

were found between men and women on all the reported issues related to children, except for concerns about drug treatment affecting custody of their children for those in methadone treatment. In general, the women were approximately twice as likely as the men to have children in their household and to have custody of them. Nearly half of these women reported childcare problems, while only low percentages of men reported having childcare problems. More than half of the women in all modalities except residential reported having custody, while a much smaller proportion of men in all modalities reported having custody. Across modalities, women were much more concerned than men that drug treatment would affect custody, and they reported other custody concerns more frequently than men as well.

CONCLUSION

A number of the differences found between men and women are consistent across all four modalities, and these findings, in general, are also consistent with the results of previous studies. We summarize the most important of these differences here.

- The women were younger and less educated than the men and had been employed less prior to admission.
- The men consistently reported more alcohol use, while the women in general reported more daily use of cocaine.
- A greater percentage of women than men had public health insurance, and the women consistently reported more problems related to depression and other health issues (e.g., more hospital stays, current health impairing ability to go to work or school).
- More women than men reported prior drug treatment.
- Men had been arrested more often and reported more criminal justice involvement than women, but women in general had higher rates of illegal activity than men.
- Large differences were found between men and women in the reported incidence of physical and sexual abuse, both current and past. The majority of men reported no abuse at all, while a higher percentage of women reported both types of abuse in their past.
- Women had children in the household and had legal custody of children more often than men. Both men and women who had custody showed concern that drug treatment might affect their custody, but most other issues related to children are still primarily women's issues.

IMPLICATIONS

Because the DATOS study is one of the largest studies of clients entering substance abuse treatment, the implications of this analysis are particularly important. Although the selection of programs was not random, this sample can be considered typical of women and men who enter treatment in medium and large metropolitan areas of the U.S.

We chose not to collapse data from the modalities into totals by gender because collapsed totals obscured important differences in the clients by modality. The gender differences we have highlighted can help practitioners to become more sensitive to their clients' needs and better able to address treatment issues raised by these needs. For example, comparison by modality reveals that the women who entered short-term inpatient programs were older, newer to treatment, had more education, were likely to be African American, and more likely to have legal jobs and insurance, yet they also reported suicidal symptoms more frequently. The characteristics of this group suggest that these women may have a level of functioning that will allow them to build upon a more solid foundation. On the other hand, women who entered long-term residential treatment were

TABLE 7. Self-Reported Issues Related to Children, by Treatment Modality and by Gender

Self-Reported Issues	Short-term Inpatient		Outpatient Methadone		Outpatient		Long-term Residential	
	Female (926) %	Male (1,860) %	Female (526) %	Male (814) %	Female (716) %	Male (1,456) %	Female (803) %	Male (1,654) %
Children under 18 years old in household	52.7	27.3	51.5	29.5	49.9	22.1	37.0	16.3
Childcare problems	17.7	6.9	19.4	9.5	22.1	5.3	8.7	2.5
Legal custody of children	52.0	22.6	52.9	24.9	52.9	20.5	34.4	13.1
Any concern drug treatment will affect custody[1]	25.7	15.0	17.8	16.1	36.1	17.3	37.0	14.3
Other concern about losing custody[2]	18.6	4.8	9.8	3.7	22.2	4.1	14.3	3.2

[1] Includes responses of "yes" and "maybe" drug treatment will affect custody.
[2] Has concern about losing custody but not that drug treatment will affect custody.

younger, reported the least education and employment, greater criminal activity, and more episodes of previous treatment. They are likely to require more assistance in developing the basic skills that will allow them to function as responsible adults.

Previous studies have noted the complexity of the internal and external world of the substance abusing woman and reinforced the idea that multiple issues often must be addressed before recovery can be a reality (Wechsberg, 1995). This study confirms that idea and reinforces it by demonstrating that women and men come to treatment with contextual differences that must be addressed in treatment planning if successful outcomes are to be achieved. Thus, one of the most important implications of the study is that substance abusers cannot be considered a homogeneous group. Significant differences exist between women and men entering treatment, and significant differences exist within both sexes according to the type of treatment sought.

In the past, substance abuse treatment was most responsive to the white male alcoholic and drug addict, and little attention was paid to cultural and gender differences. More recently, however, the emphasis shifted toward more sensitive programming that addresses women's issues (e.g., same gender counseling, women's groups, educating women about co-dependency and parenting, providing women's housing and daycare). Unfortunately, the climate supporting such comprehensive substance abuse treatment appears to be changing as managed care influences and capitation rates threaten to curtail broader and more sensitive treatment services. This trend makes it all the more important to develop and test sensitive interventions that can efficiently address the differences found among women and men entering different treatment modalities. A better understanding of these differences is an important prerequisite for more effective treatment interventions leading to positive and lasting outcomes.

REFERENCES

Adair, E.B.G., Craddock, S.G., Miller, H.G., & Turner, C.F. (1996). Quality of treatment data: Reliability over time of self-reports given by clients in treatment for substance abuse. *Journal of Substance Abuse Treatment.*

Anderson, M.D. (1980). Medical needs of addicted women and men and the implications for treatment: Focus on women. In A.J. Schacter (Ed.), *Drug dependence and alcoholism, vol. 1.* New York: Plenum Press.

Annis, H.M., & Liban, C.B. (1980). Alcoholism in women: Treatment modalities and outcomes. In O. Kalant (Ed.), *Research advances in alcohol and drug problems,* (Vol. 5, pp. 385-422). New York: Plenum Press.

Beckman, L.J. (1978). Psychological characteristics of alcoholic women. *Drug Abuse and Alcoholism Review 1*(5/6), 1-12.

Blume, S.B. (1986). Women and alcohol: A review. *Journal of American Medical Association, 256*(11), 1467-1470.

Boyd, C.J., Blow, F., & Orgain, L.S. (1993). Gender differences among African-American substance abusers. *Journal of Psychoactive Drugs, 25*(4), 301-305.

Brady, K.T., Grice, D.E., Dustan, L., & Randall, C. (1993). Gender differences in substance abuse disorders. *American Journal of Psychiatry, 150,* 1707-1711.

Bray, R.M., Schlenger, W.E., Craddock, S.G., Hubbard, R.L., & Rachal, J.V. (1982). *Approaches to the assessment of drug use in the Treatment Outcome Prospective Study.* Research Triangle Park, NC: Research Triangle Institute.

Brown, V., & Weissman, G. (1993). Women and men injection drug users: An updated look at gender differences and risk factors. In B.S. Brown, & G.M. Beschner with the National AIDS Research Consortium (Eds.), *Handbook on risk of AIDS. Injection drugs users and sexual partners* (pp. 173-194). Westport, CT: Greenwood Press.

Brown, B.S., Garvey, S.K., Meyers, M.B., & Stark, S.D. (1971). In their own words: Addicts' reasons for initiating and withdrawing from heroin. *International Journal of Addictions, 6,* 635-645.

Burt, M.R., Glynn, T.J., & Sowder, B.J. (1979). *Psychosocial characteristics of drug-abusing women*, NIDA, Services Research Monograph Series, Bethesda, MD: Burt Associates.

Cottler, L.B., Compton, W.M., Mager, D., Spitznagel, E.L., & Janca, A. (1992). Posttraumatic stress disorder among substance users from the general population. *American Journal of Psychiatry, 149*(5), 664-670.

Craddock, S.G., Hubbard, R.L., Bray, R.M., & Ginzburg, H.M. (1981). *Sex differences in drug use and implications for treatment.* Unpublished manuscript.

Craddock, S.G., Rounds-Bryant, J., Flynn, P.M., & Hubbard, R.L. (in press). Characteristics and pretreatment behaviors of clients entering drug abuse treatment: 1969 to 1993. *American Journal of Drug and Alcohol Abuse.*

De Leon,G., & Jainchill, N. (1986). Circumstance, motivation, readiness and suitability as correlates of treatment tenure. *Journal of Psychoactive Drugs, 18*, (3), 203-208.

Fornari, V., Kent, J., Kabo, L., & Goodman, B. (1994). Anorexia nervosa: Thirty something. *Journal of Substance Abuse Treatment, 11*, (1), 45-54.

Griffin, M.L., Weiss, R.D., Mirin, S.M., & Lange, U. (1989). A comparison of male and female cocaine abusers. *Archives of General Psychiatry, 46*, 122-126.

Harrison, P.A., & Belille, C.A. (1987). Women in treatment: Beyond the stereotype. *Journal of Studies on Alcohol, 48*(6), 574-578.

Hser, Y., Anglin, M.D., & McGlothin, W. (1987). Sex differences in addict careers: Initiation of use. *American Journal of Drug and Alcohol Abuse, 13*(1&2), 33-57.

Hser, Y., Anglin, M.D., & Booth, M.W. (1987). Sex differences in addict careers: Addiction. *American Journal of Drug and Alcohol Abuse, 13*(3), 231-251.

Hubbard, R.L., Marsden, M.E., Rachal, J.V., Harwood, H.J., Cavanaugh, E.R., & Ginzburg, H.M. (1989). *Drug abuse treatment: A national study of effectiveness.* Chapel Hill, NC: University of North Carolina Press.

Hubbard, R.L., Cavanaugh, E.R., Craddock, S.G., Bray, R.M., Rachal, J.V., Collins, J.J., & Allison, M. (1986). *Drug abuse treatment client characteristics and pretreatment behaviors* (Research Monograph DHHS Publication No. ADM 86-1480) Rockville, MD: National Institute on Drug Abuse.

Hubbard, R.L. (1995). Drug Abuse Treatment Outcome Study (DATOS). In J.H. Jaffe (Ed.), *Encyclopedia of Drugs and Alcohol* (pp. 394-396). New York: Simon & Schuster Macmillan.

Karuntzos, G.T., Caddell, J.M., & Dennis, M.L. (1994). Gender differences in vocational needs and outcomes for methadone treatment clients. *Journal of Psychoactive Drugs, 26*(2), 173-180.

Ladwig, G.B., & Andersen, M.D. (1989). Substance abuse in women: Relationship between chemical dependency of women and past reports of physical and/or sexual abuse. *International Journal of Addictions, 24*(8), 739-754.

Marsh, K.L., & Simpson, D.D. (1986). Sex differences in opioid addiction careers. *American Journal of Drug and Alcohol Abuse, 12*(4), 309-329.

Mondanaro, J. (1989). *Chemically dependent women: Assessment and treatment.* Lexington, MA: Lexington Books.

Peluso, E., & Peluso, L.S. (1988). *Women and drugs: Getting hooked, getting clean.* Minneapolis: Compcare Publishers.

Prather, J. (1981). Women's use of licit and illicit drugs. In J.H. Lowinson & P. Ruiz (Eds.), *Substance abuse: Clinical problems and perspectives* (pp. 729-739). Baltimore, Maryland: Williams and Wilkins.

Prather, J., & Fidell, L. (1978). Drug use and abuse among women: An overview. *International Journal of Addictions, 13,* 863-885.

Rohsenow, D.J., Corbett, R., & Devine, D. (1988). Molested as children: A hidden contribution to substance abuse. *Journal of Substance Abuse Treatment, 5,* 13-18.

Ross, H.E., Glaser, F.B., & Stiasny, S. (1988). Sex differences in the prevalence of psychiatric disorders in patients with alcohol and drug problems. *British Journal of Addiction, 83,* 1179-1192.

Thom, B. (1987). Sex differences in help-seeking for alcohol problems: Entry into treatment. *British Journal of Addiction, 82,* 989-997.

Wallen, J. (1992). A comparison of male and female clients in substance abuse treatment. *Journal of Substance Abuse Treatment, 9,* 243-248.

Wechsberg, W.M. (1995). Strategies for working with female substance abuse clients. In B. Brown (Ed.), *Substance abuse treatment in the era of AIDS* (pp. 119-152). Rockville, MD: Center for Substance Abuse Treatment.

Wechsberg, W.M., Craddock, S.G., & Hubbard, R.L. (1994). *Preliminary findings: Gender differences among those entering methadone treatment.* Presented at the National Methadone Conference, Washington, DC, April 21.

Weisner, C. (1993). The epidemiology of combined alcohol and drug use within treatment agencies: A comparison by gender. *Journal of Studies on Alcohol, 54*(3), 268-274.

Weissman, G., Sowder, B., Young, P., & the National AIDS Research Consortium. (1990). The relationship between crack cocaine and other risk factors among women in a national AIDS prevention program. [Abstract]. *Sixth International AIDS Conference.* San Francisco, CA: June 20-24, *6*(3), 126.

Yang, S.S. (1990). The unique treatment needs of female substance abusers in correctional institutions: The obligation of the criminal justice system to provide parity of services. *Medicine and Law, 9,* 1018-1027.

III. SPECIAL ISSUES OF DRUG USING WOMEN: SEXUALLY TRANSMITTED DISEASE AND INCIDENTS OF VIOLENCE

Gender Differences in Risk Factors for Gonorrhea Among Alaskan Drug Users

David M. Paschane, BS
Henry H. Cagle, BS
Andrea M. Fenaughty, PhD
Dennis G. Fisher, PhD

SUMMARY. This study developed separate models predicting risk for gonorrhea infection among female and male drug users in An-

David M. Paschane, Henry H. Cagle, Andrea M. Fenaughty, and Dennis G. Fisher are all affiliated with the Department of Psychology, University of Alaska Anchorage.

Address correspondence to: Dennis G. Fisher, Psychology Department-IVDU Project, University of Alaska Anchorage, 3211 Providence Drive, Anchorage, AK 99508 (E-mail: AFDGF@uaa.alaska.edu).

This work was funded in part by grants from the National Institute on Drug Abuse grant (U01-DA07290, F32-DA05599, R01-DA10181).

[Haworth co-indexing entry note]: "Gender Differences in Risk Factors for Gonorrhea Among Alaskan Drug Users." Paschane, David M. et al. Co-published simultaneously in *Drugs & Society* (The Haworth Press, Inc.) Vol. 13, No. 1/2, 1998, pp. 117-130; and: *Women and Substance Abuse: Gender Transparency* (ed: Sally J. Stevens, and Harry K. Wexler) The Haworth Press, Inc., 1998, pp. 117-130. Single or multiple copies of this article are available for a fee from The Haworth Document Delivery Service [1-800-342-9678, 9:00 a.m. - 5:00 p.m. (EST). E-mail address: getinfo@haworthpressinc.com].

chorage Alaska. Data were collected with the Risk Behavior Assessment, a structured interview that was administered to 728 male and 321 female adult participants who were currently not in drug treatment. History of gonorrhea infection was self-reported and coded as ever or never. The risk factors for women are trading sex for money, being American Indian or Alaska Native, perceiving oneself as homeless, and trading sex for drugs. For men the risk factors are injecting or snorting cocaine, being Black, being older, acquiring illegal income excluding prostitution, and using amphetamines. Results are useful for guiding public health intervention and policy development in drug using populations in Alaska. *[Article copies available for a fee from The Haworth Document Delivery Service: 1-800-342-9678. E-mail address: getinfo@haworthpressinc.com]*

Gonorrhea (GC) is historically the most frequently reported communicable disease in the United States, with over 440,000 cases reported in 1993 (Centers for Disease Control and Prevention [CDC], 1994) and an estimated annual cost of one billion dollars (National Institute of Allergy and Infectious Diseases, 1992). The infection rates contribute to a sizable morbidity and place an additional burden on medical services. The absence of GC treatment can lead to serious sequelae, including more complicated infections of the genitourinary and reproductive systems. Among women, the untreated disease can eventually result in tubal infertility or ectopic pregnancy (Zenilman, 1993).

The potential for reinfection makes GC fundamentally different from most reportable diseases, in which reinfection is either uncommon or impossible (Beller, Middaugh, Gellin, & Ingle, 1992). Factors contributing to the prevalence of GC are (a) the host's lack of acquired immunity, (b) the potential for asymptomatic infection, and (c) the bacteria's ability to evade the host's immune system (National Institute of Allergy and Infectious Diseases, 1992). Asymptomatic infected persons are believed to contribute disproportionately to the perpetuation of GC and may constitute a core group of transmitters (Upchurch, Brady, Reichart, & Hook, 1990). Beller and colleagues found that persons who had multiple infections accounted for nearly 17% of GC infections during a 5-year period. These may represent a core group of infected individuals. Moreover, the dramatic increases of penicillin-resistant strains occurring in certain regions of the United States may increase the rates of GC prevalence (CDC, 1994; Gorwitz, Nakashima, Moran, & Knapp, 1993; Handsfield, Rice, Roberts, & Holmes, 1989).

In addition to biological factors that contribute to the high prevalence of GC, behavioral characteristics have been reported to be associated with

GC (Handsfield et al., 1989; Schwarcz et al., 1992; Upchurch et al., 1990) and other sexually transmitted diseases (STDs; Booth, Watters, & Chitwood, 1993; Chirgwin, DeHovitz, Dillon, & McCormack, 1991; Kim, Marmor, Dubin, & Wolfe, 1993; Marx, Aral, Rolfs, Sterk, & Kahn, 1991; Richert et al., 1993). A collection of ethnographic reports (Ratner, 1993) describes the relationship between trading sex for drugs or money and smoking cocaine, and illustrates the multitude of risk profiles for STDs within drug using populations. Behaviors associated with acquiring STDs can be both direct (e.g., deliberate unprotected sexual contact) and indirect (e.g., drug use leading to unprotected sexual contact). The covariation of drug use and sexual behavior is often due to the context in which drugs are obtained and the extent of the drug user's perceived need for those drugs (Ratner).

In Alaska, GC rates are an important surrogate indicator of HIV risk. Where chlamydia is not reported and syphilis rates (1.34 per 100,000) are too low to be reliable indicators, GC rates are the most reliable long-term indicators of unsafe sexual behavior. GC rates have declined since their peak in the 1970s consistent with changes in the population. In 1993, a total of 676 cases of GC were reported with an overall rate of 115 per 100,000; highest rates were among 15-19 year old women, 834 per 100,000, and Blacks, 894 per 100,000 (State of Alaska HIV Prevention Planning Group, 1995). The average number of times individuals were infected with GC at the Alaska site ($M = 2.00$; $SD = 2.24$; $n = 394$) of the Cooperative Agreement (CA) closely represents the CA sites overall ($M = 1.96$; excluding Rio de Janeiro). The highest mean number of times infected with GC was at the St. Louis site ($M = 2.65$; $SD = 3.25$; $n = 103$) and the lowest was at the Puerto Rico site ($M = 1.35$; $SD = 0.89$; $n = 229$).

Where previous studies describing risk for GC utilize data from participants who are seeking STD treatment, this design is unique because data were collected at a non-clinical setting of drug users who were not in drug treatment. In addition to clinical studies, surveillance data is a primary source of GC information, however, both sources of data do not reflect the correlates of STDs as they are found among specific high-risk populations (Anderson, McCormick, and Fichtner, 1994). The aim of this study was to develop separate models enumerating GC risk factors for female and male drug users. Exploratory modeling suggested inclusion of a variety of health, socioeconomic, and behavioral factors as possible indicators of GC infection. The advantage of sample survey studies, as this one, is that it allows for more precise targeting measures where resources are limited. A limitation to such design is that it is cross-sectional and may not respond accurately to temporal effects.

METHOD

Report of current drug use behavior (i.e., smoking cocaine or injecting drugs) was confirmed by either positive urinalysis (ONTRAK Roche Diagnostics) for cocaine metabolites, morphine, or it was demonstrated by needle track marks. Participants self-reported sexual behaviors, sources of income, history of drug use, demographic information, history of incarceration, and number of times a doctor or nurse told them they had STD infection(s). The data collection instrument used was the Risk Behavior Assessment (RBA), a structured interview used throughout the CA. The RBA has been demonstrated to have substantial reliability and validity (Fisher et al., 1993; Needle et al., 1995; Dowling-Guyer et al., 1994; Weatherby et al., 1994).

GC infection was assessed by responses to two items: (a) the number of times participants report being told by a doctor or nurse that they had GC, and (b) the year they report last being treated. Utilizing the Dowling-Guyer et al. (1994) data, separate reliability analyses for number of times ($n = 222$) and year treated ($n = 64$) were performed. Test-retest reliability coefficients for number of times ($r = .94$) and year treated ($r = .93$) were both substantial. Test-retest reliability analyses were also conducted by gender. Among women, reliability coefficients for number of times ($r = .95$; $n = 57$) and year treated ($r = .99$; $n = 15$) were only slightly greater than number of times ($r = .94$; $n = 164$) and year treated ($r = .91$; $n = 48$) for men. Number of times had GC was recoded as ever or never because of the nonnormality of the distribution and similar use of the variable in previous research (Kim et al., 1993; Schwarcz et al., 1992; Upchurch et al., 1990).

Results of earlier studies suggest that separate models by gender better describe risk profiles because of interactions between gender and other factors (Paschane, Fenaughty, Cagle, & Fisher, 1995), and the difference in risk factors for hepatitis B infection between men and women (Kuhrt-Hunstiger & Fisher, 1994). Separate models were developed for identifying risk related to GC infection among drug users. Bivariate analyses included chi-square tests for categorical variables and Student's t tests for continuous variables. The SAS procedure PROC LOGISTIC (SAS Institute Inc., 1990) was used to analyze indicators of ever having had GC and model building was based on empirical findings. The fit of the model to the data was tested using appropriate regression diagnostics. Estimated odds ratios (*OR*) with 95% confidence intervals (*CI*) are reported for both models.

RESULTS

The study sample ($N = 1049$) consisted of 69% men and 31% women. The mean age was 35.2 years ($SD = 7.52$) for men and 32.9 years ($SD = $

7.35) for women. A summary of selected characteristics of the study sample, by gender, is reported in Table 1. More Whites (44%) participated than other race groups; however, a greater proportion of Blacks (36%) and American Indians/Alaska Natives (AI/ANs; 20%) participated than are represented in the Municipality of Anchorage, 6% each (Municipality of Anchorage, Community Planning & Development Department, 1993). A majority of the men (56%) and 42% of the women were single (never married and not living with a sex partner). The living situations for men and women often included living with another adult (frequently a sexual partner). Injection drug use within the last thirty days, a risk factor associated with the prevalence of the HIV, was reported by 33% of the men and 25% of the women. History of GC infection was equal for men and women (37%).

Table 2 contains a summary of STDs and sex-related behaviors included in the RBA for men and women. Both gender groups contain a greater number of individuals reporting infection with GC than any other

TABLE 1. Demographic Characteristics of Male and Female Drug Users in Alaska

Characteristic	Men (n = 728)		Women (n = 321)	
	n	%	n	%
Ethnicity				
White, not Hispanic	333	46	128	40
Black, not Hispanic	281	38	98	30
AI/AN	114	16	95	30
Marital Status				
Married	50	7	34	11
Single	405	56	136	42
Other	272	37	151	47
Education (years)				
< 12	236	33	133	42
12	264	36	109	34
> 12	228	31	78	24
Perceived homelessness	259	36	72	23
Injection drug user	238	33	79	25

Note. AI/AN refers to American Indian/Alaska Native. Missing values may reduce total *n*.

TABLE 2. Sexually Transmitted Diseases and Sex-Related Risk Behaviors Among Alaskan Drug Users

	Men			Women		
	M	SD	n	M	SD	n
History of disease						
Hepatitis B	1.50	2.00	103	1.31	1.09	48
Gonorrhea	2.18*	2.64	268	1.68	1.42	119
Syphilis	1.25	0.74	40	1.19	0.40	16
Genital warts	1.05	0.22	59	1.02	0.15	44
Chlamydia	1.33*	0.81	79	1.64	0.98	70
Genital herpes	1.07	0.38	27	1.09	0.30	21
Sexual activities (past 30-days)						
Traded sex for drugs	1.77*	1.09	13	5.17	7.10	35
Traded drugs for sex	5.19*	6.96	84	2.33	1.53	3
Traded sex for money	2.06*	1.44	16	38.26	116.68	53
Traded money for sex	2.82	4.29	22	3.00	.00	1
Number of sex partners	2.00*	2.33	559	5.84	23.63	276
Times without a condom	21.82	26.82	498	20.87	33.51	255

*$p < .05$.

disease (men, $n = 268$; women, $n = 119$). Among men and women, GC had the highest mean number of reinfections (men, $M = 2.18$, $SD = 2.64$; women, $M = 1.68$, $SD = 1.42$). There was a significant gender difference for number of infections for GC, $t(385) = 1.94$, $p = .05$, and chlamydia, $t(147) = 2.14$, $p = .03$. Where trading sex is a recent sex-related risk behavior, the most commonly reported activity among women is trading sex for money ($n = 53$) and among men is trading drugs for sex ($n = 84$). Significant differences ($p < .05$) between men and women were identified for all sex trading behaviors where such behaviors were present. The elevated number of times having had sex without a condom for both genders in the last 30-days ($M > 20$) indicates a potential risk for STDs and HIV among this sample of drug users. Women reported a significantly greater number of recent sex partners ($M = 5.84$, $SD = 23.63$) than did men ($M = 2.00$, $SD = 2.33$; $t(833) = 3.80, p < .01$).

Results of the multivariate logistic regression indicate that risk factors for GC among women ($n = 321$) were (a) ever traded sex for money ($OR = 2.68$; $CI = 1.53, 4.69$), (b) being AI/AN ($OR = 2.58$; $CI = 1.52, 4.39$), (c) perceiving oneself homeless ($OR = 1.94$; $CI = 1.10, 3.42$), and (d) ever traded sex for drugs ($OR = 1.66$; $CI = 0.91, 3.02$). Trading sex for drugs was retained even though it was not a significant parameter; removing this factor would cause a significant change in the estimated model fit. The main effects model with estimated coefficients, odds ratios, and 95% confidence intervals for predicting GC infection among female drug users is reported in Table 3.

Among men ($n = 728$), the risk factors for GC were (a) ever injected or snorted cocaine ($OR = 3.32$; $CI = 1.44, 7.64$), (b) being Black ($OR = 3.25$; $CI = 2.26, 4.68$), (c) being older (adjusted for an increase of 10 years at a time; $OR = 1.86$; $CI = 1.48, 2.35$), (d) acquiring illegal income excluding prostitution during the last 30 days ($OR = 1.83$; $CI = 1.25, 2.67$), and (e) ever using amphetamines ($OR = 1.69$; $CI = 1.13, 2.54$). Table 4 includes the estimated coefficients, odds ratios, and 95% confidence intervals of the main effects model for male drug users. The model describes the likelihood of men in the sample ever having had GC infection.

Age in years associated with history of GC infection is an expected artifact in this analyses; however, age was not significantly associated with GC among women (infected and not-infected, $M = 32.7$). Among men, age was significantly associated with history of GC infection (infected, $M = 37.5$; not-infected, $M = 33.8$; $t(726) = 6.49$, $p < .01$). No interactions were identified among factors in either models. The Hosmer-Lemeshow goodness-of-fit tests (Hosmer & Lemeshow, 1989) for women, $\chi^2 (8) = 10.91$, $p = .21$, and for men, $\chi^2 (8) = 8.83$, $p = .36$, demonstrate adequate model fit.

TABLE 3. Logistic Regression Model for Predicting Gonorrhea Among Drug Users ($n = 321$) in Alaska

Factor	β	$SE(\beta)$	OR	95% *CI*
Traded sex for money	0.98***	0.29	2.68	1.53, 4.69
AI/AN	0.95***	0.27	2.58	1.52, 4.39
Perceived homeless	0.66*	0.29	1.94	1.10, 3.42
Traded sex for drugs	0.51	0.31	1.66	0.91, 3.02
Constant	−1.53***	0.21		

Note. AI/AN refers to American Indian/Alaska Native.
*$p < .05$. ***$p < .001$.

TABLE 4. Logistic Regression Model for Predicting Gonorrhea Among Drug Users (*n* = 728) in Alaska

Factor	β	$SE(\beta)$	OR	95% CI
Used cocaine	1.20**	0.43	3.32	1.44, 7.64
Blacks	1.18***	0.19	3.25	2.26, 4.68
Age	0.06***	0.01	1.86	1.48, 2.35
Illegal income	0.60**	0.19	1.83	1.25, 2.67
Used amphetamines	0.52*	0.21	1.69	1.13, 2.54
Constant	−4.91***	0.61		

Note. The *OR* and 95% *CI* for age are adjusted for an increase of 10 years.
*$p < .05$. **$p < .01$. ***$p < .001$.

DISCUSSION

This study includes some limitations due to the structure of the variables included in the modeling. The outcome variable is self-reported history of GC and this may introduce undesirable measurement error to the model. Even though reliability of self-report is believed to be high where the RBA instrument is applied (see method; Dowling-Guyer et al., 1994; Fisher et al., 1993; Needle et al., 1995), validity of self-reported infection may be a problem and require further investigation. The same problem may be present for variables describing history of drug use or history of trading sex for money or drugs. Many of the methodological recommendations identified by Marx et al. (1991) in their review of previous studies reporting associations between sex, drugs, and STDs risk (e.g., comparison to uninfected group, specification of drugs used, gender differences, nonminorities, and rural populations) are addressed in this study. Due to small sample size, this model could not be replicated within this sample; therefore, it is recommended that similar modeling be applied among other samples of drug users.

The differences identified between models further describe what has been called a "core group" phenomenon (Rothenberg, 1983; Yorke, Hethcote, & Nold, 1978), a condition where GC prevalence is clustered sociodemographically among distinct subgroups of the population. Core groups maintain the potential for increased prevalence of GC and can contribute to the spread of treatment-resistant strains of GC, as well as the introduction of other STDs (Gershman & Rolfs, 1991). These findings are comparable with earlier reports that drug use is consistently associated with STDs, specifically, the link between chronic cocaine use and GC (Marx et al., 1991). The risk profile for men is consistent with data reported by local STD treatment centers, in that Blacks were more likely than Whites or AI/ANs to report history of GC infection. The risk profile for women is consistent with findings reported previously (Fisher, Cagle, & Wilson, 1993) that suggest Alaska Native women disproportionally engage in behaviors associated with risk for HIV infection. Not only are Alaskan women practicing behaviors associated with HIV infection, necessary HIV screening is infrequent among this population when accessing health care services. Queen, Cagle, Fisher, and Haverkos (1994) found that, of those women who access primary care providers and are drug users, 66% were not assessed for drug use or offered HIV testing.

The increased risk among AI/AN women (OR = 2.58) as compared to non-Native women suggest an ongoing need for STD prevention in this population. Earlier Alaskan based reports describing the association of race with GC identify AI/ANs at greatest risk (Blackwood, 1981, 1982). Compared to the national objective of 225 per 100,000 (CDC, 1994), the most dramatic results reported is a 5-year mean rate for AI/ANs as 1,470 per 100,000 (Toomey, Oberschelp, & Greenspan, 1989). Beller et al. (1992) compared single and multiple infection cases in Alaska over a 5-year period and identified AI/ANs as most likely to have multiple infections. The AI/AN population has access to free screening and treatment of STDs, and this may account for high prevalence rates of GC when it was first being reported in Alaska. Identifying AI/AN as a risk factor compared to other race groups parallels findings of Hart (1993) who reported that the indigenous population in Australia (aborigines) account for 31% of GC cases even though they comprise less than 2% of the population.

History of trading sex for money or drugs is considered a behavioral risk for GC. In this sample of drug users, a woman who has traded sex for money is over two and a half times more likely to have had a history of GC infection than a woman who has not traded sex for money. Likewise, a woman who has traded sex for drugs is over one and a half times more likely to have had GC. Prostitution has received little attention in Alaska, especially among AI/ANs. This may be due to the belief that high-risk sexual behaviors are primarily a characteristic of urban populations (Forney, Inciardi, & Lockwood, 1992). In addition, AI/ANs are stereotypically thought of as members of isolated communities where trading sex is not relied upon for economic survival. This sample of AI/AN women is often separated from their traditional community norms found outside the Municipality of Anchorage. The AI/AN women in this cohort often report several sex partners, unsafe sex, and high-risk drug using behaviors (Fenaughty, Fisher, MacKinnon, Wilson, & Cagle, 1994; Fisher et al., 1993). The risk factors identified illustrate that among drug using women, the greatest potential for GC infection lies among AI/ANs who perceive themselves to be homeless and are trading sex for money or drugs.

The Municipality of Anchorage has a substantial number of homeless who leave Anchorage for seasonal employment and return during the winter (Parker, Huelsman, Fisher, & Reynolds, 1995; Reynolds et al., 1994). The instability of homelessness may affect the individual's sense of safety or well-being, thereby compromising effective negotiations over sex behaviors and leading to greater exposure to STDs (Leonardo & Chrisler, 1992). Women who perceived themselves as homeless were almost twice as likely to have had history of gonorrhea infection. Identifying perceived homelessness as an indicator of GC among women and not men suggests a unique risk associated with homelessness in women and warrants further investigation. A woman who reports a self-perception of homelessness may also report recent living arrangements that do not fit an operational definition of homelessness. It seems that self-perception, however, has some significant association with behavior. It is important to emphasize that homelessness, in this case, is a matter of personal perception and that those women who have this view of themselves may have other characteristics that are cofactors that are not identified herein. Perceived homelessness has not previously been identified as associated with GC and may require further research.

The model for men is completely different from that for women. Previous studies have discussed the frequency of high-risk behaviors among Black men (Kim et al., 1993; Upchurch et al., 1990) and the association of cocaine use with the transmission of STDs (Schwarcz et al., 1992). The model for men includes two factors reported in the literature, history of cocaine use ($OR = 3.32$) and being Black compared to White or AI/AN ($OR = 3.25$). A review of 16 epidemiological studies (Marx et al., 1991) reported 14 studies that found an association between cocaine use and STDs. Recent findings in Alaska suggest a dramatic risk among Blacks, with GC infection rates of 894 per 100,000 compared to 115 per 100,000 for the overall population in Alaska (State of Alaska HIV Prevention Planning Group, 1995). Gershman and Rolfs (1991) suggest that race may be a surrogate marker for high-risk behavior, and if better defined, the core transmitters of a disease can be more clearly identified.

The model for men also included three main effects not previously reported as factors of GC: (a) older age, (b) amphetamine use, and (c) illegal income (excluding prostitution). For every ten additional years of age, men were almost twice as likely to have ever had GC. As an individual gets older they have more opportunity for GC infection, and these findings may be due to limitations identified in the methodology of this study. History of amphetamine use has not been described specifically as a factor of GC; however, Marx et al., (1991) does report one study identifying an association between amphetamines and syphilis infection. History of amphetamine use may characterize those drug users who prefer a greater variety of risk-taking behaviors or it may be a proxy for a specific social network. The illegal income variable is specific to income acquired during the last thirty days prior to interview. Among male drug users, illegal income is most likely to be related to the selling of drugs or other illegal activity in order to obtain money for purchasing drugs. The relationship between this behavior and GC is unclear. A risk prone personality may underlie both risky sexual behavior and participation in illegal activity, accounting for the covariation between history of GC and illegal income sources.

As the number of available disease screening resources decrease in the United States (Yankauer, 1994) and GC prevalence increases (CDC, 1994), more precise methods for targeting core groups of potentially infected people are needed. The models reported here better describe gender differences of risk factors for GC in a sample commonly believed to be at high-risk for HIV and other STDs. Haverkos (1991) argues that the integration of drug abuse and STD treatments would improve the effectiveness of interventions designed for targeting those individuals participating in high-risk behaviors. Support for this argument has been tested by clinical trials among injection drug users (Umbricht-Schneiter, Ginn, Pabst, & Bigelow, 1994). If implemented, this approach may have a substantial effect on GC rates in Alaska. Having unique risk profiles for GC may benefit public health professionals developing HIV/STD interventions in Alaska. At a minimum, HIV screening among drug using women should increase where such population is seeking treatment for GC infection. In addition, the main effects reported in this study suggest the existence of covariates not previously discussed in the literature. Future studies should investigate the strength of these covariates as they may provide additional insights into the prevention of disease transmission.

AUTHOR NOTE

For their supportive efforts the authors wish to acknowledge the assistance of the staff of the Drug Abuse Research Field Station; Bonnie Long and staff of the Municipality of Anchorage Sexually Transmitted Disease Clinic; Jeri van den Top and the staff of the Alaska Health Sciences Information Service, University of Alaska Anchorage; and the Department of Psychology, University of Alaska Anchorage.

REFERENCES

Anderson, J. E., McCormick, L., & Fichtner, R. (1994). Factors associated with self-reported STDs: Data from a national survey. *Sexually Transmitted Diseases, 21,* 303-308.

Beller, M., Middaugh, J., Gellin, B., & Ingle, D. (1992). The contribution of reinfection to gonorrhea incidence in Alaska, 1983 to 1987. *Sexually Transmitted Diseases, 19,* 41-46.

Blackwood, L. (1981). Epidemiology of gonorrhea in Native Alaskans. *British Journal of Venereal Disease, 57,* 372-375.

Blackwood, L. G. (1982). Repeated infections with Neisseria gonorrhoeae in a population of Alaska Natives. *Sexually Transmitted Diseases, 9,* 89-92.

Booth, R. E., Watters, J. K., & Chitwood, D. D. (1993). HIV risk-related sex behaviors among injection drug users, crack smokers, and injection drug users who smoke crack. *American Journal of Public Health, 83,* 1144-1148.

Center for Disease Control and Prevention. (1994). *Sexually transmitted disease surveillance, 1993.* Atlanta, GA: Author.

Chirgwin, K., DeHovitz, J. A., Dillon, S., & McCormack, W. M. (1991). HIV infection, genital ulcer disease, and crack cocaine use among patients attending a clinic for sexually transmitted diseases. *American Journal of Public Health, 81,* 1576-1579.

Dowling-Guyer, S., Johnson, M. E., Fisher, D. G., Needle, R., Watters, J., Anderson, M., Williams, M., Kotranski, L., Booth, R., Rhodes, F., Weatherby, N., Estada, A. L., Fleming, D., Deren, S., & Tortu, S. (1994). Reliability of drug users' self-reported HIV risk behaviors and validity of self-reported recent drug use. *Assessment, 1,* 383-392.

Fenaughty, A. M., Fisher, D. G., MacKinnon, D. P., Wilson, P. J., & Cagle, H. H. (1994). Predictors of condom use among Alaskan Native, White, and Black drug users in Alaska. *Arctic Medical Research, 53,* 704-711.

Fisher, D. G., Cagle, H. H., & Wilson, P. J. (1993). Drug use and HIV risk in Alaska Natives. *Drugs & Society, 7,* 107-117.

Fisher, D. G., Needle, R., Weatherby, N., Brown, B., Booth, R., Williams, M. et al. (1993). Reliability of drug user self-report [abstract]. *Proceedings of the IXth International Conference on AIDS, 9 (2),* 776.

Forney, M. A., Inciardi, J. A., & Lockwood, D. (1992). Exchanging sex for crack-cocaine: A comparison of women from rural and urban communities. *Journal of Community Health, 17,* 73-85.

Gershman, K. A., & Rolfs, R. T. (1991). Diverging gonorrhea and syphilis trends in the 1980s: Are they real? *American Journal of Public Health, 81,* 1263-1267.

Gorwitz, R. J., Nakashima, A. K., Moran, J. S., & Knapp, J. S. (1993). Sentinel surveillance for antimicrobial resistance in *Neisseria gonorrhoeae*–United States, 1988-1991. *Morbidity and Mortality Weekly Report, 42,* 29-39.

Handsfield, H. H., Rice, R. J., Roberts, M. C., & Holmes, K. K. (1989). Localized outbreak of penicillinase-producing Neisseria gonorrhoeae. *Journal of the American Medical Association, 261,* 2357-2361.

Hart, G. (1993). Risk profiles and epidemiologic interrelationships of sexually transmitted diseases. *Sexually Transmitted Diseases, 20,* 126-136.

Haverkos, H. W. (1991). Infectious diseases and drug abuse. *Journal of Substance Abuse Treatment, 8,* 269-275.

Hosmer, D. W., Jr., & Lemeshow, S. (1989). *Applied Logistic Regression.* New York: John Wiley & Sons.

Kim, M. Y., Marmor, M., Dubin, N., & Wolfe, H. (1993). HIV risk-related sexual behaviors among heterosexuals in New York City: Associated with race, sex, and intravenous drug use. *AIDS, 7,* 409-414.

Kuhrt-Hunstiger, T. I., & Fisher, D. G. (1994). Hepatitis B: How unique is Alaska? [Abstract]. *Abstracts of the 122nd Annual Meeting and Exhibition of the American Public Health Association*, Washington, DC (3106-310).

Leonardo, C., & Chrisler, J. C. (1992). Women and sexually transmitted diseases. *Women & Health, 18,* 1-15.

Marx, R., Aral, S. O., Rolfs, R. T., Sterk, C. E., & Kahn, J. G. (1991). Crack, sex, and STD. *Sexually Transmitted Diseases, 18,* 92-101.

Municipality of Anchorage, Community Planning & Development Department. (1993). *Anchorage indicators.* Anchorage, AK: Author.

National Institute of Allergy and Infectious Diseases. (1992). *Sexually transmitted diseases.* Bethesda, MD: Author.

Needle, R., Fisher, D. G., Weatherby, N., Chitwood, D., Brown, B., Cesari, H., Booth, R., Williams, M. L., Watters, J., Andersen, M., & Braunstein, M. (1995). The reliability of self-reported HIV risk behaviors of drug users. *Psychology of Addictive Behaviors, 9* (4), 242-250.

Parker, B., Huelsman, M. D., Fisher, D. G., & Reynolds, G. (1995). Predictors of homeless persons purchasing alcoholic beverages. [Abstract]. *Abstracts of the 123rd Annual Meeting and Exhibition of the American Public Health Association*, San Diego, CA (2010.2-116).

Paschane, D. M., Fenaughty, A. M., Cagle, H. H., & Fisher, D. G. (1995). Predictors for Gonorrhea Infection in Alaskan Drug Users. [Abstract]. *Abstracts of the 123rd Annual Meeting and Exhibition of the American Public Health Association*, San Diego, CA (3004-291).

Queen, P. J., Cagle, H. H., Fisher, D. G., & Haverkos, H. (1994). Female drug users: Provider assessment of AIDS risk [Abstract]. *Tenth International Conference on AIDS*, Yokohama, Japan (PD0505).

Ratner, M. (Ed.). (1993). *Crack pipe as pimp: An ethnographic investigation of sex-for-crack exchanges.* New York: Lexington Books.

Reynolds, G., Huelsman, M. D., Fisher, D. G., Parker, W., Jones, J., & Beirne, H. (1994). A 14-year comparison of Alaska homeless. *Arctic Medical Research, 53,* 209-212.

Richert, C. A., Peterman, T. A., Zaidi, A. A., Ransom, R. L., Wroten, J. E., & Witte, J. J. (1993). A method for identifying persons at high risk for sexually transmitted infections: Opportunity for targeting intervention. *American Journal of Public Health, 83,* 520-524.

Rothenberg, R. B. (1983). The geography of gonorrhea: Empirical demonstration of core group transmission. *American Journal of Epidemiology, 117*, 688-694.

SAS Institute Inc. (1990). *SAS/STAT user's guide, version 6, fourth edition, volume 1*. Cary, NC: Author.

Schwarcz, S. K., Bolan, G. A., Fullilove, M., McCright, J., Fullilove, R., Kohn, R., & Rolfs, R. T. (1992). Crack cocaine and the exchange of sex for money or drugs. *Sexually Transmitted Diseases, 19*, 7-13.

State of Alaska HIV Prevention Planning Group. (1995). *HIV prevention plan*. Anchorage, AK: Author.

Toomey, K. E., Oberschelp, A. G., & Greenspan, J. R. (1989). Sexually transmitted diseases and Native Americans: Trends in reported gonorrhea and syphilis morbidity, 1984-88. *Public Health Reports, 104*, 566-572.

Umbricht-Schneiter, A., Ginn, D. H., Pabst, K. M., & Bigelow, G. E. (1994). Providing medical care to methadone clinic patients: Referral vs. on-site care. *American Journal of Public Health, 84*, 207-210.

Upchurch, D. M., Brady, W. E., Reichart, C. A., & Hook, E. W., III. (1990). Behavioral contributions to acquisition of gonorrhea in patients attending an inner city sexually transmitted disease clinic. *Journal of Infectious Diseases, 161*, 938-941.

Weatherby, N. L., Needle, R., Cesari, H., Booth, R., McCoy, C. B., Watters, J. K., Williams, M., & Chitwood, D. D. (1994). Validity of self-reported drug use among injection drug users and crack cocaine users recruited through street outreach. *Evaluation and Program Planning, 17*, 347-355.

Yankauer, A. (1994). Sexually transmitted diseases: A neglected public health priority. *American Journal of Public Health, 84*, 1894-1897.

Yorke, J. A., Hethcote, H. W., & Nold, A. (1978). Dynamics and control of the transmission of gonorrhea. *Sexually transmitted diseases, 5*, 51-56.

Zenilman, J. M. (1993, February 28). Gonorrhea: Clinical and public health issues. *Hospital Practice*, 29-50.

Women and Violence:
A Different Look

Bridget S. Murphy, CSAC
Sally J. Stevens, PhD
Robin A. McGrath, CSAC
Harry K. Wexler, PhD
Deborah Reardon

SUMMARY. The incidents of violence involving women and the use of alcohol and other drugs (AOD) among women has increased at an alarming rate. In spite of this, little research has been conducted on the role (i.e., perpetrator vs. victim) that drug using women assume in different episodes and/or settings of violence, and with whom these violent encounters occur. This study describes the self reported life experience of violent encounters of 98 women enrolled in a residential drug treatment center in Tucson, Arizona. Results of the study indicate that many of the women were both the perpetrators and victims of violence. Additionally, the results indicate that aggressive acts from or against others may, in part, be related to the amount of power or control that women had in the relationship as

---

Bridget S. Murphy is Evaluation Coordinator; Sally J. Stevens, Quality Assurance; Robin A. McGrath is Project Director; Harry K. Wexler is Project Evaluator; and Deborah Reardon is Research Assistant, all at the National Development and Research Institutes, Desert Willow Project.

The authors would like to acknowledge the work of the National Development and Research Institute Desert Willow Evaluation Department for assistance in preparing this paper including: Mary Cuadrado, MA; Elizabeth Loman, BA; and Ralph Wilson, BA.

Funding for this project was provided by the Center for Substance Abuse Treatment (1 H86 SFO 5696).

[Haworth co-indexing entry note]: "Women and Violence: A Different Look." Murphy, Bridget S. et al. Co-published simultaneously in *Drugs & Society* (The Haworth Press, Inc.) Vol. 13, No. 1/2, 1998, pp. 131-144; and: *Women and Substance Abuse: Gender Transparency* (ed: Sally J. Stevens, and Harry K. Wexler) The Haworth Press, Inc., 1998, pp. 131-144. Single or multiple copies of this article are available for a fee from The Haworth Document Delivery Service [1-800-342-9678, 9:00 a.m. - 5:00 p.m. (EST). E-mail address: getinfo@haworthpressinc.com].

131

well as the setting in which the violence occurred. *[Article copies available for a fee from The Haworth Document Delivery Service: 1-800-342-9678. E-mail address: getinfo@haworthpressinc.com]*

INTRODUCTION

The increase in violence in the past decade has become a concern to most people living in the United States. Every night on the local and national news most people hear reports of at least one or two murders in their city. Gang related crime, domestic violence, and many displays of random violence have moved into our cities, townships, and rural communities. Researchers and law makers have begun to try to explain the apparent increase in violence and define ways to remedy this epidemic. Many studies have looked at the relationship between violence and alcohol and other drug (AOD) use (Norris & Cubbins, 1992; Goldstein, Bellucci, Spunt, & Miller, 1991, Stevens & Arbiter, 1995). A consistent finding demonstrates a positive correlation between AOD use and level of violence. Stevens and Arbiter (1995) note that in a sample of women enrolled in a residential substance abuse treatment program (N = 61), 90% reported having been physically assaulted and 95% reported having been raped in their lifetime.

Paralleling the observed increase in violence, AOD use among women has increased. In 1990 the New York Times reported that of the 9.5 million drug users in the United States, 5.5 million were women. Daily use of highly addictive drugs by women is not uncommon. In one study of injection drug users, women were more likely than men to report daily injection of heroin and "speedballs" (Brown & Weissman, 1993). The use of crack cocaine has been linked to a rise in illegal drug use among women (Forbes, 1993) and has been found to be the drug of choice for many injection drug using women who were not enrolled in drug treatment (Weissman, Sowder, Young, and the National AIDS Research Consortium, 1990). Additionally, Stevens (1996) found an increase in amphetamine use by in treatment and out of treatment female drug users; a drug that has been associated with increased levels of violence (Bowden, 1996).

Along with the upward trend in AOD use among women, researchers have begun to more closely examine the role women play in different episodes and/or settings of violence; are women becoming more violent, and, if so, against whom and in what settings?

The research regarding aggression in men and women has more often than not confirmed that men are more aggressive than women. However, there have been studies in which the authors have argued that "men are always more aggressive than women" cannot be substantiated (Eagly &

Steffen, 1986; Frodi, Macaulay, & Thome, 1977; Hyde & Linn, 1986; White, 1983). Harris (1991) reported that while women have been found to physically abuse men about as often as men abuse women, the degree of injury sustained was higher for the women. Results of one spousal abuse national survey indicated women were more likely than men to report physically abusing their spouses; "wives committed an average of 10.3 acts of violence against their husbands whereas their husbands averaged only 8.8 acts against their wives" (Steinmetz & Lucca, 1988, pp. 237-238). Self-reports of violent actions toward an intimate partner indicate that physical violence of women toward their husbands or boyfriends is similar to men's toward their wives or girlfriends (Sorenson, Upchurch, & Shen, 1996). In a Bureau of Justice study, Dawson and Langan, (1994) reported that a third of family murders involved a female as the killer. In sibling murders, females were 15% of the killers, and in murders of parents, 18%. In spouse murders, women represented 41% of killers. In murders of their offspring, women predominated, accounting for 55% of killers. An interesting theory presented in an article by White and Kowalski (1994) is that women are more aggressive in environments like the home due to "gender roles." "The resultant opportunity to engage in violence against husbands and children was greater than the opportunity to aggress in the public sphere" (White & Kowalski, 1994, pp. 495). Perhaps women may be as aggressive as men, but because women's aggression more often takes place in the home, it is not as visible and consequently may be more difficult to detect and study. While there is evidence that women can be violent, particularly in the home setting, the level of violence exhibited by women may be greater than what has been documented as women may be reluctant to admit that they engage in violence in the home for fear of loosing custody of their children.

Literature written about women substance abusers as perpetrators of violence is limited. How "type of violence" (e.g., verbal vs. physical vs. sexual) might differ depending upon with whom (e.g., father, sex partner, stranger) the violent encounter occurs has not been adequately investigated. Studies regarding the situation and/or setting in which women may more often be the perpetrators of violence versus the victim of violence are also limited. However, based on White and Kowalski (1994), we hypothesized that women would be the perpetrator of violence against sibling(s), sex partner(s), and their children (i.e., in a "home setting" in which they might feel more power and/or control) more often than a perpetrator of violence against a stranger. Moreover, it is thought that while women would frequently report being a victim of violence from family member(s), many women would also report being the victim of violence from a stranger.

METHODOLOGY

Instruments and Procedures

The National Development and Research Institutes (NDRI) Desert Willow Evaluation Department in conjunction with clinicians from NDRI Desert Willow and other treatment programs developed the Violence Questionnaire. The questionnaire examines whether the participant was a victim or a perpetrator of violence. It asked what type of violence the participant encountered; verbal, physical, sexual or a combination of any/ or all three. The questionnaire contained a list of possible people with whom the participant could have encountered any of these types of violence. These people included: mother, father, siblings, sexual partner, other relatives, children, friends, strangers, authority figures, and gang related crimes. The participants were asked whether or not a weapon was used for those who encountered physical or sexual violence and how disturbing the encounter was at the time of the incident. The questionnaire asked about the age of first rape, whether or not the rape was reported to authorities, and whether the participant pursued prosecution. The participants were asked their age of first sexual encounter, and whether their first sexual experience was a rape. Additionally, the participants were asked how many sexual partners they had in their lifetime.

The Violence Questionnaire was administered during the baseline interview. This interview occurred within the first two weeks of treatment entry and was conducted in a private, individual session with a trained interviewer. Prior to the administration of the instrument, the interviewer explained to the women that the information gathered during the interview would be kept confidential: (1) that an identification number would be assigned to her; (2) that her data would not be shared with the clinical staff; and (3) all reports written about the data would only include aggregated data in which there would not be any identifying information. During the baseline interview the women also completed additional instruments including, but not limited, to the: Addictions Severity Index; Beck Depression Inventory; Beck Hopelessness Scale; and the SCL-90.

RESULTS

The sample included 98 adult women. All women were enrolled in the NDRI Desert Willow residential substance abuse treatment program funded by the Center for Substance Abuse Treatment. Basic demographics of this group were as follows: in self reports of their ethnic group 64.3% were White; 16.3% were African American; 12.2% were Hispanic; and 7.1% were Native American. In regard to their marital status, 51.0% had never been married, 25.5% were married, 14.3% divorced, 8.2% separated, and 1.0% remarried. The average age of these women was 30.7 years old and the average number of years in school was 11.9 (Table 1).

The substance that the women self reported as having caused them most difficulty was as follows: 40.8% cocaine/crack; 19.4% amphetamines; 14.3% heroin; 13.3% alcohol; 7.1% marijuana; 3.1% other opiates; and 2.0% reported no AOD problem. The average number of years these women used drugs (not including alcohol) was 13.5 years. Additionally, 34% of the women reported that they had overdosed on drugs at least once in their lifetime (Table 2).

TABLE 1. Demographic Characteristics: Ethnicity, Age, Education, and Marital Status (N = 98)

	%	N
Ethnicities		
White	64.3	63
African American	16.3	16
Native American	7.1	7
Hispanic	12.2	12
	%	N
Age*		
18-25	22.4	22
26-33	52.0	51
Over 33	25.5	25
	%	N
Education**		
11 years or less	29.6	29
GED or high school grad	37.8	37
More than high school	32.7	32
	%	N
Marital Status		
Never married	51.0	50
Married	25.5	25
Divorced	14.3	14
Separated	8.2	8
Remarried	1.0	1

* Mean age 30.7
** Mean education 11.9

TABLE 2. Primary Drug of Choice (N = 98)

	%	N
Cocaine/Crack	40.8	40
Amphetamines	19.4	19
Heroin	14.3	14
Alcohol	13.3	13
Marijuana	7.1	7
Other opiates	3.1	3
No problem	2.0	2

In relation to the criminal justice system 52% were on probation or parole at the time of enrollment and 51% reported that their entry into the treatment program was prompted or suggested by the criminal justice system, including prompting from Child Protective Services. Furthermore, 89% of the women reported having been arrested at least once with an average number of arrests of 11 times. The average age of first arrest was 18.7 years. Sixty-three percent of the women reported being incarcerated for one month or longer. The average number of months incarcerated was 20.1. The last charge for which the women were incarcerated included: 35.5% parole/probation violations; 21.1% drug charges; 6.7% assault; 6.7% burglary/larceny; 5.3% forgery; 5.3% shoplifting; 3.9% prostitution; 2.6% child abuse/neglect; 1.3% weapons offense; 1.3% robbery; and 10.4% other charges (DWI, contempt of court, and major driving violations) (Table 3).

Data from the Violence Questionnaire is best illustrated by reporting not only the mean but the median and mode scores as well given the extreme range of responses. Seventy-one percent of the women reported being assaulted at least once in their life with the average number of times being 354 (median = 17.5 and mode = 2.0). The average age of first assault was 11.5 years. Sixty-five percent of the women reported being the victim of rape at least once in their life with the average being 60 (median = 3 and mode = 1). The average age of first rape was 13.0 years. Additionally, 48.4% of the women reported that their first sexual experience was a rape.

Women as Perpetrators

The women were asked about violent encounters in which they were the perpetrators against family members. Table 4 shows that: 28.6% were a perpetrator of violence against their mother with a average number of times at 170 (median = 5 and mode = 1). The most frequent type of violence against their mother was verbal violence at 82.1%. Of the women

TABLE 3. Charge for Last Incarceration (N = 76)

	%	N
Parole/Probation Violations	35.5	27
Drug Charges	21.1	16
Burglary/Larceny	6.7	5
Assault	6.7	5
Shoplifting	5.3	4
Forgery	5.3	4
Prostitution	3.9	3
Child Abuse/Neglect	2.6	2
Weapons Offense	1.3	1
Robbery	1.3	1
Other Charges	10.4	8

who reported some type of physical violence, 40% stated that they used a weapon. In relation to perpetrating violence against their father 20% of the women reported they had at least one instance of violence against their father. The average number of times was 98 (median = 6.5 and mode = 2). Again, the most frequent type of violence against their father was verbal at 45%. Of the women who encountered physical or sexual violence against their father, 18% stated that they used a weapon. Forty-nine percent reported having at least one violent encounter against their sibling(s). The average number of times was 39.5 (median = 5 and mode = 2). Interestingly, the most frequent type of violence against siblings was verbal/physical at 62.5%. Of the women who reported physical violence, 23.1% stated that they had used a weapon. In relation to the women who reported violence as the perpetrator against their sexual partner, 58.2% of the women reported at least one instance of violence. The average number of times was 208 (median = 6 and mode = 1). The most frequent type of violence against their sexual partner was verbal/physical at 66.7%. Of the women who reported physical or sexual violence, 48.9% stated that they used a weapon. Just over 21% reported being a perpetrator of violence at least once against their children. The average number of times was 32 (median = 10 and mode = 3). The most frequent type of violence against their children was verbal only at 47.6%. Of the women who reported physical violence against their children 27.3% stated that they used a weapon.

The women were asked about violent encounters in which they were the perpetrators against strangers. Thirty-one percent of the women reported perpetrating violence against a stranger at least once. The average number of times was 64 (median = 8 and mode = 3). The most frequent type of violence against a stranger was physical/verbal at 56.6%. Of the women who reported physical violence, 57.7% reported that they used a weapon (Table 4). As expected women more frequently reported being the perpetrator of violence against siblings (49.0%) and sexual partners (58.2%) than against strangers (30.6%). However, a smaller percentage of women reported violence against their children (21.4%) than originally anticipated.

Women as Victims

The women were asked the same set of questions only with reference to victimization. Table 5 shows that 49% stated that they had been a victim of violence from their mother. The average number of times was 471 (median = 20 and mode = 1). The most frequent type of violence encountered from their mother was verbal/physical at 54.0%. Of the women who reported physical violence, 52% stated that a weapon was used. In relation to their father, 41.8% stated they had been the victim of violence from their father. The average number of times was 271 (median = 20 and mode = 1). The most frequent type of violence encountered from their father was verbal/physical at 41.5%. Of the women who were victimized physically or sexually by their father, 48.4% stated that a weapon was used. Almost 50% of the women reported being the victim of violence from their sibling(s). The average number of times was 110 (median = 10 and mode = 1). The most frequent type of violence encountered from their sibling(s) was verbal/physical at 56.5%. Of the women who reported physical or sexual violence, 51.4% reported that a weapon was used. In relation to their sexual partners, 78.6% of the women reported being a victim of violence. The average number of times was 104 (median = 20 and mode = 1). The most frequent type of violence encountered from their sexual partners was verbal/physical at 45.5%. Of the women who were the victims of physical and/or sexual violence from their sexual partners, 52.8% reported that a weapon was used.

Victimization from a stranger, was reported by 52% of the women. The average number of times was 105 (median = 5 and mode = 1). The most frequent type of violence encountered from a stranger was verbal/physical/sexual at 45.1%. Of the women that reported physical and/or sexual violence from a stranger 58.8% reported that a weapon was used (Table 5). As expected, the women in this study reported being the victim of violence

TABLE 4. Women as Perpetrators of Violence (Lifetime) (N = 98)

Association	Mean Times	% reported	% used weapon*	% verbal only	% physical only	% sexual only	% physical/ verbal	% verbal/ sexual	% physical/ sexual	% verbal/ physical/ sexual
Against Mother	170	28.00	40.00	82.10	7.10	0.00	10.70	0.00	0.00	0.00
Against Father	98	20.00	18.00	45.00	0.00	0.00	0.00	40.00	15.00	0.00
Against Sibling(s)	40	49.00	23.10	18.80	18.80	0.00	62.50	0.00	0.00	0.00
Against Sex Partner	208	58.20	48.90	17.50	8.80	0.00	66.70	0.00	0.00	7.00
Against Children	32	21.40	27.30	47.60	9.50	0.00	42.90	0.00	0.00	0.00
Against Stranger	64	30.60	57.70	13.30	30.00	0.00	56.60	0.00	0.00	0.00

* Excludes women who reported only verbal violence

TABLE 5. Women as Victims of Violence (Lifetime) (N = 98)

Association	Mean Times	% reported	% used weapon*	% verbal only	% physical only	% sexual only	% physical/ verbal	% verbal/ sexual	% physical/ sexual	% verbal/ physical/ sexual
From Mother	471	49.00	52.00	31.30	14.60	0.00	54.00	0.00	0.00	0.00
From Father	271	41.80	48.40	24.40	7.30	4.90	41.50	4.90	2.40	14.60
From Sibling(s)	110	46.90	51.40	19.60	10.90	2.20	56.50	2.20	2.20	6.50
From Sex Partner	104	78.60	52.80	9.10	5.20	2.60	45.50	1.30	1.30	35.10
From Children	15	1.00	0.00	100.00	0.00	0.00	0.00	0.00	0.00	0.00
From Stranger	105	52.00	58.80	2.00	13.70	11.80	13.70	2.00	11.70	45.10

* Excludes women who reported only verbal violence

from numerous people including, those in the "home setting" who might have more power/control in the relationship (mother = 49.0%; father = 41.8%; sibling(s) = 46.9%; sex partners = 78.6%). Also as expected, a large percentage (52.0%) of the women reported being the victims of violence from a stranger.

DISCUSSION

Data from this study presents some enlightening information. First, almost all of women in this study experienced violence in some form; either as the perpetrator and/or the victim of violence. More than half of the women reported being the perpetrator of violence against someone. While this may seem like a high percentage, perhaps more astounding is the frequency of violent occurrences that the women reported. In other words, if women reported being the perpetrator of violence, then it often followed that they were the perpetrator of violence on numerous occa- sions. This same pattern held for those who reported being the victim of violence. At least 78% of the women reported being the victim of some type of violence. Those who reported being the victim of violence often reported many incidences in which they were the victim. For a few of the women, the number of incidences involving perpetration or victimization of violence was extreme. This is indicated by the differences in the mean, median, and mode scores for the various types of perpetration and victimization experiences. For some of the women, violence, in some form, occurred almost daily over a period of several years.

As can be seen from the data the large percentage of women who reported being the perpetrators of violence against their mother, father, and sibling(s) was similar to the large percentage of women who reported victimization, suggesting that violence, for some women, may have been part of a family dynamic. As one woman stated: "violence is the way we communicated; we use our fists whereas other people talk."

Women in the "home setting" typically have power over their children. Consequently, it was thought that given this power differential women would report perpetrating violence against their children more frequently than against people with whom this power differential does not exist. Unexpectedly, data from this study shows that fewer women (21%) reported being the perpetrator of violence against their children, compared to 30% who reported being the perpetrators of violence against a stranger. It should be noted, however, that the stated percentage of violence against children may be underreported as the women may have been reluctant to report aggressive acts toward their children for fear of loosing custody of them.

While women reported being the perpetrator of violence against their sexual partner less often (58.2%) than being the victim of violence by their sexual partner (78.2%), this difference is accounted for by the high percentage of male partners violating their female partner sexually. Over 35% of the women were the recipients of verbal/physical/sexual violence from their sexual partner. This high percentage of sexual violence toward female partners substantiates previous studies that report increased levels of sexual violence against women by their male sex partners.

As expected, women were less likely to be the perpetrator of violence toward a stranger (30.6%) as opposed to the recipient of violence (52.0%). This supports the White and Kowalski (1994) hypothesis that women may be just as aggressive or violent as men, but, "gender roles" impact the situation or circumstance in which violence occurs. Women generally do not have as much power or control in a more public setting as compared to the home setting. Consequently they may more often be the recipient of a violent encounter from a stranger.

Given this data, several treatment recommendations are indicated. First, substance abuse treatment programs must address the issue of the violence that the women have encountered in their lives. For women who have experienced a violent encounter (that may or may not have included having been raped) evaluation of, and treatment for, Post Traumatic Stress Disorder may be necessary. For women who have encountered violence on a daily or weekly basis over a period of several years, additional psychological help and communication training may be called for. These women may need counseling to "de-role" from their "norm" of violence. They may need additional assistance in learning new, less aggressive ways to communicate. Because many women have experienced violence as children and now, as adults, engage in aggressive acts against their own children, treatment programs must address the cycle of violence. Exploration into how one's childhood experiences influence present behavior may help to identify patterns of abuse which may, in turn, lead to positive behavior change.

While treatment programs may already focus on issues regarding victimization, programs may not be addressing the issues of women as perpetrators of violence. Treatment providers should address the harm that women may have done to others as well as negative feelings that they might have regarding not protecting others (e.g., their children) from other abusers. Issues of guilt and shame must be dealt with in an emotionally safe and confidential environment. Providing a way in which the women can make "amends" for their past aggressive behavior is important for their recovery process. Additionally, treatment programs should educate and assist women in developing more positive ways of handling their frustration and anger. Role playing situations that have previously led to violence and providing alternative solutions may help women in developing alternative and more appropriate communication skills.

At the NDRI Desert Willow program, the clinical staff have facilitated curriculum on violence for the past four years. Screening for the level and type of violence occurs within two weeks of intake and is ongoing throughout the women's treatment stay. Additionally, how the experience of violence has affected the psychosocial, physical, and daily functioning of the women is also assessed. Degrees of violence including victimization (i.e., assault, rape, molestation) perpetration (i.e., assault, hate crimes, child abuse) and witnessing (i.e., gang rapes, murders, child torture) are addressed in individual sessions with trained counselors, in therapeutic groups, and in workshops.

While this study supports the need for treatment for issues involving both perpetration and victimization of violence, further study is called for. Investigators may want to examine the relationship of background variables such as ethnicity, age, and primary drug of choice with frequency of perpetration and victimization of violence. Additionally, numerous research questions need to be addressed. Can the findings reported in this study on the perpetration of violence by women be replicated? Is there a correlation between being victimized as a child and being a perpetrator of violence as an adult? Who initiates violence in the household, men or women? In regards to incidents of violence between partners, do women become violent in response to an already aggressive male partner? What are most violent episodes caused by (i.e., financial problems, obtaining drugs, infidelity, child care)? Are women more likely to be violent against their children than are men, given equal child interaction time of mothers and fathers?

Finally, further research is needed on what treatment approaches might work best for sensitive issues such as violence. How can treatment providers help substance abusing women who have had histories of violence, understand the role violence has played in their lives and unravel their experience so that they can go on to lead productive non-violent lives?

REFERENCES

Bowden, K. (1996). *Street Drugs & Methamphetamine.* Presented at the Interagency Council on Alcohol and Drug Addictions Training Conference, March 28, 1996. Tucson, Arizona.

Brown, V., & Weisman, G. (1993). Women and men injection drug users: An updated look at gender differences and risk factors. In B.S. Brown & G.M.

Beschner with the National AIDS Research Consortium (Eds.), *Handbook on risk of AIDS. Injection drug users and sexual partners.* Westport, CT: Greenwood Press.

Dawson, J.M., & Langan, P.A. (1994). Bureau of Justice Statistics: Special Report. Washington, D.C.: United States Department of Justice.

Eagly, A.H., & Steffen, V.J. (1986). Gender and aggressive behavior: A meta-analytic review of the social psychological literature. *Psychological Bulletin, 100,* 309-330.

Forbes, A. (1993). Crack cocaine and HIV: How the national drug-addiction-treatment deficits fan the pandemic's flames. *AIDS and Public Policy Journal, 8,* 44-52.

Frodi, A., Macaulay, J., & Thome, PR. (1977). Are women less aggressive than men? A review of the experimental literature. *Psychological Bulletin, 84,* 634-680.

Goldstein, P.J., Bellucci, P.A., Spunt, B.J., and Miller, T. (1991). Volume of cocaine use violence: A comparison between men and women. *Journal of Drug Issues, 21* (2), 345-367.

Harris, M.B. (1991). Effects of sex of aggressor, sex of target, and relationship on evaluations of physical aggression. *Journal of Interpersonal Violence, 6* (2), 174-186.

Hyde, J.S., & Linn, M.C., (1986). *The psychology of gender: Advances through meta-analysis.* Baltimore: Johns Hopkins Press.

New York Times, (January 1990). Ideas & trends: Drug treatment is scarcer than ever for women: pp. 26-27.

Norris, J., & Cubbins, L.A. (1992). Dating, drinking, and rape; Effects of victim's and assailant's alcohol consumption and judgments of their behavior and traits. *Psychology of Women Quarterly, 16,* 179-191.

Sorenson, S.B, Upchurch, D., & Shen, H. (1996). Violence and injury in marital arguments: Risk patterns and gender differences. *American Journal of Public Health 86* (1), 35-40.

Steinmetz, S.K., & Lucca, J.S. (1988). Husband battering. In V.B. Van Hasselt, R.L. Morrison, A.S. Bellack, & M. Hersen (Eds.), *Handbook of family violence* (pp. 233-246). New York: Plenum Press.

Stevens, S.J. (1996). *The increase in methamphetamine use in Southern Arizona.* Presented at the Interagency Council on Alcohol and Drug Addictions Training Conference, March 28, 1996. Tucson, Arizona.

Stevens, S.J., & Arbiter, N., (1995). A therapeutic community for substance abusing pregnant women and women with children: Process and outcome. *Journal of Psychoactive Drugs, 27* (1), 49-57.

Weissman, G., Sowder, B., Young, P., & National AIDS Research Consortium. (1990). The relationship between crack cocaine and other risk factors among women in a national AIDS prevention program. [Abstract]. Sixth International AIDS Conference. San Francisco, June 20-24, *6* (3), 126.

White, J.W. (1983). Sex and gender issues in aggression research. In R.G. Geen & E.I. Donnerstein (Eds.), *Aggression: Theoretical and empirical reviews.* New York: Academic Press.

White, J.W, & Kowalski, R.M. (1994). Deconstructing the myth of the non aggressive woman: A feminist analysis. *Psychology of Women Quarterly, 18,* 487-508.

IV. PHYSICIANS' ASSESSMENT, PRENATAL CARE AND PREGNANCY OF FEMALE SUBSTANCE ABUSERS

Physicians' Assessment of Drug Use and Other HIV Risk Behavior: Reports by Female Drug Users

Christiane Brems, PhD
Dennis G. Fisher, PhD
Patricia J. Queen, MSN

SUMMARY. With epidemiological trends indicating that Acquired Immune Deficiency Syndrome (AIDS) is the third leading cause of

Christiane Brems is Professor (E-mail: AFCB@UAA.ALASKA.EDU) and Dennis G. Fisher is Professor (E-mail: AFDGF@UAA.ALASKA.EDU) University of Alaska Anchorage, Anchorage, AK 99508. Patricia J. Queen is Executive Director, Alaskan AIDS Assistance Association, Anchorage, AK 99501.

Address correspondence to: Dr. Dennis G. Fisher, Department of Psychology, 3211 Providence Drive, University of Alaska Anchorage, Anchorage, AK 99508.

This research was funded in part by Grant U01-DA-07290 from the National Institute on Drug Abuse.

The authors express their appreciation to Harry W. Haverkos, M.D. Stein, and Henry H. Cagle for their assistance with this manuscript.

[Haworth co-indexing entry note]: "Physicians' Assessment of Drug Use and Other HIV Risk Behavior: Reports by Female Drug Users." Brems, Christiane, Dennis G. Fisher, and Patricia J. Queen. Co-published simultaneously in *Drugs & Society* (The Haworth Press, Inc.) Vol. 13, No. 1/2, 1998, pp. 145-159; and: *Women and Substance Abuse: Gender Transparency* (ed: Sally J. Stevens, and Harry K. Wexler) The Haworth Press, Inc., 1998, pp. 145-159. Single or multiple copies of this article are available for a fee from The Haworth Document Delivery Service [1-800-342-9678, 9:00 a.m. - 5:00 p.m. (EST). E-mail address: getinfo@haworthpressinc.com].

death among women ages 25 to 44 in the United States, it is becoming increasingly important to deal with the issue of Human Immunodeficiency Virus (HIV) prevention for women. Recommendations for primary and secondary prevention strategies tailored to the needs of women have been formulated. Such calls have included the recommendation that prevention efforts be intensified in medical settings regularly frequented by women. One setting identified is that of gynecological and obstetric services where HIV risk assessment, testing, and counseling would be an excellent means of reaching a maximum number of women of child-bearing age. Despite calls by the American College of Obstetricians and Gynecologists for OB/GYN service providers to engage in HIV prevention, research has shown that physicians remain reluctant to address the issue with patients. This study explored the likelihood of physicians and other health service providers to engage in HIV prevention through risk behavior assessment, HIV testing, and HIV counseling by requesting information from female drug abusers not currently in substance abuse treatment. Sixty percent of the drug abusing women in this study did not receive HIV information from their health care provider, 70% did not receive HIV counseling, 68% were not offered HIV testing, and 66% were not asked to provide a drug history. Of those participants who had not been asked to provide a drug history, almost half indicated that they would have been willing to provide truthful answers had they been asked. These findings indicate that a prime opportunity for HIV prevention is being missed by women's health care providers. Neglecting to ask female patients about their drug use history and to explore their risk for HIV infection can have dire consequences for these women. Early intervention is less likely if the topic is not broached by service providers, increasing the likelihood of infection and the spread of the disease. *[Article copies available for a fee from The Haworth Document Delivery Service: 1-800-342-9678. E-mail address: getinfo@haworthpressinc.com]*

Epidemiological trends indicate that acquired immune deficiency syndrome (AIDS) is the third leading cause of death among women between the ages of 25 and 44 in the United States (Center for Disease Control [CDC], 1996). Reported incidence of HIV/AIDS is increasing particularly rapidly among women, individuals of low socioeconomic status, people of color, and persons without education (Stuntzner-Gibson, 1991). As of 12/31/1995, the Center of Disease Control had identified 71,818 women as being infected with the human immunodeficiency virus nationwide (CDC, 1996). In the State of Alaska, where the current study was conducted, the reported incidence of women with AIDS doubled in the first six months of 1993 (Alaska Department of Health and Social Services,

1993a), with a reported rate of infection of 5.3 women and adolescents per 100,000 population. In 1992, the HIV seroprevalence rate among child-bearing women in Alaska was the same as Washington state, with women comprising 10% of all AIDS cases diagnosed between 1982 and June 30, 1993 (Alaska Department of Health and Social Services, 1993b). Through the year 1994, of 272 confirmed AIDS cases in Alaska, 31 were women (Alaska Department of Health and Social Services, 1995).

Primary vectors of transmission for women have been identified to include high risk sexual behaviors, injection drug use, and sexual relation-ships with male partners who themselves are injection drug users (IDUs) or engage in high risk sexual behavior. Contrary to popular beliefs, statis-tics from the CDC (1993) reflected that the number of women diagnosed with AIDS who were infected through heterosexual contact exceeded those infected through personal injection drug use. In fact, heterosexual transmission may be a primary vector of transmission for women, as 60% of diagnosed women aged 20 to 29 were infected through heterosexual contact, a proportion significantly higher than for any older age group of women (CDC, 1993). Further corroborating this hypothesis is the finding that the majority of women (56.8%) have male IDUs as sexual partners. Nevertheless, injection drug use remains an important vector of transmis-sion and the relationship between crack cocaine use and increased inci-dence of sexually transmitted diseases and human immunodeficiency vi-rus (HIV) infections has been demonstrated repeatedly and consistently (Booth, Watters, & Chitwood, 1993; Chirgwin, Dehovistx, Dillon, & McCormack, 1991; Ellerbrock, Lieb, & Harrington, 1992; Schwartz et al., 1992; Seigal, Carlson, & Falck, 1992).

Higher levels of HIV/AIDS infection among women also translates direct-ly into higher risk for their children. Specifically, in 83% of pediatric AIDS cases, HIV is transmitted perinatally (CDC, 1993). Tragically, many women become aware of their seropositive status only after one or more of their children are diagnosed with HIV infection, passing on the infection unwit-tingly. Given the reality of these statistics, it becomes clear that a concerted effort at prevention of HIV/AIDS targeted specifically at women is necessary to curb the spread of the disease. Such efforts are best multi-faceted, involv-ing both primary and secondary prevention strategies (CDC, 1987).

Primary prevention strategies can be defined as being geared toward promoting health and preventing infection. As such, they include increas-ing women's perceptions of their own risk, identifying and educating women about high-risk behaviors, and conducting educational programs about HIV/AIDS designed specifically for women. Primary prevention has been the partial focus and goal of a multi-site research project funded by the National Institute on Drug Abuse (NIDA) since 1984. This project was designed to target drug users not in treatment and their sexual partners, a hidden population that has been hard to reach through conventional prevention strategies. The effectiveness of this project has been documented through a reduction of HIV-related risk behavior in this population associated with outreach and standard HIV counseling interventions (Liebman & Mulia, 1993; McCoy, Rivers, & Khoury, 1993).

Secondary prevention requires detection of infection and is closely linked to the assessment of risk behavior. With regard to detection, the CDC has maintained that primary care physicians are in the best position to prevent the spread of AIDS through early detection of and education about risk behaviors among their patients (Prevention Practices of Primary Care Physicians, 1994). Even more recently, the Centers for Disease Control and Prevention have called for HIV/AIDS testing of all pregnant women regardless of risk-group status (Hostetler, 1995). Similarly, policy makers have targeted women in family planning and obstetrical settings for HIV screening and counseling programs (Minkoff, McCalla, & Delke, 1990). The American College of Obstetricians and Gynecologists, recognizing this opportunity for prevention, has called for offering HIV testing to all women and encouraging testing particularly for those women known to be at risk for acquiring the virus (1991). This recommendation is based on the fact that OB/GYN service providers are at the forefront of women's medical care and are frequently the only providers whom women consult during their childbearing years (Klapholz, 1993).

With regard to assessment of risk behavior, the belief that universal adoption of HIV risk assessment and counseling are essential to the containment of HIV/AIDS is reflected in the Healthy People 2000 goal of increasing the proportion of primary and mental health care providers who provide HIV and other sexually transmitted disease prevention counseling to at least 75% of their patients (US Department of Health and Social Services, 1991). The U.S. Preventive Services Task Force has recommended that every primary care physician assess the risk of sexually transmitted disease (STD) and HIV infection among all adolescent and adult patients through a complete sexual practice and drug use history (US Preventive Services Task Force, 1989). This recommendation makes particular sense in light of the fact that female IDUs seek out primary care physicians on an average of 4.1 times per year (Selwyn, Budner, & Arno, 1993)! A number of guidelines have been developed that can be used by primary and mental health care providers to assess patients' drug use and sexual behavior history (American Medical Association, 1979; Cyr, 1988; Ende, Rockwell, & Glasgow, 1984; Nolte, Sohn, & Koons, 1992). For example, more than 500 health care experts from across the nation formulated a health care reform proposal outlining a screening for substance abuse usable with all patients, even those who present for non-substance abuse reasons in primary health care settings (Flinchbaugh, & Vollinger, 1993). Similarly, guidelines for sensitive inquiries into patients' sexual histories and practices have been provided (Ende, Rockwell, & Glasgow, 1984; Nolte, Sohn, & Koons, 1992). A plethora of studies outlines factors that may signal the presence of high risk behaviors that typically precede and are associated with HIV infection (Chiasson, Stoneburner, & Hildebrandt, 1991; Diaz & Chu, 1992; Haverkos, Genser, Grace, & Smeriglio, 1991; Haverkos & Lange, 1990; Marx, Aral, & Rolfs, 1992; Streissguth, Grant, & Barr, 1991). Such information about correlated diseases and behaviors that serve as red flags for potential high risk can easily be solicited during standard physical or gynecological exams.

Despite these recommendations and the availability of clear and simple guidelines for data collection, few physicians inquire about risk behaviors when women (or men) present for medical services. Boekeloo et al. (1991) reported that over 60% of physicians in Washington, DC (a high prevalence area for STD and HIV) did not "always or often" ask single men, single women, recent divorcees, new adult patients, or continuing adult patients about their sexual practices. Approximately 25% of these physicians, when asked about HIV positive, homosexual, or IDU patients, stated they "did not have this type of patient" in their practice. Stereotypes about the typical substance abuser as derelict, dirty, and riddled with communicable diseases hinder effective detection (Iber, 1991) because the typical abuser who seeks medical services has the same features as the average patient in that practice; namely, over 90% are employed and reasonably healthy. Gerbert, Maguire and Coates (1990) found that if patients themselves did not broach the topic of AIDS or reveal their high risk status, it was unlikely that physicians would address the potential for sexual risk of STD or HIV infection. According to researchers, such failure to deal with topics of drug use and other risk behaviors and transmission of infectious disease is related to physicians' lack of confidence in their ability to help prevent HIV, discomfort with discussing patients' sexual practices, and misconceptions about STD and HIV as presenting problems in their practice (Boekeloo et al., 1991).

Despite these reports of hesitation among physicians to deal with the topic of HIV/AIDS, it is critical that prevention of HIV/AIDS be emphasized at the local and community level as federal budgets and federal services are being reduced (Stuntzner-Gibson, 1991). Access to HIV counseling, testing, and treatment services is problematic for many high risk populations, including women, in many communities (Marks, 1992; Myers, 1992). Hence, it is imperative that prevention strategies are incorporated into existing services for women and minorities (Fullilove & Fullilove, 1992).

To assess where frequently used services are located and how they are delivered, the current study addressed several specific questions to a sample of high-risk injection drug-using women. Specifically, the current project assessed whether women who are currently using cocaine and opiates access obstetrical and gynecological health care providers in their local community, and if so, where and why. Further, they were asked whether they were assessed for risk of HIV infection and asked to provide a drug history, and if so, whether they did or would answer truthfully.

METHOD

Participants and Procedures

Participants were drawn from a subject pool of over 1000 individuals obtained via targeted sampling (Watters & Biernacki, 1989) for a National Institute on Drug Abuse (NIDA) funded project designed to provide HIV/AIDS educational counseling to injection and other drug users not currently in treatment. Eligibility criteria for participation in this project were (1) age 18 or older, (2) no drug abuse treatment within the last 30 days, and (3) either a positive urinalysis for morphine, cocaine metabolites, or amphetamine; and/or visible needle injection tracks. All clients gave informed consent to participate voluntarily in the study and a federal Certificate of Confidentiality was obtained which forbids release of information to other agencies. Clients receive monetary compensation for time spent in research participation.

For the purposes of this study, a subsample was drawn from the larger study between June 1992 and July 1993. This subsample was chosen specifically to answer the question of this study and intended to be a representative sample of the overall study sample. The sample, not needing to be as large as the entire sample used for the Cooperative agreement, consisted of the 148 women who participated in the project between the specified dates during which this study was to be carried out. Of these women 35.2% were White, 33.1% African American, 26.2% Alaska Native or American Indian, 2.1% Hispanic, and 3.5% of other ethnic backgrounds. With regard to drug use patterns in the past 30 days, 75% of the women reported that they had smoked cocaine (crack), but did not inject drugs; 21% had smoked cocaine and injected drugs; and 4% injected drugs exclusively. Of those who did not report current needle use, 25% had a history of needle use. The women ranged in age from 19 to 53, with a mean age of 33.6 (*SD* = 7.3). Average number of children was 2.24 (*SD* = 1.87; Mode = 2; *Mdn* = 2), with 23.3% of the women having no children and 12.3% having five or more. Almost half (44.7%) of the women reported they had a sexual partner who was a current drug user.

Instruments

All participants in the NIDA project respond to the Risk Behavior Assessment (RBA; NIDA, 1991), a structured interview developed by NIDA grantees that addresses high risk behaviors such as drug use, needle sharing, and sexual behaviors. The RBA has good reliability and the questions regarding drug use have good reliability and validity (Dowling-Guyer et al., 1994; Fisher et al., 1993; Needle et al., in press). The focus of the RBA is assessment of high risk behaviors for HIV transmission. Using a structured interview format, this questionnaire elicits information about lifetime drug use, current drug use practices, sexual practices, condom use, medical history, and demographic characteristics.

For the purposes of the current study, a supplemental questionnaire was used to gather information about risk assessment during visits to health care providers for obstetrical and gynecological health concerns. First, women were asked whether and where they sought such services and for what reasons. Second, information was elicited about physicians' offers of HIV testing, HIV counseling, and tendency to take drug histories.

Statistical Analyses

Descriptive statistics are provided about where and for what reasons the women sought OB/GYN services. Further descriptive statistics about the women's reports of physicians' questions and practices around HIV/AIDS are reported. Data were also subjected to Chi-Square analyses to assess whether women of different ethnic groups had different experiences with regard to the types of settings in which they sought services and the types of services offered to them or required of them by their health care providers.

RESULTS

Of the 148 participants, all had received some form of OB/GYN services since 1964 and almost all had received services within the past decade (95%). The majority (42.5%) sought OB/GYN services at a public clinic (e.g., women's health centers, municipal STD screening clinics, Alaska Native Health Center). Other places of service, in order of frequency, were private physicians (25.3%), hospitals and hospital based practices (15.1%), emergency or first care facilities (10.3%), and nurse practitioners (2.7%). The remaining 4.1% received services elsewhere (e.g., through the Department of Correction or corporate franchises). Most participants reported more than one reason for their visit. The most common presenting concern of women seeking OB/GYN services was cervical cancer screening (PAP test), with 99.3% of the women having received such services at least once and 85.5% having received such services between 1990 and 1993. This figure compares well with statewide data that indicate that approximately 83% of women sought cervical cancer screens in the last two years (Alaska Department of Health and Social Services, 1991). The figure is higher, however, than that reported for female IDUs across the country. This discrepancy is most likely explained by the fact that Alaska has excellent availability of medical services for Alaska Native women through Indian Health Services (IHS), along with excellent IHS outreach programs that encourage women to avail themselves of these preventive medical services. PAP test services were followed by treatment for sexually transmitted disease (75%), birth control services (71%), and obstetric/prenatal care services (70%). Of the women who had been screened for cervical cancer, 32% were offered HIV testing during the visit. Of the women seeking treatment of a sexually transmitted disease, 37% were offered HIV testing. Of the women seeking birth control, 38% were offered HIV testing and of the women making prenatal visits, 36% were offered testing. Considering all types of OB/GYN services, only 37.7% of the women had received HIV information from a health provider, 28.1% had received HIV counseling, and only 30.8% had been offered testing.

Drug use history taken by the physician was reported by only 32.9% of the women. Of these women, 86.4% claimed to have provided the health care practitioner with accurate information. Of the women who indicated that no drug use history was taken by their care provider, 59.3% indicated that, if asked, they would have provided accurate information. Many women revealed anecdotally that they felt it was important to share drug use information with their care provider, regardless of whether the questions were asked. It is not clear why so few physicians requested drug history information, especially given the willingness of the women to provide it. It is possible that physicians assume that women would not provide accurate information and hence do not bother to ask. Alternatively, it is possible that even though physicians have been made aware of the relevance of drug and alcohol use, they do not know how to inquire about it in a manner they find sensitive and effective, a possible explanation that has training implications for physicians.

When analyzed separately by ethnic group (using only African American [*n* = 48], White [*n* = 51], and Alaska Native women [*n* = 38] due to group sizes), few differences emerged in the data. Only the setting in which services were sought differed, c^2(2, N = 137) = 35.71, *p* < .0001. Specifically, Alaska Native Women were less likely than either White or African American women to seek services from private physicians. However, they were more likely to seek services at a public clinic (specifically, at the Alaska Native Medical Center). This finding is not surprising as health care is free for Alaska Native women at the Alaska Native Medical Center. However, despite differences in setting where services were received, none of the Chi-Square analyses for offers of HIV testing, information, counseling, or for drug history reached significance. This reveals that not any particular group of women had a different experience regarding these issues with their care providers. Setting and service data broken down by ethnic group are presented in Tables 1 and 2.

DISCUSSION

Results reveal that OB/GYN services are indeed accessed with great frequency by drug using women, at least in the Anchorage Alaska area where medical services are somewhat more abundant than in most cities of similar size (population of approximately 250,000). Hence, this medical setting would be an excellent place where secondary (and primary) HIV/AIDS prevention could take place. Virtually all women had received OB/GYN services in the form of PAP smears, suggesting that a combination of HIV/AIDS screening with such a test would reach most women who abuse drugs.

When interpreting the results of this study, it must be remembered that corresponding self-report data from physicians were not collected. However, results show that at least according to the self report of the women in this sample, the opportunity for secondary HIV prevention through detection and assessment is not taken advantage of by most health care providers. Less than a third of the women received actual HIV testing, counseling, or information; and only about a third were asked to provide drug use histories (Table 3). These data suggest that previous research indicating that physicians are not comfortable broaching the topic of drug abuse and HIV risk may be accurate and replicable for this sample. The fact that only 32.9% of the women were asked to provide drug histories means

TABLE 1. Demographic Characteristics

Demographic Variable	n	%
Ethnicity		
White	52	35.2
African American	49	33.1
Alaska Native/American Indian	39	26.3
Hispanic	3	2.1
Other	5	3.4
Drug Use Type		
Crack Only	111	75.0%
Crack and IDU	31	21.0%
IDU Only	6	4.0%
Women with IDU Sex Partner	66	44.7%
Age		
Mean	33.6	
Standard Deviation	7.3	
Range	19-53	
Children		
Mean	2.24	
Standard Deviation	1.87	
Mode	2	
Range	0-9	

that the health care providers failed to detect this HIV risk behavior in 67.1% of the participants. This staggeringly high lack of detection suggests that despite being the best health care providers potentially to engage in HIV prevention, OB/GYN providers fail to do so. This is despite the fact that the American College of Obstetricians and Gynecologists has called for HIV testing of all patients presenting for OB/GYN services.

The findings of this study, though somewhat crude, have several implications. First, they suggest that OB/GYN settings are indeed prime targets for the implementation of HIV/AIDS primary and secondary prevention services. Gynecological services are accessed by women of childbearing age with sufficient regularity that most women in a given community could be reached through this avenue. Second, the study suggests that

TABLE 2. Health Care Providers Consulted by Patients of Different Ethnicities

		Ethnicity		
		African American	White	Alaska Native	Total
Health Care Provider Consulted					
Public Clinics					
	n	21	17	20	58
	%	43.75	33.33	52.63	42.5
Private Physicians					
	n	14	19	2	35
	%	29.17	37.25	5.26	25.3
Hospitals or Hospital-Based Services					
	n	3	4	13	20
	%	6.25	7.84	34.21	15.1
Emergency or First Care Facilities					
	n	8	5	1	14
	%	16.67	9.80	2.63	10.3
Other (e.g., Corrections)					
	n	1	5	0	6
	%	2.08	9.80	0.00	4.1
Nurse Practitioners					
	n	1	1	2	4
	%	2.08	1.96	5.26	2.7

most health care providers remain reluctant to deal with the topic of HIV/AIDS either directly through offering testing or counseling, or indirectly through the assessment of related risk behaviors, such as drug use. Third, results revealed that a surprisingly large proportion of women would not only be willing to disclose drug use information, but indeed

TABLE 3. Service Delivered to Patients of Different Ethnicities by Health Care Providers

Service Delivered	African American	White	Alaska Native	Total
		Ethnicity		
HIV/AIDS Information Provided				
n	17	22	14	53
%	35.42	43.14	36.84	37.7
HIV/AIDS Counseling Offered				
n	12	16	11	39
%	25.00	31.37	28.95	28.1
HIV Testing Offered				
n	14	17	12	43
%	29.17	33.33	31.58	30.8
Drug History Taken				
n	15	17	14	46
%	31.25	33.33	36.84	32.9

consider the disclosure of such information to their health care provider as an important aspect of their medical care.

Given these findings, it is necessary to repeat the call for increased attention among gynecological service providers to deal with the issues of drug use and HIV/AIDS. Not only should testing be offered on a regular or routine basis, but it should be accompanied by the thorough assessment of correlated risk behaviors. While sexual histories are a familiar and often a routine part of obstetrical and gynecological examinations, drug-use histories are much less common. It is likely that fears of offending the patient, frustration with the lack of treatment alternatives, time constraints, and other barriers still persist and prevent care providers from approaching this topic openly and willingly with their patients. The sad reality is that unless these barriers are identified and overcome, care providers will continue to miss out on the opportunity for prevention of a deadly disease. In fact, failure on the part of women's health care providers to discuss HIV/AIDS and drug use means that detection of the virus will take place later in the disease process and women will die sooner. Further, it almost assures the continued spread and proliferation of HIV, a preventable disease, within our communities.

REFERENCES

Alaska Department of Health and Social Services. (1995). 1995 Annual AIDS Alaska report. *State of Alaska Epidemiology Bulletin, January 31,* 1.

Alaska Department of Health and Social Services. (1991). *Behavioral Risk Factor Survey: Executive Summary.* Juneau, AK: Author.

Alaska Department of Health and Social Services. (1993a). AIDS-Alaska. *State of Alaska Epidemiology Bulletin, July 3,* 26.

Alaska Department of Health and Social Services. (1993b). Survey of HIV prevalence in childbearing women. *State of Alaska Epidemiology Bulletin, August 3,* 33.

American College of Obstetricians and Gynecologists. (1991). Voluntary testing for HIV. *ACOG Committee Opinion, 97.*

American Medical Association. (1979). *AMA guidelines for physical involvement in the care of substance abusing patients.* Washington, DC: AMA Council on Scientific Affairs.

Boekeloo, B. O., Marx, E. S., Kral, A. H., Coughllin, S. C., Bowman, M., & Rabin, D. L. (1991). Frequency and thoroughness of STD/HIV risk assessment by physicians in a high-risk metropolitan area. *American Journal of Public Health, 81,* 1645-1648.

Booth, R. E., Watters, J. K., & Chitwood, D. D. (1993). HIV risk-related behaviors among injection drug users, crack smokers, and injection drug users who smoke crack. *American Journal of Public Health, 83,* 1144-1148.

Centers for Disease Control. (1987). Public health service guidelines for counseling and antibody testing to prevent HIV infection and AIDS. *Morbidity and Mortality Weekly Report, 36,* 509-514.

Centers for Disease Control. (1993). Update: Acquired Immunodeficiency Syndrome–United States. *Morbidity and Mortality Weekly Report, 42,* 547-557.

Centers for Disease Control. (1996). Update: Mortality attributable to HIV infection among persons aged 25 to 44 years–United States, 1994. *Morbidity and Mortality Weekly Report, 45 (6).*

Chiasson, M. A., Stoneburner, R. L., & Hildebrandt, D. S. (1991). Heterosexual transmission of HIV-1 associated with the use of smokable freebase cocaine (crack). *AIDS, 5,* 1121-1126.

Chirgwin, K., Dehovistx, J. A., Dillon, S., & McCormack, W. M. (1991). HIV infection, genital ulcer disease, and crack cocaine use among patients attending a clinic for sexually transmitted diseases. *American Journal of Public Health, 81,* 1576-1579.

Cyr, M. G. (1988). The effectiveness of routine screening in the detection of alcoholism. *Journal of the American Medical Association, 267,* 1106-1108.

Diaz, T., & Chu, S. Y. (1992). Crack cocaine use and sexual behavior among people with AIDS. *Journal of the American Medical Association, 269,* 2845-2846.

Dowling-Guyer, S., Johnson, M. E., Fisher, D. G., Needle, R., Watters, J., Andersen, M., Williams, M., Kotranski, L., Booth, R., Rhodes, F., Weatherby, N., Estrada, A. L., Fleming, D., Deren, S., & Tortu, S. (1994). Reliability of drug users' self-reported HIV risk behaviors and validity of self-reported recent drug use. *Assessment, 1,* 383-392.

Ellerbrock, T. V., Lieb, S., & Harrington, P. E. (1992). Heterosexually transmitted human immunodeficiency virus infection among pregnant women in a rural Florida community. *New England Journal of Medicine, 327,* 1704-1709.

Ende, J., Rockwell, S., & Glasgow, M. (1984). The sexual history in general medicine practice. *Archives of Internal Medicine, 144,* 558-561.

Fisher, D., Needle, R., Weatherby, N., Brown, B., Booth, R., Williams, M. et al. (1993). Reliability of drug user self-report [Abstract] (PO-C35-3355). *IXth International Conference on AIDS Abstract Book, Vol II,* 776. Berlin, Germany.

Flinchbaugh, L. J., & Vollinger, B. (Eds.). (1993). Special report on health care reform and substance abuse. *Alcohol, Tobacco & Other Drugs Section Newsletter, September.* (Available from the American Public Health Association, 1015 Fifteenth Street, NW; Washington, DC 20005).

Forney, M. A., Inciardi, J. A., & Lockwood, D. (1992). Exchanging sex for crack-cocaine: A comparison of women from rural and urban communities. *Journal of Community Health, 17,* 73-85.

Fullilove, M. T., & Fullilove, R. E. (1992). HIV risk in multi-ethnic neighborhoods. *Focus: A Guide to AIDS Research and Counseling, 7,* 5-6.

Gerbert, B., Maguire, B. T., & Coates, T. J. (1990). Are patients talking to their physicians about AIDS? *American Journal of Public Health, 80,* 467-468.

Haverkos, H. W., & Lange, W. R. (1990). Serious infections other than human immunodeficiency virus among intravenous drug abusers. *Journal of Infectious Disease, 61,* 894-902.

Haverkos, H. W., Genser, S. G., Grace, W. C., & Smeriglio, V. L. (1991). Complications of drug misuse. *Current Opinion in Psychiatry, 4,* 454-459.

Hostetler, A.J. AIDS test urged for all pregnant women. (1995, July 7). *Anchorage Daily News,* A6.

Iber, F. L. (1991). *Alcohol and drug abuse as encountered in office practice.* Boca Raton, FL: CRC.

Klapholz, J. (1993). *Collaborative strategy to train OB/GYN's: AIDS Project Los Angeles* [Abstract] (PO-B23-1942). IXth International Conference on AIDS Abstract Book, Vol I., 459. Berlin, Germany.

Liebman, J., & Mulia, N. (1993). An office-based AIDS prevention program for high risk drug users. *Drugs & Society, 7,* 205-223.

Marks, R. (1992). The changing epidemic. *Focus: A Guide to AIDS Research and Counseling, 7,* 2.

Marx, R., Aral, S., & Rolfs, R. T. (1991). Crack, sex, and STD. *Sexually Transmitted Diseases, 18,* 92-101.

McCoy, C. B., Rivers, J. E., & Khoury, E.L. (1993). An emerging public health model for reducing AIDS-related risk behavior among injecting drug users and their sexual partners. *Drugs & Society, 7,* 143-159.

Minkoff, H. L., McCalla, S., & Delke, I. (1990). The relationship of cocaine use to syphilis and human immunodeficiency virus infection among inner city parturient women. *American Journal of Obstetrics and Gynecology, 163,* 521-526.

Myers, M. T. (1992). The African-American experience with HIV disease. *Focus: A Guide to AIDS Research and Counseling, 7,* 3-4.

National Institute on Drug Abuse. (1991). *Risk behavior assessment.* Rockville, MD: National Institute on Drug Abuse (Community Research Branch).

Needle, R., Fisher, D. G., Weatherby, N., Chitwood, D., Brown, B., Cesari, H., Booth, R., Williams, M. L., Watters, J., Andersen, M., & Braunstein, M. (in press). The reliability of self-reported HIV risk behaviors of drug users. *Psychology of Addictive Behaviors.*

Nolte, W., Sohn, M. A., & Koons, B. (1992). Prevention of HIV infection in women. *Journal of Gynecological & Neonatal Nursing, 22,* 128-134.

Prevention Practices of Primary-Care Physicians–United States. (1994). *Morbidity and Mortality Weekly Report, 42,* 988-992.

Schwartz, S. K., Bolan, G. A., Fullilove, M., McCright, J., Fullilove, R., Kohn, R., & Rolfs, R. T. (1992). Crack cocaine and the exchange of sex for money or drugs: Risk factors for gonorrhea among black adolescents in San Francisco. *Sexually Transmitted Diseases, 19,* 7-13.

Seigal, H. A., Carlson, R. G., & Falck, R. (1992). High-risk behaviors for transmission of syphilis and human immunodeficiency virus among crack cocaine-using women: A case study from the Midwest. *Sexually Transmitted Diseases, 19,* 266-270.

Selwyn, P.A., Budner, N.S., & Arno, P.S. (1993). Utilization of on-site primary care services by HIV seropositive and seronegative drug users at a methadone maintenance program. *Public Health Reports, 108,* 492-500.

Streissguth, A. P., Grant, T. M., & Barr, H. M. (1991). Cocaine and the use of alcohol and other drugs during pregnancy. *American Journal of Obstetrics and Gynecology, 164,* 1239-1243.

Stuntzner-Gibson, D. (1991). Women and HIV disease: An emerging social crisis. *Social Work, 36,* 22-27.

US Department of Health and Human Services. (1991). *Healthy People 2000* (PHS 91-50212). Washington, DC: US Government Printing Office.

US Preventive Services Task Force. (1989). *Guide to Clinical Preventive Services.* Baltimore, MD: Williams & Wilkins.

Watters, J. K., & Biernacki, P. (1989). Targeted sampling: Options for the study of hidden populations. *Social Problems, 36,* 416-430.

Revealing Drug Use to Prenatal Providers: Who Tells or Who Is Asked?

Brian W. Weir, BA
Michael J. Stark, PhD
David W. Fleming, MD
Haiou He, MBA
Helen Tesselaar, BS

SUMMARY. *Objective:* Health risks associated with prenatal drug use can be effectively reduced through targeted medical and counseling services. However, the delivery of these services depends on the providers knowing which women are using drugs. The purpose of this retrospective study is to determine factors associated with substance using women revealing their drug use to their prenatal providers. *Methods:* The study subjects were injection drug users (IDUs) or crack users, recruited in Portland, OR., from 3/92 to 12/95, as part of a National Institute on Drug Abuse-sponsored HIV risk reduction project. Women were eligible if during their last pregnancy they: (1) used cocaine, methamphetamines, or heroin; (2) had at least

---

Brian W. Weir, Michael J. Stark, Haiou He, and Helen Tesselaar are with Program Design and Evaluation Services, Multnomah County Health Department and Oregon Health Division. David W. Fleming is with the Oregon Health Division.

Address correspondence to: Brian W. Weir, Oregon Health Division, 800 N.E. Oregon Street, Suite 550, Portland, OR 97232 (E-mail: brian.w.weir@state.or.us).

This research was conducted at the Portland site of the Cooperative Agreement for AIDS Community-Based Outreach/Intervention Research Program, supported by the National Institute on Drug Abuse, Community Research Branch (1-U01-DA-07302-02).

[Haworth co-indexing entry note]: "Revealing Drug Use to Prenatal Providers: Who Tells or Who Is Asked?" Weir, Brian W. et al. Co-published simultaneously in *Drugs & Society* (The Haworth Press, Inc.) Vol. 13, No. 1/2, 1998, pp. 161-176; and: *Women and Substance Abuse: Gender Transparency* (ed: Sally J. Stevens, and Harry K. Wexler) The Haworth Press, Inc., 1998, pp. 161-176. Single or multiple copies of this article are available for a fee from The Haworth Document Delivery Service [1-800-342-9678, 9:00 a.m. - 5:00 p.m. (EST). E-mail address: getinfo@haworthpressinc.com].

161

one prenatal visit; and (3) did not have an induced abortion. Of the 97 women meeting these criteria, the mean age at their last pregnancy was 28 years (range 19-42); 45% were White and 44% were African American; 32% had less than a high school education; and 50% had their last pregnancy between 1990-95. *Results:* Only 52% of the respondents reported telling their prenatal providers of their drug use. Variables independently associated with revealing of prenatal drug use were: African American race (p < .01); less than a high-school education (p < .05); and older age at last pregnancy (p < .05). *Conclusions:* Prenatal providers are not identifying a large portion of their drug using clients. Furthermore, White or more educated women who do not fit the stereotype of a drug user are even less likely to be identified. By asking all pregnant clients about drug use, whether they look the "type" or not, many more drug using women and their newborns can benefit from needed perinatal services. *[Article copies available for a fee from The Haworth Document Delivery Service: 1-800-342-9678. E-mail address: getinfo@haworthpressinc.com]*

Substance use during pregnancy is known to have serious consequences for the health of mothers and their fetuses. While medical treatments for drug-exposed infants continue to improve, drug use prevention and rehabilitation must be recognized as the foremost solutions to the problem of prenatal substance use. While the prenatal visit provides a propitious opportunity to intervene with substance using pregnant women, interventions can be effectively delivered to drug using women only if their drug use is known to their prenatal providers.

Identification of cocaine, amphetamine, and heroin use is particularly problematic as the use of these substances carries strong stigma; prenatal providers may be uneasy about inquiring about "hard" drug use, and women may be reluctant about revealing such use. The use of these drugs during pregnancy can have direct effects on in utero development of the fetus. In utero exposure to cocaine has been associated with increased rates of fetal death, abrupto placentae, premature births and low birth weight (Bell & Lau, 1995; Chasnoff, Burns, Schnoll & Burns, 1985; Oro & Dixon, 1987). In utero amphetamine exposure is associated with increased prematurity and perinatal mortality (Oro & Dixon, 1987). Following in utero heroin exposure, the majority of neonates will have narcotic withdrawal symptoms (Kaltenbach & Finnegan, 1986; Olofsson, Buckley, Andersen & Friis-Hansen, 1983a). Heroin exposure is associated with low birth weight, prematurity, and seizures (Bell & Lau, 1995; Olofsson et al., 1983a; Oro & Dixon, 1987).

In utero drug exposure has also been linked to developmental and behavioral deficiencies in infants. In utero exposure to cocaine has been associated with a multitude of neurobehavioral disorders (Chasnoff et al., 1985; Kain, Rimar & Barash, 1993), in utero amphetamine exposure has neurobehavioral effects similar to cocaine, and has been associated with behavior and social problems (Eriksson, Billing, Steneroth & Zetterstrom, 1989), and heroin exposure is implicated in long term psychosocial problems (Olofsson, Buckley, Andersen & Friis-Hansen, 1983b). Other long term effects of in utero drug exposure for children, adolescents, and adults have not been clearly elucidated (Behnke & Eyler, 1993), and some studies indicate that the long term effects may not be as pernicious as once thought (Carta & McEvoy, 1996).

Direct causal relationships between in utero drug exposure and poor birth outcomes have also been difficult to establish. Many cocaine, amphetamine, and heroin users often use more than one of these substances, and alcohol, marijuana, and tobacco use are also common (Robins & Mills, 1993). Furthermore, drugs may be "cut" with other substances themselves which might have deleterious effects. Poor birth outcomes can also result from sexually transmitted diseases, inadequate prenatal care, hepatitis, and AIDS, all of which are associated with substance use (Kain et al., 1993; Mann, Battagin, Cooper & Mahan, 1992). Substance using pregnant women are more likely to be of lower socioeconomic status, suffer from violence, lack social support or emotional stability, and be less able to fulfill basic needs of food, clothing, and shelter (Amaro, Fried, Cabral & Zuckerman, 1990; Marcenko, Spence & Rohweder, 1994). These factors have adverse effects on the health of the woman and fetus during pregnancy, and also on the future physical and psychosocial development of the newborn. Mothers who continue to use drugs postpartum have an impaired ability to nurture and provide for their children, as reflected in the high rates of removal of drug-exposed infants from their biological parents (Eriksson et al., 1989; Kelley, Walsh & Thompson, 1991).

Prenatal providers are learning how to manage the effects of in utero drug exposure to neonates, and the provision of adequate prenatal care to drug using women is associated with more favorable birth outcomes (Kain et al., 1993). Through connecting drug using pregnant women with social services, providers can help ensure that the basic needs of food, clothing, and shelter and freedom from violence are met. However, the best method for reducing the harm associated with prenatal substance use is helping pregnant women reduce or quit their drug use, which is predicated upon knowledge of their use.

While toxicologic screens can be effective in identifying substance using women, they can only detect recent drug use, and the use of toxicologic screens can also erode client-physician trust. In contrast, the need is well recognized for providers to question women about prenatal substance use in a professional, nonjudgmental manner, with the clear purpose of protecting the health of the fetus rather than punishing the woman (ACOG Committee Opinion, 1991; United States Public Health Service, 1989). Women may value discussing prenatal drug use, as pregnancy provides a unique opportunity for women to reevaluate the costs associated with their continued drug use, and the desire to have a healthy baby can be a powerful motivator for behavior change (Reed, 1985).

Unfortunately, many providers only ask patients about drug use when they feel that there is an increased likelihood that the woman is using drugs. Providers may selectively ask women about substance use depending on pregnancy complications, poor pregnancy outcomes, clinical criteria, or symptomatologies of drug use exhibited by their clients. However, pregnancy complications and poor pregnancy outcomes caused by substance use can be more effectively prevented when identification of drug use and intervention occurs before complications become evident.

The likelihood of a pregnant woman being screened for drug use may also be affected by other client characteristics. Provider bias may influence the application of clinical criteria for assessing who is more likely to use drugs and who should be asked about drug use. Chasnoff, Landress and Barrett (1990) investigated factors associated with the identification of drug using women in Pinnas County, Florida, where providers have been required to report to state health authorities any woman known to have used illicit drugs during her pregnancy. When provider reports were matched against blind toxicologic screens, African American women were 10 times more likely to have been reported as drug users than White women, despite similar rates of drug use. Women with positive toxicologic screens were also more likely to have been reported by their provider if they were of lower socioeconomic status. Chasnoff et al. offered several possible explanations for the socioeconomic and racial differences in reporting of prenatal drug use, which will be discussed subsequently.

Other studies indicate that the identification of prenatal drug use may also be influenced by provider characteristics. Women seen by public versus private providers are more likely to receive information on the adverse effects of prenatal cocaine and marijuana use and on the importance of not using drugs during pregnancy (Freda, Andersen, Damus & Merkatz, 1993; Kogan, Alexander, Kotelchuck, Nagey & Jack, 1994). As public providers are more willing to address the sensitive issue of prenatal substance use, women may be more likely to reveal their drug use when they are seen by public providers.

Factors associated with revealing drug use to providers need to be further investigated to assess the extent to which providers are recognizing prenatal drug users and if there are biases in whom is recognized. This retrospective study examines the revealing of substance use to providers by injection drug and crack using women who report using cocaine, methamphetamines, or heroin during their last pregnancy. It is hypothesized that the drug use of many of these women goes unrecognized by their prenatal providers, and that African American women are more likely to be targeted for screening.

METHODS

Subjects

The subjects for this study were participants in a National Institute on Drug Abuse-sponsored HIV risk reduction project, recruited in Portland, OR, from March 1992 through December 1995. The recruitment for the risk reduction project followed a targeted sampling approach (Watters & Biernacki, 1989), in which geographic areas of Portland containing concentrations of injection drug users were identified by mapping of HIV risk-related databases (e.g., AIDS, syphilis, and hepatitis cases, illicit drug use in women giving birth, death due to drug overdose or where drugs contributed to death, drug abuse among clients visiting the local health department and hospitals, and drug-related arrests). Subjects were recruited through street outreach, flyers, and word-of-mouth. To be eligible for the HIV risk reduction study, subjects had to: (1) have injected drugs or smoked crack within 30 days prior to recruitment, confirmed by fresh track marks and/or positive urinalysis; (2) not have participated in formal drug treatment in the last 30 days; and (3) be 18 years of age or older.

Women were included in this sub-study on revealing prenatal drug use if they reported that during their last pregnancy they: (1) used cocaine, methamphetamines, or heroin; (2) had at least one prenatal visit; and (3) did not have an induced abortion.

Procedures

Participants in the HIV risk reduction project were recruited for HIV counseling and testing and were informed and gave consent prior to their participation. During the pretest counseling session, respondents completed a standard risk behavior assessment questionnaire (RBA), and were then counseled and tested for HIV. Two weeks later, they returned for their

HIV test results. After post-test counseling, women were interviewed about past pregnancies, and in particular about the circumstances of their last pregnancy. Both the HIV risk assessments and the pregnancy questionnaires were administered by trained interviewers in private, one-on-one sessions.

Measurement

The analysis for this study examines the data from the baseline RBA and the pregnancy questionnaire. The RBA examines sexual and drug use behaviors, and has been shown to be both reliable and valid (Needle, Fisher, Weatherby, Brown, Cesari, Chitwood, Booth, Williams, Watters, Andersen & Braunstein, 1995; Weatherby, Needle, Cesari, Booth, McCoy, Watters, Williams & Chitwood, 1994). Data derived from the RBA included race/ethnicity, age at last pregnancy, education level, and years of drug use. All other data were derived from the pregnancy questionnaire. The dependent variable is revealing of drug use to one's prenatal provider, as determined by the question, "Did you tell your provider you were using illicit (street) drugs at the time you were pregnant?"

Demographic and pregnancy related variables include: race/ethnicity; level of education; age at last pregnancy; and year of last pregnancy. Variables reflecting substance use during last pregnancy include: type of drug use (i.e., methamphetamines only, cocaine only, heroin only, or two or more of these drugs); years of drug use before last pregnancy; cessation of drug use during pregnancy; alcohol use; tobacco use; and marijuana use. Variables regarding prenatal care include: adequate prenatal care (i.e., five or more prenatal visits and prenatal care during the first trimester); and public provider (i.e., provider practicing in a publicly funded setting or midwife provider) versus private provider.

Analysis

Univariate analyses of categorical and ordinal variables were conducted with the Pearson and Mantel-Haenszel χ^2 statistics, respectively, with revealing of drug use to prenatal providers as the dependent variable. Variables found in univariate analyses to be associated with revealing prenatal drug use at $p < .20$ were entered into a forward stepwise logistic regression. A second multivariate analysis was carried out to examine possible interactions between variables independently associated with revealing substance use. Adjusted odds ratios and 95% confidence intervals were calculated for variables independently associated with revealing of drug use from the beta coefficients and standard errors from the logistic analysis. All analyses were executed using SPSS 6.1 for Windows (Norušis, 1994).

RESULTS

Of the 443 women enrolled in the HIV risk reduction project, data on previous pregnancies were available for 407 (91.9%). One hundred and five women (23.7%) met the inclusion criteria. Data on revealing drug use to their provider were available for 97 of these women.

The mean age of the 97 women at the time of the interview was 33 years (SD = 6.4, range: 19-49) and the mean age at their last pregnancy was 28 years (SD = 5.2, range: 19-42). Study participants were predominantly White (45%) or African American (44%); the other women were either Native American (6%) or of mixed race/ethnicity (4%). Thirty-two percent had less than a high school education, while 32% had some college education.

The median number of prior pregnancies was 4 (range: 0-13). Half of the women were last pregnant between 1990 and 1995. Although all women had to have had some prenatal care to be eligible for the study, 39% of the women did not have adequate prenatal care, as measured by either no prenatal care during the first trimester (30%) or fewer than 5 total prenatal visits (21%). The median number of prenatal visits was 10 (range 1-40). Fifty-nine percent of women were seen by public prenatal providers.

Sixty-seven percent of women reported cocaine use during their last pregnancy, 22% reported methamphetamine use, and 53% reported heroin use; 40% of women reported using at least two of these drugs. The types of drugs used varied by race/ethnicity. African American women were more likely to report having used cocaine (χ^2 = 12.7, p < .001), and less likely to report having used methamphetamines (χ^2 = 13.2, p < .001) compared to women who were not African American. Heroin use did not differ significantly by race/ethnicity. The mean number of years women used drugs before their last pregnancy was 9 (SD = 5, range: 0-13). Thirty-one percent of the women reported quitting drug use during their first trimester of pregnancy, and 40% used drugs throughout their pregnancy. Many of the women also reported use of tobacco (90%), alcohol (51%), and marijuana (37%) during their last pregnancy.

Of the 97 women in this study, only 50 (52%) reported revealing their drug use to their prenatal providers. In univariate analysis, compared to women who did not reveal their drug use to their prenatal providers, those who did reveal their drug use were significantly more likely to be African American, to have been older at the time of their last pregnancy, to have had their last pregnancy between 1990-95, and to have less than a high school education (see Table 1). In univariate analysis, several factors were found to be unrelated to revealing drug use, including type of drug use, adequacy of prenatal care, public versus private prenatal care provider, tobacco use, alcohol use, and marijuana use.

Factors entered into the conditional forward stepwise multiple logistic regression analysis included race/ethnicity, level of education, age at last pregnancy, and year of last pregnancy. Factors found to be independently associated with revealing drug use to prenatal providers are: African American race ($p < .01$), less than high school education ($p < .05$), and older age at last pregnancy ($p < .05$) (see Table 2). Factors entered into the second logistic regression included the three variables found to be independently associated with revealing drug use and all possible two-way interactions between these three variables. No interaction terms were found to be significant.

DISCUSSION

In this cohort of female out-of-treatment drug users who reported using cocaine, methamphetamines, or heroin during their last pregnancy, nearly half reported that they did not tell their prenatal providers of their drug use. The rate of revealing prenatal drug use is unacceptably low, and is likely to be overestimated for two reasons. First, due to the stigma and shame associated with prenatal substance abuse, women may have denied their prenatal drug use when asked by the study interviewer. These women, who would have been less inclined to reveal their drug use to their prenatal providers as well, would have been excluded from the study on the basis of no self-reported drug use during their last pregnancy, resulting in an underrepresentation of women who did not reveal their drug use to their providers. Second, some women may not have clearly recalled whether or not they told their provider of their substance use. These women may have been inclined to tell the study interviewer that they did reveal their substance use to their prenatal providers, as it is the socially desirable response. This would result in an overestimate of the rate of revealing drug use to prenatal providers in this cohort. As prenatal cocaine, methamphetamine, and heroin use in this population has serious consequences for the health of the fetus and the future health of the child, the drug use of these women must be brought into the open so that effective interventions can be delivered to these women. The low rate of revealing substance use in this cohort demonstrates the necessity for prenatal providers to question all women about substance use.

TABLE 1. Characteristics of Women Who Did Not (n = 47) and Did (n = 50) Reveal Their Substance Use to Their Prenatal Providers

| | Reveal Drug Use | | | | |
| | No | | Yes | | |
Variable	n	%	n	%	χ^2
Race/ethnicity**					
African American	13	30.2	30	69.8	
Non-African American	34	63.0	20	37.0	10.27
Age at last pregnancy**					
18-24	19	73.1	7	26.9	
25-29	15	44.1	19	55.9	
30-34	11	42.3	15	57.7	
35+	2	18.2	9	81.8	9.36
Education*					
Less than high school	12	38.7	19	61.3	
High school	15	42.9	20	57.1	
Some college	20	64.5	11	35.5	4.09
Year of last pregnancy*					
1973-82	12	75.0	4	25.0	
1983-89	17	51.5	16	48.5	
1990-95	18	37.5	30	62.5	6.94
Drugs used during last pregnancy					
Methamphetamines only	7	70.0	3	30.0	
Cocaine only	13	44.8	16	55.2	
Heroin only	10	52.6	9	47.4	
Multiple drug use	17	43.6	22	56.4	2.51
Years of drug use					
0-5	19	59.4	13	40.6	
6-10	13	41.9	18	58.1	
11-15	12	48.0	13	52.0	
16+	3	33.3	6	66.7	1.73
Quit drug use during pregnancy[†]					
Yes	22	56.4	17	43.6	
No	25	43.1	33	56.9	1.65
Marijuana use during pregnancy					
No	27	44.3	34	55.7	
Yes	20	55.6	16	44.4	1.16

TABLE 1 (continued)

	Reveal Drug Use				
	No		Yes		
Variable	n	%	n	%	χ^2
Alcohol use during pregnancy					
No	22	45.8	26	54.2	
Yes	25	51.0	24	49.0	0.26
Tobacco use during pregnancy					
No	5	50.0	5	50.0	
Yes	42	48.3	45	51.7	0.01
Adequate prenatal care					
No	18	47.4	20	52.6	
Yes	29	49.2	30	50.8	0.03
Prenatal provider (n = 83)					
Private	23	46.9	26	53.1	
Public	14	41.2	20	58.8	0.27

*p < .05
**p < .01
†p < .20

TABLE 2. Factors Associated with Revealing Substance Use to Prenatal Providers in Multiple Regression

Variable	OR	(95% CI)
Race/ethnicity		
African-American (vs. Non-African American)	4.0	1.3, 15.1
Education		
Less than high school (vs. some college)	5.5	1.5, 20.6
High school (vs. some college)	3.6	1.1, 11.6
Age at last pregnancy		
25-29 (vs. 18-24)	2.9	0.9, 9.8
30-34 (vs. 18-24)	5.4	1.4, 21.9
35+ (vs. 18-24)	13.7	2.0, 94.3

The high rates of reported prenatal tobacco (90%) and alcohol (51%) use in conjunction with prenatal drug use are consistent with the findings of other studies. In an examination of reports from Oregon birth attendants, Slutsker, Smith, Higginson and Fleming (1993) found that recognized prenatal tobacco and alcohol use were strongly associated with recognized prenatal drug use. Because many of the cocaine, methamphetamine, and heroin using women in this study used more than one of these substances and because many of them also used tobacco, alcohol, or marijuana, the threats to the health of the mother and fetus are compounded. These high rates of polysubstance use further demonstrate the urgency of identifying and intervening with drug using pregnant women.

Whether or not women reveal their drug use to their providers may be influenced by the willingness of women to reveal their drug use and by whom providers ask about drug use. In the multivariate analysis, a higher rate of revealing was found for women who were older during their last pregnancy. This difference in revealing may result from younger drug using women being more reticent or recalcitrant about revealing their drug use. Alternatively, the detrimental effects of a drug using lifestyle on a woman's health and behavior may be more apparent in older women, thus alerting providers to suspect and to inquire about drug use. Further investigation is needed to clarify the relationship between age at last pregnancy and revealing of substance use.

The multivariate analysis also showed that African American and less educated women were more likely to have revealed their prenatal substance use to their providers. These results are very similar to the previously described findings of Chasnoff et al. (1990); drug using women were more likely to be reported to health authorities by their prenatal providers if the women were African American or of lower socioeconomic status. The consistency between the predictors of revealing of drug use to prenatal providers found in this study and the predictors of provider reporting of drug use found by Chasnoff et al. indicates that the findings of these two studies may be manifestations of the same underlying factors. Chasnoff et al. offer several explanations for the different rates of reporting by prenatal providers which are salient for the current study.

First, as Chasnoff et al. found that White women were more likely to have used marijuana and African American women were more likely to have used cocaine, they hypothesized that African American women may have been more frequently screened for drug use because of the more severe symptoms associated with cocaine intoxication. The current study also demonstrated differences in type of drug use by ethnicity, with African Americans more likely to have used cocaine, and less likely to have used methamphetamines. Nevertheless, the explanation that the higher rate of revelation by African American women is an artifact of the type of drug used is unlikely; women in this study who did not use cocaine during their last pregnancy used either methamphetamines or heroin. The markers of methamphetamine and heroin use would be as likely to prompt providers' concern as the markers of cocaine use.

Second, Chasnoff et al. offer that the differences in revealing of drug use may be associated with the type of provider a woman sees. Because private providers may be more likely to associate with their patients outside of the patient-provider relationship and because they may be concerned about maintaining their client bases, they may be less willing to potentially offend their patients by bringing up the question of substance use. Consequently, if White and more educated drug users are more likely to be seen by private providers, they may be less likely to be asked about their drug use. In the current study, however, while women seen by public providers were somewhat more likely to reveal their drug use than women seen by private providers, the difference was not statistically significant. Thus, the higher rate of revealing prenatal substance use by African American women is not explained by differences in the type of providers they saw.

Third, Chasnoff et al. hypothesize that the higher rate of reporting of drug use for African American women and women of lower socioeconomic status may be driven by physician bias in whom they ask about prenatal drug use due to "the preconception that substance abuse, especially during pregnancy, is a problem that affects minority groups, urban populations, and lower socioeconomic groups" (Chasnoff et al., 1990, p. 1206). As much of the current concern about prenatal substance use arose out of the crack epidemic, and as crack use has been more prevalent among African American, urban, and less educated populations, the preconception may have developed that African American and less educated women are more likely to use drugs harmful to their fetuses. Providers who only ask their patients when there is a suspicion of drug use face the dilemma of being unsure which of their clients are likely to be drug users, and they may be more likely to ask women who are more like their preconceived image of the "typical" drug user: African American and less educated.

Provider bias has serious implications for the identification of prenatal substance use and the delivery of needed services. In the recent investigation into the identification of drug using women by Oregon birth attendants, Slutsker et al. (1993) found that African American women were more likely than women of other races to be identified for drug use other than marijuana (Odds Ratio = 7.9). The results from the current study indicate that this odds ratio may be appreciably inflated by provider bias. Furthermore, even if the true rate of prenatal drug use in Oregon is highest among African Americans, African Americans still constitute only 4% of the Oregon population. Because the majority of the risk for prenatal substance use in Oregon is among White women, specifically targeting African American pregnant women would deny the majority of drug using women and their newborns the benefit of addressing their prenatal substance use.

The possibility of substance use by pregnant women should be addressed regardless of risk factors, as substance use is common in women of all race/ethnicities and education levels (Wheeler, 1993). The American College of Obstetricians and Gynecologists has recently recommended that all patients should be asked about substance use during their first prenatal visit (Welch & Sokol, 1994), and in 1989, the Public Health Service Expert Panel on the Content of Prenatal Care recommended that prenatal care providers should conduct an alcohol, tobacco, and drug use history with all clients, provide advice to all clients on cessation and avoidance of alcohol, tobacco, and drugs, and provide appropriate referrals to substance use cessation interventions (United States Public Health Service, 1989). In the Oregon birth attendant survey, practitioners who routinely asked their patients about drug use were more than twice as likely to identify drug use than those who did not (Slutsker et al., 1993), and in a national survey, hospitals with preexisting protocols to detect prenatal substance use had an incidence of diagnosis of substance use three times greater than hospitals without preexisting protocols (Chasnoff, 1989).

Several aspects of the study design may influence the accuracy of the results. Because drug use was not confirmed through toxicologic screens and because chart audits were not conducted to confirm revealing drug use to providers, the accuracy of the data cannot be confirmed. Although recollection of substance use during pregnancy has been shown to have test-retest reliability (Blumhagen & Little, 1985), on average five years had elapsed between the time of last pregnancy and the time of the study interview, and recall of events during pregnancy for some women may be inaccurate. The sampling method for this study also limits the ability to generalize the results to other populations, as all subjects were out-of-treatment drug users at the time of the interviews. Because these women continued to use drugs after their pregnancy, their behaviors and experiences during their pregnancy may have been different from other cocaine, methamphetamine, and heroin using women who were able to discontinue their drug use.

Despite these limitations, the finding that many women who use drugs do not reveal their drug use to their prenatal providers is consistent with other studies (Chasnoff et al., 1990; Gillogley et al., 1990). Because of the association between prenatal drug use and poor birth outcomes, identifying and intervening with these women is imperative. The finding that African American and less educated women are more likely to reveal their drug use probably reflects preferential screening of women who look like "typical" drug users. However, prenatal substance abuse is a preventable and treatable problem which affects women in all demographic groups. Data from this study confirm the need for universal verbal screening for prenatal substance use. For substance using pregnant women to receive needed prenatal care, all prenatal providers must address the problem of substance use with all of their clients.

REFERENCES

ACOG Committee Opinion: Committee on Obstetrics: Cocaine abuse: Implications for pregnancy. (1991). *International Journal of Gynecology and Obstetrics, 36* (20), 164-166.

Amaro, H., Fried, L. E., Cabral, H., & Zuckerman, B. (1990). Violence during pregnancy and substance use. *American Journal of Public Health, 80* (5), 575-579.

Behnke, M., & Eyler, F. D. (1993). The consequences of prenatal substance use for the developing fetus, newborn, and young child. *International Journal of the Addictions, 28* (13), 1341-1391.

Bell, G. L., & Lau, K. (1995). Prenatal and neonatal issues of substance abuse. *Pediatric Clinics of North America, 42* (2), 261-281.

Blumhagen, J. M., & Little, R. E. (1985). Reliability of retrospective estimates of alcohol consumption during pregnancy by recovering women alcoholics. *Journal of Studies on Alcohol, 46* (1), 86-88.

Carta, J. J., & McEvoy, M. A. (1996, May). *Research update on substance exposure: Myths versus facts.* Paper presented at Alcohol, Tobacco & Other Drugs Update 1996 Teleconference, Tucson, AZ.

Chasnoff, I. J. (1989). Drug use and women: Establishing a standard of care. *Annals of the New York Academy of Sciences, 562,* 208-210.

Chasnoff, I. J., Burns, W. J., Schnoll, S. H., & Burns K. A. (1985). Cocaine use in pregnancy. *New England Journal of Medicine, 313* (11), 666-669.

Chasnoff, I. J., Landress, H. J., & Barrett, M. E. (1990). The prevalence of illicit-drug or alcohol use during pregnancy and discrepancies in mandatory reporting in Pinellas County, Florida. *The New England Journal of Medicine, 322* (17), 1202-1206.

Eriksson, M., Billing, L., Steneroth, G., & Zetterstrom, R. (1989). Health and development of 8-year-old children whose mothers abused amphetamine during pregnancy. *Acta Paediatricia Scandinavica, 78* (6), 944-9.

Freda, M. C., Andersen, F., Damus, K., & Merkatz, I. R. (1993). Are there differences in information given to private and public prenatal patients? *American Journal of Obstetrics and Gynecology, 169* (1), 155-160.

Kain, Z. N., Rimar, S., & Barash, P. G. (1993). Cocaine abuse in the parturient and effects on the fetus and neonate. *Anesthesia and Analgesia, 77* (4), 835-45.

Kaltenbach, K., & Finnegan, L. P. (1986). Neonatal abstinence syndrome, pharmacotherapy and developmental outcome. *Neurobehavioral Toxicology and Teratology, 8* (4), 353-5.

Kelly, S. J., Walsh, J. H., & Thompson, K. (1991). Birth outcomes, health problems, and neglect with prenatal exposure to cocaine. *Pediatric Nursing, 17* (2), 130-6.

Kogan, M. D., Alexander, G. R., Kotelchuck, M., Nagey, D. A., & Jack, B. W. (1994). Comparing mothers' reports on the content of prenatal care received with recommended national guidelines for care. *Public Health Reports, 109* (5), 637-646.

Mann, T., Battagin, J., Cooper, S., & Mahan, C. S. (1992). Some of my patients use drugs. *Journal of Florida Medical Association, 79* (1) 41-45.

Marcenko, M. O., Spence, M., & Rohweder, C. (1994). Psychosocial characteristics of pregnant women with and without a history of substance abuse. *National Association of Social Workers, 19* (1), 17-22.

Needle, R., Fisher, D., Weatherby, N., Brown, B., Cesari, H., Chitwood, D., Booth, R., Williams, M. L., Watters, J., Andersen, M., & Braunstein, M. (1995). The reliability of self-reported HIV risk behaviors of drug users. *Psychology of Addictive Behaviors, 9* (4), 242-250.

Norušis, M. J. (1994). *SPSS Advanced Statistics 6.1.* Chicago: SPSS Inc.

Olofsson, M., Buckley, W., Andersen, G. E., & Friis-Hansen, B. (1983a). Investigation of 89 children born by drug-dependent mothers. I. Neonatal course. *Acta Paediatrica Scandinavica, 72* (3), 403-6.

Olofsson, M., Buckley, W., Andersen, G. E., & Friis-Hansen, B. (1983b). Investigation of 89 children born by drug-dependent mothers. II. Follow-up 1-10 years after birth. *Acta Paediatrica Scandinavica, 72* (3), 407-10.

Oro, A. S., & Dixon, S. D. (1987). Perinatal cocaine and methamphetamine exposure: Maternal and neonatal correlates. *Journal of Pediatrics, 111* (4) 571-8.

Reed, B. G. (1985). Drug misuse and dependency in women. *International Journal of the Addictions, 20* (1), 13-62.

Robins, L. N., & Mills, J. L. (Eds.). (1993). Effects of in utero exposure to street drugs. *American Journal of Public Health, 83* (supplement), 1-32.

Slutsker, L., Smith, R., Higginson, G., & Fleming, D. (1993). Recognizing illicit drug use by pregnant women: Reports from Oregon birth attendants. *American Journal of Public Health, 83* (1), 61-64.

United States Public Health Service. (1989). *Caring for our future: A report of the Public Health Service expert panel on the content of prenatal care.* Washington, D.C.: United States Public Health Service.

Watters, J. K., & Biernacki, P. (1989). Targeted sampling: Options for the study of hidden populations. *Social Problems, 36,* 416-430.

Weatherby, N. L., Needle, R., Cesari, H., Booth, R., McCoy, C. B., Watters, J. K., Williams, M., & Chitwood, D. D. (1994). Validity of self-reported drug use among injection drug users and crack cocaine users recruited through street outreach. *Evaluation & Program Planning, 17* (4), 347-355.

Welch, R. A., & Sokol, R. J. (1994). ACOG technical bulletin. Substance abuse in pregnancy. *International Journal of Gynecology and Obstetrics, 47,* 73-80.

Wheeler, S. F. (1993). Substance abuse during pregnancy. *Primary Care: Clinics in Office Practice, 20* (1), 191-207.

Pregnancy Among Women
with a History of Injection Drug Use

Mary Comerford, MSPH
Dale D. Chitwood, PhD
Karen McElrath, PhD
John Taylor, MA

SUMMARY. The reproductive histories of women who use drugs have received little attention in spite of risks associated with drug use during pregnancy and the high risk settings in which children of drug users are raised. This study describes the epidemiology of pregnancy and related drug use among African-American and White women injection drug users. Almost all of the study sample had been pregnant and most used drugs during pregnancy. Treatment programs should provide multifaceted interventions that include family planning, prenatal care, and parenting skills to reduce the negative effects of drug use on mothers and children in this population.

Mary Comerford is Senior Research Associate, and Dale D. Chitwood is Professor of Medical Sociology, Department of Sociology, and Health Services Research Center, University of Miami, 5665 Ponce de Leon Boulevard, Room 126, Coral Gables, FL 33146-0719. Karen McElrath is Associate Professor of Criminology, Department of Sociology, University of Miami and Visiting Professor, Department of Sociology and Social Policy, Queen's University, Belfast BT7 1NN, Ireland. John Taylor is a graduate student in the Department of Sociology, University of Miami.

This research was supported by NIDA grants RO1DA04433 and 1P50DA10236 and by a supplemental grant from the Office of Research for Women's Health (ORWH).

[Haworth co-indexing entry note]: "Pregnancy Among Women with a History of Injection Drug Use." Comerford, Mary et al. Co-published simultaneously in *Drugs & Society* (The Haworth Press, Inc.) Vol. 13, No. 1/2, 1998, pp. 177-192; and: *Women and Substance Abuse: Gender Transparency* (ed: Sally J. Stevens, and Harry K. Wexler) The Haworth Press, Inc., 1998, pp. 177-192. Single or multiple copies of this article are available for a fee from The Haworth Document Delivery Service [1-800-342-9678, 9:00 a.m. - 5:00 p.m. (EST). E-mail address: getinfo@haworthpressinc.com].

177

At least 8 million women of childbearing age in the United States are estimated to be substance abusers (Adams, Gfroerer, & Rouse, 1989). Recent increases in the number of young women who initiate use will further increase this population (Kokotailo, Langhough, Cox, Davidson, & Fleming, 1994; National Institute on Drug Abuse, 1994). These women constitute a pool for potentially high risk pregnancies that frequently require special resources for both the mother and child.

The prevalence of alcohol and other drug abuse among pregnant women has received considerable attention in recent years (Burke & Roth, 1993). National estimates indicate that more than 700,000 infants each year are prenatally exposed to at least one illicit drug (Gomby & Shiono, 1991), and women who use heroin give birth to an estimated 10,000 children every year (Bashore, Ketchum, Staisch, Barrett, & Zimmerman, 1981).

Most published studies of pregnancy and drug use focus on the impact of prenatal alcohol (Abel, 1990a; Abel, 1990b) and other drug use on the health of the fetus and neonate (Chasnoff, Keith, & Schnoll, 1986; Bashore et al., 1981; Stern, 1984; Center for Substance Abuse Prevention, 1996), and less frequently, on the mother's health (Chasnoff et al., 1986; Kroll, 1986; Stern, 1984). There is widespread agreement that women who use drugs, particularly alcohol, opiates, or cocaine, are at high risk for complications during pregnancy and childbirth and infants born to these women are at high risk for a variety of adverse outcomes.

Less consensus exists about the specific contribution that drug use makes in the determination of those adverse outcomes. We know that nutrition, lifestyle, and prenatal care (Kroll, 1986; McCalla, Feldman, Webbeh, Ahmadi, & Minkoff, 1995; Melnikow & Alemagno, 1993) play a large role in pregnancy outcome. Lack of prenatal care has been associated with infant mortality and low birth weight (Leveno, Cunningham, Roark, Nelson, & Williams, 1985; Melnikow & Alemagno, 1993). We also know that women who abuse alcohol and drugs are likely to suffer from poor nutrition, lead unhealthy lifestyles, and receive little or no prenatal care (Kroll, 1986; Leveno et al., 1985; Melnikow, Alemagno, Rottmen, & Zyzanski, 1991). The mother who abuses drugs often is in poor health prior to pregnancy and brings these pre-existing conditions to her pregnancy (Bashore et al., 1981; Kroll, 1986). Consequently, the effects of these factors upon maternal and perinatal outcome often are difficult to separate from the pharmacological effects of drug use (Frank et al., 1988; Richardson, Day, & McGauhey, 1995; Stern, 1984). The HIV/AIDS epidemic adds an additional dimension to the problem. Women who inject drugs or use crack are at high risk for HIV infection which can be transmitted to the fetus or neonate (Brown, Mitchell, DeVore, & Primm, 1989; Ellerbock et al., 1995; Lindsay et al., 1992). Polydrug use, which is quite common among drug users, further complicates our understanding of the impact that individual drugs such as cocaine or heroin have upon the fetus, the newborn, and the mother. In spite of these questions, there is a broad consensus that women who abuse alcohol and other drugs and become pregnant place both themselves and their fetus/neonate at high risk for a variety of health and social problems.

In light of this awareness, it is surprising that little attention has been given to the reproductive histories of women who are heavy users of alcohol and other drugs (Bashore et al., 1981). One brief report of pregnancy among clients of a methadone maintenance program suggested that female injection drug users are a fertile population (Brown et al., 1989). For the most part, however, medical issues have dominated the research arena, and these questions have focused attention upon the individual drug-use-during-pregnancy event to the exclusion of broader questions of women and health. Public health programs have expended enormous resources and money to care for individual infants who have major medical problems but only recently have begun to invest in drug treatment and specialized prenatal care for women drug users who are pregnant. Most studies that have examined the pharmacological impact of drug use during pregnancy have been much less concerned with the reproductive histories of women who use drugs (Cartwright, Schorge, & McLaughlin, 1991; McCalla et al., 1995; Wiemann, Berenson, & Landwehr, 1995).

The purpose of this study is to investigate the history of pregnancy among women who use drugs to obtain information that is relevant for the development and implementation of effective treatments and interventions.

METHODS

As a supplement to a longitudinal study of drug use and risk factors for HIV infection among injection drug users (IDUs), 117 women were asked to describe their reproductive histories. These data are reported in this article. All of the women were IDUs who had been recruited originally from treatment centers in Dade County, Florida (Chitwood, Rivers, Comerford, & McBride, 1993). Most of the women had been treated for opiate addiction; 87.4% had been recruited from methadone maintenance clinics.

The women had been followed for 72 months when the supplemental questionnaire was administered. Items included: the number of pregnancies in lifetime; outcome and ending date of each pregnancy; and history of drug use. Since these data were based on recall, we did not attempt to determine which specific drugs were used with each specific pregnancy. Rather, we determined which drugs had been used during any pregnancy and which drugs had been used during the last pregnancy. All interviews were administered by a trained interviewer and confidentiality of the data was assured. These data were combined with data from baseline and follow-up collection instruments which contained demographic and drug use information for each individual.

RESULTS

Of the 117 women IDUs, 111 (94.9%) had been pregnant at least once. Only data from these 111 women were used in the analysis. The majority (65.8%) were White non-Hispanic, 27.9% were African-American, and 6.3% were White Hispanic. Because of the small number of Hispanic women, ethnicity was dichotomized into African-American and White, which included the 7 Hispanic women. The mean age of the sample was 39.5 with a range from 28 to 58. The African-American women were older (mean 41.3 years) than the white women (mean 39.1 years) (p < .05). More than two-thirds (69.4%) of the sample had graduated from high school. At the time of interview, 19 (17.1%) of the women were positive for antibodies to HIV. As described in Table 1, women who were African-American IDUs (41.9%) were significantly more likely than White women IDUs (7.5%) to be HIV positive (p < .00002).

There were 464 pregnancies among the 111 women including 227 live births, 161 therapeutic abortions, 57 spontaneous abortions, 10 stillbirths, and 3 ectopic pregnancies. Six of the pregnancies were not characterized. Pregnancy outcome by ethnicity of the 460 pregnancies with a known

TABLE 1. HIV Serostatus by Ethnicity

	n	% Positive*
African-American Women	31	41.9
White Women	80	7.5

*p < .00002

outcome is presented in Table 2. African-Americans had more live births and fewer therapeutic abortions than Whites (p < .001).

More than half (52.9%) of the women had their first pregnancy while in their teens. The mean age for first pregnancy was 20.0. There was no significant difference at age of first pregnancy between African-American women (19.2) and White women (20.3). The age range for first pregnancy was 11 to 36.

Polydrug use was the norm for the study sample. Almost all of the women (99.1%) reported using an opiate at some time in their life and 98.2% reported cocaine use. All women had used marijuana. First use of most drugs occurred before age 21. Exceptions to this were speedball (an injected mixture of an opiate, usually heroin and cocaine), methadone, and crack. The later age of methadone use reflects a time lag between the time of first use of opiates to treatment. Crack use was initiated later than any of the other drugs, at a mean age of 29.8. This is indicative of the age of the sample; the crack use phenomenon appeared relatively late in their drug use careers.

A little more than half (51.9%) had initiated injection prior to their first pregnancy. Table 3 describes the drug use patterns of these women during their cumulative pregnancies. An overwhelming majority of African-American (77.4%) and White (82.5%) women used illicit drugs either alone or in

TABLE 2. Pregnancy Outcome by Ethnicity

	African-Americans (N = 31)			Whites (N = 80)		
	No.	Mean	Range	No.	Mean	Range
Live Births*	108	3.5	0-7	119	1.5	0-8
Therapeutic Abortions*	14	0.5	0-4	147	1.8	0-8
Spontaneous Abortions	20	0.6	0-4	37	0.5	0-5
Stillbirths	4	0.1	0-1	6	0.1	0-3
Ectopic Pregnancies	1	0.03	1	2	0.02	1
Total Pregnancies	147	4.7	1-9	311	3.9	1-10

*p < .001

TABLE 3. Drug Use During Pregnancy

	African-American (N = 31) %		White (N = 80) %	
	Any Pregnancy	Last Pregnancy	Any Pregnancy	Last Pregnancy
No Alcohol, No Other Drugs	16.1	25.8	15.0	28.8
Alcohol, No Other Drugs	6.5	9.7	2.5	2.5
No Alcohol, Other Drugs	38.7	38.7	42.5	41.3
Alcohol, Other drugs	38.7	25.8	41.3	27.4

combination with alcohol during any pregnancy. Just over 15% of the women used neither alcohol nor any other drug during at least one pregnancy. Among the African-American women, 6.5% used alcohol but no other drugs during their pregnancies. Less than 3% of the White women used alcohol only. Table 3 also presents data on drug use during the women's most recent pregnancy. There was a minor increase in the number of women who reported no alcohol or drug use. Nevertheless, approximately 3 out of every 4 women reported drug use during their last pregnancy with no difference between African-American and White women.

The majority of these women were polydrug users during their most recent pregnancy. Alcohol, heroin, other opiates, crack, other cocaine, barbiturates, and tranquilizers were the most frequently used substances. Whites were more likely than African-Americans to have used marijuana ($p < .05$) while African-American women were more likely to have used speedball ($p < .001$).

DISCUSSION

Drug Treatment and Reproductive Health Education

Drug treatment programs are an ideal place to provide comprehensive education on all aspects of reproduction and reproductive health. Almost every woman in this study had experienced at least one pregnancy and most had two or more pregnancies. Considering the multiple ramifications of pregnancy and childbirth for chronic drug using women, education is imperative and interventions must be multifaceted.

Treatment programs should provide multidisciplinary counseling and related services to reduce the risk of drug use during pregnancy. The need is obvious. Four out of five women in our study had used one or more illicit drugs during pregnancy, and fewer than one out of six had been alcohol and drug free during any of their pregnancies. These services ideally would reach women before pregnancy but are equally valuable for those who have already had a pregnancy or those with a current pregnancy.

Simply stated, drug use during pregnancy affects the health of the mother and neonate. The obvious role of treatment programs is to alert women to the high risk that drug use during pregnancy has for both the mother and the child. Some of the more common problems include pre-term and precipitous labor, breech presentation, pre-mature rupture of membranes, need for a c-section, and post partum hemorrhage (Chasnoff et al., 1986; Kroll, 1986; Stern, 1984). Injection drug using women such as those in this study have additional complications such as infections caused by injection or the increased risk of infection associated with the use of subclavical veins which may be necessary when medical personnel cannot locate usable veins (Silver, Wapner, Loriz-Vega, & Finnegan, 1987). Infants born to IDUs also have more frequent infections than do infants born to women drug users who do not inject (Chasnoff et al., 1986).

Prenatal and Neonatal Effects of Drug Use

Prenatal and neonatal effects of drug use have been reported by several studies. There are numerous reports of fetal distress and fetal abnormalities attributed to cocaine and/or heroin use during pregnancy. Most often reported are fetal death, abrupto placentae, and ammionitis, (Acker, Sachs, Tracey, & Wise, 1983; Bingol, Fuchs, Diaz, Stone, & Gromisch, 1987; MacGregor et al., 1987). Neonates of drug using women frequently have been reported to exhibit low birth weight, low-gestational age, smaller head circumferences, and congenital abnormalities (Bingol et al., 1987; Chasnoff et al., 1986; Chouteau, Namerow, & Leppert, 1988; MacGregor et al., 1987). Babies born to women who are opiate addicts are born addicted to opiates and must go through detoxification (Bashore et al., 1981). Babies born to mothers who used cocaine during pregnancy have been described as jittery, tremulous, without normal sleep patterns, and prone to excessive crying (Chasnoff, Burns, Schnoll, & Burns, 1985).

Treatment programs are a logical place to develop and implement interventions which can reduce drug use during pregnancy.

Importance of Prenatal Care

These interventions also must emphasize the importance of prenatal care. Adequate nutrition and health care during pregnancy are particularly important for the welfare of both mother and child when the mother is a drug user (Neuspiel, 1994; Richardson et al., 1995). In spite of the known advantages of prenatal care, drug users are less likely to receive prenatal care than other populations (Bashore et al., 1981; Funkhouser, Butz, Feng, McCaul, & Rosenstein, 1993). Financial barriers, attitude toward pregnancy, and attitude toward health professionals may be deterrents for prenatal care. The more powerful factor may be fear of criminal prosecution or loss of custody of the baby if a women presents for care and is found to use drugs (Baciewcz, 1993; Poland, Dombrowski, Ager, & Sokol, 1993). As more states enact punitive laws toward drug abuse during pregnancy, drug users may become even less willing to receive prenatal care.

In spite of these barriers, intervention is possible. The model PACE project in New York City, where comprehensive prenatal care was given to pregnant drug users, indicates that prenatal care can achieve a significant reduction in maternal and perinatal adverse outcomes (LaFrance et al., 1994). A study in Philadelphia has concluded that if drug dependent women are provided with specialized care, they may experience intrapartum and perinatal outcomes that are similar to those of non-drug dependent women (Silver et al., 1987).

Since prenatal care may be able to counteract many adverse effects that drug use during pregnancy can impose (Paltrow, 1990), prenatal care for substance abusers is extremely important. Adequate prenatal care for drug abusing women may require special services of obstetricians, pediatricians, nutritionists, and social workers and require special assistance to access those services (Kroll, 1986; Stern, 1984). Drug treatment programs ideally will incorporate these interdisciplinary services into their systems to insure that drug users receive adequate prenatal care.

Family Planning and Birth Control

A comprehensive intervention also will include family planning and birth control services. Treatment must move beyond crisis management of women who are pregnant to provide care that extends to the woman's entire reproductive life. A survey of 115 women who were heroin addicts found that those women (25.8%) were much less likely than a national sample of women (48.5%) to use any type of contraception (Ralph & Spigner, 1986). Rosenbaum (Rosenbaum, 1979; 1981) also has noted that several women heroin users erroneously believed that drug use prevented pregnancy. Heroin and methadone contribute to dysmenorrhea and thus pregnancy may be masked by what is perceived to be a symptom of drug use.

Drug treatment programs have the opportunity to give comprehensive education on birth control measures and to help women and men with family planning. Information about birth control techniques and assertiveness training to allow the women to gain control over their own reproduction should be a central facet of the program. Some women experience pressure from sex partners to not use birth control. Many women who inject drugs fail to use condoms primarily because of partners' preference (Stevens, Erickson, & Estrada, 1993). Additional reasons why women who inject drugs give for not using condoms include a belief that partners do not have HIV, lack of knowledge about where to get condoms and how to use them, and discomfort discussing condom use with their partners (Nyamathi, Lewis, Leake, Flaskerud, & Bennett, 1995). Women IDUs who are not knowledgeable or are unwilling or unable to use birth control methods such as birth control pills or intradermal application of birth control substances, may experience partner dissatisfaction with other barrier methods. Education on birth control also must include training on the prevention of sexually transmitted diseases. Failure to use condoms increases the risk of transmission of HIV infection to the woman from her sex partner, particularly if that partner is also an IDU (King et al., 1994).

Two striking dissimilarities in our study include (1) the differential rates of live births and therapeutic abortions of White IDUs and their African-American counterparts and (2) the significantly greater number of African-American women who are infected with HIV. Whites had significantly more therapeutic abortions than did African-Americans. In fact, White women reported more therapeutic abortions than live births. Conversely, African-Americans had more live births, with a relatively low percentage of abortions. The reasons for this difference are unknown. Two possible explanations include financial/access issues and cultural norms and values. African-American women may have less access to abortion because of financial considerations. In our sample, household income of African-American women was significantly lower than that of White women. Since Medicaid will not pay for abortions except when the life of the mother is in danger, ability to pay may play a role in the lower rate of abortion among African-Americans. A second possible explanation focuses on sub-cultural values that support or ostracize the abortion alternative. It is possible that African-American women have greater social support for having a child, particularly as a single mother, and the baby is viewed as a source of status. Some pregnant teenagers view a child as the only thing of their lives that they can create, and thus choose not to abort (Deisher, Farrow, & Litchfield, 1989).

Judging from the number of pregnancies and subsequent abortions among this group of drug using women as a whole, and among White IDUs in particular, it appears that abortion may be used as a primary birth control technique by several women. Comprehensive interventions in treatment must include information about the total spectrum of birth control techniques. Therapeutic abortions are not entirely safe, and multiple abortions may put the mother at high risk for a variety of medical problems. Women who use therapeutic abortion as their primary birth control technique may benefit from an educational program that expands their knowledge about the variety of effective birth control methods that are available to them.

The prevalence of HIV infection among women drug users in general and African-American women in particular has risen in recent years. Drug treatment programs can serve as a vital resource to educate women drug users about the danger of HIV infection during pregnancy. We found a significantly higher percentage of African-American women to be infected with HIV than non-African-American women. This is consistent with other studies which have described increased risk of HIV infection among African-American IDUs (D'Aquila, Peterson, Williams, & Williams, 1989; Brunswick et al., 1993; Hahn, Onorato, Jones, & Dougherty, 1989; Novick et al., 1989). While we have no data to indicate the HIV status of these women during their past pregnancies, it is reasonable to presume that African-American women are at higher risk for a pregnancy concurrent with HIV infection. Thus, while education and intervention programs must serve all women, programs particularly sensitive to African-American IDUs need to be developed (Airhihenbuwa, DiClemente, Wingood, & Lowe, 1992).

HIV infection during pregnancy presents a myriad of problems for both the mother and the baby. Drug treatment programs should teach women about effects of pregnancy on HIV infection, mother-fetus transmission of HIV, and how to cope with and plan for the future of their children. Not only can the fetus become infected, but the health of the HIV infected mother can deteriorate during pregnancy and women need to be aware of this danger. A mother who is HIV positive also needs to develop special coping skills to care for herself and her baby, particularly if the baby also is infected with HIV. An important area of consideration, but one rarely dealt with, is planning for the future of the child should the mother become too sick to care for the child or should the mother die. Drug treatment centers can assist women in developing skills to assist them to cope with their own grief and to make wise decisions to prepare for the care of their child(ren).

Pregnancy as a Motivator in Eliminating or Reducing Drug Use

Drug treatment for pregnant drug using women not only is essential, it is an ideal opportunity to maximize the likelihood of successful treatment. Women may be more motivated to enter drug treatment while they are pregnant (Anderson & Grant, 1984; LaFrance et al., 1994; Rosenbaum, 1981). Many drug users attempt to reduce or eliminate alcohol and/or drug use during pregnancy because of concern for their unborn child (Anderson & Grant, 1984; Rosenbaum, 1981). Pregnancy, then, presents an opportunity to enroll and motivate women in drug treatment. Many drug treatment programs historically have refused to accept pregnant drug users, but recently more are willing to do so (Breitbart, Chavkin, & Wise, 1994). It is imperative that drug treatment programs recognize this vulnerable population of drug users and provide adequate treatment. Treatment should occur in collaboration with obstetricians, pediatricians, and other health professionals.

Controversy exists about the advisability of pregnant women undergoing detoxification because of increased risk of fetal distress (Hoegerman & Wilson, 1990) and neonate mortality (Center for Substance Abuse Treatment, 1993). If detoxification is undertaken, it must be a gradual process. Methadone offers an alternative for opiate users which is considered to be less harmful for the mother (Bashore et al., 1981; Chasnoff et al., 1986), but there is controversy as to the effect of this synthetic opiate upon the fetus and neonate. Some reports indicate that newborn withdrawal from methadone is more stressful for the infant (Bashore et al., 1981); other reports dispute this and believe fetal outcome is no worse and perhaps better (Deren, 1986). From our data, it appears that many heroin injectors are on methadone maintenance during pregnancy. Drug treatment programs should work in conjunction with other health professionals to decide if detoxification is appropriate for each client and, if so, assist in the detoxification process.

Parenting Skills Training

Parenting skills training also must be a central component of the intervention curriculum for men and women, whether or not they have a child. Training needs to focus on both newborns and older children. The behavior traits of babies born addicted to opiates who are going through detoxification and "coke" babies who are irritable and prone to excessive crying, may make it difficult for the mother to bond with the infant (Kaltenbach & Finnegan, 1992; Stern, 1984). Drug using women often lack good parenting skills (Kroll, 1986; LaFrance et al., 1994) and this lack of bonding exacerbates the mother's inadequate proficiency in child rearing. While the majority of drug users who have children love their children and want to be good mothers, the addiction often gets in the way, leaving the children with a lack of care, love, and role models (Rosenbaum, 1981). This can have very damaging effects on the child. Drug users tend to give birth to more than one child, and parental drug use can place all children in the home at risk for abuse and neglect. For example, in 1989, 675,000 (75%) of the 900,000 substantiated reports of child abuse or neglect involved care givers who abused alcohol and/or other drugs (Daro & Mitchell, 1990). Other studies have found that children raised in substance abusing families are more likely than other children to suffer physical abuse (Davis, 1990) and sexual abuse (Miller, Downs, Gondoli, & Keil, 1987). Reports have documented the staggering costs that arise from foster care placement and preparing these children for school (Kusserow, 1990). An additional concern is the labeling of drug-exposed infants, e.g., "crack kids," and "cocaine babies." Neuspiel (1994) suggested that these labels might lead to a self-fulfilling prophecy: the label itself could contribute to a child's failure.

Comprehensive education and training that includes all of these aspects of the reproductive life of women who use drugs can be offered on an out-patient basis which will make them available to all drug users and their families, whether in treatment or not. Classes must be accessible and offered at times and days that permit the target populations to participate. Where target populations are not in treatment, access can be greatly enhanced if transportation is provided or made affordable. Most important, the program must provide for child care.

CONCLUSION

Our study indicates that childbearing can span several years during the woman's drug using career. The study does not purport to represent all women who use drugs, although our review of existing data suggests that the need for education and skills training is relevant for all women who use drugs. Interventions must move beyond crisis treatment for pregnant women, important as this is, to a prevention oriented perspective that intervenes with drug using women before they are pregnant or with women of child bearing age who are at risk for alcohol and drug misuse.

REFERENCES

Abel, E.L. (1990a). Historical background. In *Fetal Alcohol Syndrome* (pp. 1-11). Oradell, NJ: Medical Economics Books.

Abel, E.L. (1990b). A spectrum of effects. In *Fetal Alcohol Syndrome* (pp. 45-54). Oradell, NJ: Medical Economics Books.

Acker, D., Sachs, B.P., Tracey, K.J., & Wise, W.E. (1983). Abruptio placentae associated with cocaine use. *American Journal of Obstetrics and Gynecology, 146*, 220-221.

Adams, E.H., Gfroerer, J.C., & Rouse, B.A. (1989). Epidemiology of substance abuse including alcohol and cigarette smoking. Annals of the New York Academy of Sciences, *Prenatal Abuse of Licit and Illicit Drugs, 562*, 14-20.

Airhihenbuwa, C.O., DiClemente, R.J., Wingood, G.M., & Lowe, A. (1992). HIV/AIDS education and prevention among African-Americans: A focus on culture. *AIDS Education and Prevention, 4*, 267-276.

Anderson, S.C., & Grant, J.F. (1984). Pregnant women and alcohol: Implications for social work. *Social Casework, 65*, 3-10.

Baciewcz, G. (1993). The process of addiction. *Clinical Obstetrics and Gynecology, 36*, 223-231.

Bashore, R.A., Ketchum, J.S., Staisch, K.L., Barrett, C.T., & Zimmerman, E.G. (1981). Heroin addiction and pregnancy. *Western Journal of Medicine, 134*, 506-514.

Bingol, N., Fuchs, M., Diaz, V., Stone, R.K., & Gromisch, D.S. (1987). Teratogenicity of cocaine in humans. *Journal of Pediatrics, 110*, 93-96.

Breitbart, V., Chavkin, W., & Wise, P.H. (1994). The accessibility of drug treatment for pregnant women: A survey of programs in five cities. *American Journal of Public Health, 84*, 1658-1661.

Brown, L.S., Jr., Mitchell, J.L., DeVore, S.L., & Primm, B.J. (1989). Female intravenous drug users and perinatal HIV transmission (Letter). *New England Journal of Medicine, 320*, 1493-1494.

Brunswick, A.F., Aidala, A., Dobkin, J., Howard, J., Titus, S.P., & Banaszak-Holl, J. (1993). HIV-1 seroprevalence and risk behaviors in an urban African-American community cohort. *American Journal of Public Health, 83*, 1390-1394.

Burke, M.S., & Roth, D. (1993). Anonymous cocaine screening in a private obstetric population. *Obstetrics & Gynecology, 81*, 354-356.

Cartwright, P.S., Schorge, J.O., & McLaughlin, F.J. (1991). Epidemiologic characteristics of drug use during pregnancy. *Southern Medical Journal, 84*, 867-870.

Center for Substance Abuse Treatment. (1993). *Improving Treatment for Drug-Exposed Infants*. Rockville, MD: U.S. Dept. of Health and Human Services.

Center for Substance Abuse Prevention. (1996). *Pregnancy and Exposure to Alcohol and Other Drug Use*. Rockville, MD: U.S. Dept. of Health and Human Services.

Chasnoff, I.J., Burns, W.J., Schnoll, S.H., & Burns, K.A. (1985). Cocaine use in pregnancy. *New England Journal of Medicine, 313*, 666-669.

Chasnoff, I.J., Keith, L., & Schnoll, S.H. (1986). Perinatal aspects of maternal addiction. *Current Problems in Obstetrics, Gynecology and Fertility, IX,* 403-440.

Chitwood, D.D., Rivers, J.R., Comerford, M., & McBride, D.C. (1993). A comparison of HIV related risk behaviors of street recruited and treatment program injection drug users. *Drugs & Society, 7,* 53-64.

Chouteau, M., Namerow, P.B., & Leppert, P. (1988). The effect of cocaine abuse on birth weight and gestational age. *Obstetrics & Gynecology, 72,* 351-354.

D'Aquila, R.T., Peterson, L.R., Williams, A.B., & Williams, A.E. (1989). Race/ ethnicity as a risk factor for HIV-1 infection among Connecticut intravenous drug users. *Journal of Acquired Immune Deficiency Syndromes, 2,* 503-513.

Daro, D., & Mitchell, L. (1990). *Current trends in child abuse reporting and fatalities: The results of the 1989 fifty-state survey.* Chicago: National Committee for the Prevention of Child Abuse.

Davis, S. (1990). Chemical dependency in women: A description of its effects and outcome on adequate parenting. *Journal of Substance Abuse Treatment, 7,* 225-232.

Deisher, R.J., Farrow, K.H., & Litchfield, C. (1989). The pregnant adolescent prostitute. *American Journal of Diseases of Children, 143,* 1162-1165.

Deren, S. (1986). Children of substance abusers: A review of the literature. *Journal of Substance Abuse Treatment, 10,* 445-448.

Ellerbock, T.V., Harrington, P.E., Bush, T.J., Scheoenfisch, S.A., Oxtoby, M.J., & Witte, J.J. (1995). Risk of human immunodeficiency virus infection among pregnant crack cocaine users in a rural community. *Obstetrics & Gynecology, 86,* 400-404.

Frank, D.A., Zuckerman, B.S., Amaro, H., Aboagye, K., Bauchner, H., Cabral, H., Fried, L., Hingson, R., Kayner, H., Levenson, S.M., Parker, S., Reece, H., & Vinci, R. (1988). Cocaine use during pregnancy: Prevalence and correlates. *Pediatrics, 82,* 888-895.

Funkhouser, A.W., Butz, A.M., Feng, T.I., McCaul, M.E., & Rosenstein, B.J. (1993). Prenatal care and drug use in pregnant women. *Drug and Alcohol Dependence, 33,* 1-9.

Gomby, D.S., & Shiono, P.H. (1991). Estimating the number of drug exposed infants. *Future of Children, 1,* 17-25.

Hahn, R.A., Onorato, I.M., Jones, T.S., & Dougherty, J. (1989). Prevalence of HIV infection among intravenous drug users in the United States. *Journal of the American Medical Association, 261,* 2677-2684.

Hoegerman, G., & Wilson, C. (1990). Drug-exposed neonates. *Western Journal of Medicine, 152,* 559-564.

Kaltenbach, K.A., & Finnegan, L.P. (1992). Studies of prenatal drug exposure and environmental research issues: The benefits of integrating research within a treatment program. In M.M. Kilbey & K. Asghar (Eds.). *Methodological Issues in Epidemiological, Prevention, and Treatment Research on Drug-Exposed Women and their Children.* National Institute on Drug Abuse Monograph 117. (pp. 259-270). Rockville, MD: U.S. Govt. Printing Office.

King, V.L., Jr., Brooner, R.K., Bigelow, G.E., Schmidt, C.W., Felch, L.J., &

Gazaway, P.M. (1994). Condom use rates for specific sexual behaviors among opioid abusers entering treatment. *Drug and Alcohol Dependence, 35,* 231-238.

Kokotailo, P.K., Langhough, R.E., Cox, N.S., Davidson, S.R., & Fleming, M.F. (1994). Cigarette, alcohol and other drug use among small city pregnant adolescents. *Journal of Adolescent Health, 15,* 366-373.

Kroll, D. (1986). Heroin addiction in pregnancy. *Midwives Chronicle & Nursing Notes, July,* 153-157.

Kusserow, R.P. (1990). *Crack Babies.* Washington, D.C.: U.S. Dept. Health and Human Services.

LaFrance, S.V., Mitchell, J., Damus, K., Driver, C., Roman, G., Graham, E., & Schwartz, L. (1994). Community-based services for pregnant substance-using women. *American Journal of Public Health, 84,* 1688-1689.

Leveno, K.J., Cunningham, F.G., Roark, M.L., Nelson, S.D., & Williams, M.L. (1985). Prenatal care and the low birth weight infant. *Obstetrics and Gynecology, 66,* 599-605.

Lindsay, M.K., Peterson, H.B., Boring, J., Gramling, J., Willis, S., & Klein, L. (1992). Crack cocaine: A risk factor for human immunodeficiency virus infection type 1 among inner-city parturients. *Obstetrics & Gynecology, 80,* 981-984.

MacGregor, S.N., Keith, L.G., Chasnoff, I.J., Rosner, M.A., Chisum, G.M., Shaw, P., & Minogue, J.P. (1987). Cocaine use during pregnancy: Adverse perinatal outcome. *American Journal of Obstetrics and Gynecology, 157,* 686-690.

McCalla, S., Feldman, J., Webbeh, H., Ahmadi, R., & Minkoff, H.L. (1995). Changes in perinatal cocaine use in an inner-city hospital, 1988 to 1992. *American Journal of Public Health, 85,* 1695-1697.

Melnikow, J., & Alemagno, S. (1993). Adequacy of prenatal care among inner-city women. *Journal of Family Practice, 37,* 575-582.

Melnikow, J., Alemagno, S., Rottmen, C., & Zyzanski, S.J. (1991). Characteristics of inner-city women giving birth with little or no prenatal care: A case-control study. *Journal of Family Practice, 32,* 283-288.

Miller, B., Downs, W., Gondoli, D., & Keil, A. (1987). The role of childhood sexual abuse in the development of alcoholism in women. *Western Journal of Medicine, 152,* 559-564.

National Institute on Drug Abuse. (1994). *National Survey Results on Drug Use from the Monitoring the Future Study, 1975-1993, Volume II,* NIH Publication No. 94-3810. Washington, D.C.: U.S. Govt. Printing Office.

Neuspiel, D.R. (1994). Behavior in cocaine-exposed infants and children: Association versus causality. *Drug and Alcohol Dependence, 36,* 101-107.

Novick, D.M., Trigg, H.L., Des Jarlais, D.C., Friedman, S.R., Vlahov, D., & Kreek, M.J. (1989). Cocaine injection and ethnicity in parenteral drug users during the early years of the human immunodeficiency virus (HIV) epidemic in New York City. *Journal of Medical Virology, 29,* 181-185.

Nyamathi, A.M., Lewis, C., Leake, B., Flaskerud, J., & Bennett, C. (1995). Barriers to condom use and needle cleaning among impoverished minority female injection drug users and partners of injection drug users. *Public Health Reports, 110*, 166-171.

Paltrow, L. (1990). When becoming pregnant is a crime. *Criminal Justice Ethics, 9*, 101-107.

Poland, M.L., Dombrowski, M.P., Ager, J.W., & Sokol, R.J. (1993). Punishing pregnant drug users: Enhancing the flight from care. *Drug and Alcohol Dependence, 31*, 199-203.

Ralph, N., & Spigner, C. (1986). Contraceptive practices among female heroin addicts. *American Journal of Public Health, 6*, 1016-1017.

Richardson, G.A., Day, N.L., & McGauhey, P.J. (1995). The impact of prenatal marijuana and cocaine use on the infant and child. *Clinical Obstetrics and Gynecology, 36*, 302-318.

Rosenbaum, M. (1979). Difficulties in taking care of business: Women addicts as mothers. *American Journal of Drug and Alcohol Abuse, 6*, 431-446.

Rosenbaum, M. (1981). *Women on Heroin.* New Brunswick, NJ: Rutgers University Press.

Silver, H., Wapner, R., Loriz-Vega, M., & Finnegan, L.P. (1987). Addiction in pregnancy: High risk intrapartum management and outcome. *Journal of Perinatology, VIII*, 178-184.

Stern, L. (1984). Drugs and other substance abuse in pregnancy. In L. Stern (Ed.). *Drug Use in Pregnancy* (pp. 148-176). Boston: AIDS Health Science Press.

Stevens, S.J., Erickson, J.R., & Estrada, A.L. (1993). Characteristics of female sexual partners of injection drug users in southern Arizona: Implications for effective HIV risk reduction interventions. *Drugs & Society, 7*, 129-142.

Wiemann, C.M., Berenson, A.B., & Landwehr, B.M. (1995). Racial and ethnic correlates of tobacco, alcohol and illicit drug use in a pregnant population. *Journal of Reproductive Medicine, 40*, 571-578.

V. EFFECTIVE DRUG TREATMENT STRATEGIES FOR FEMALE SUBSTANCE ABUSERS: PROCESS, OUTCOME AND COST EFFECTIVENESS

Developing Comprehensive Prison-Based Therapeutic Community Treatment for Women

Dorothy Lockwood, PhD
Jill McCorkel, MA
James A. Inciardi, PhD

Dorothy Lockwood is an independent consultant conducting program evaluations, organizational development and training for drug treatment and social service agencies, courts, corrections, and prevention programs. Jill McCorkel was on a fellowship with the Department of Sociology at the University of Delaware at the time of this study. James A. Inciardi is Director of the Center for Drug and Alcohol Studies at the University of Delaware; Professor in the Department of Sociology and Criminal Justice at Delaware; Adjunct Professor in the Department of Epidemiology and Public Health at the University of Miami School of Medicine; a Distinguished Professor at the State University of Rio de Janeiro; and a Guest Professor in the Department of Psychiatry at the Federal University of Rio Grande do Sul in Porto Alegre, Brazil.

[Haworth co-indexing entry note]: "Developing Comprehensive Prison-Based Therapeutic Community Treatment for Women." Lockwood, Dorothy, Jill McCorkel, and James A. Inciardi. Co-published simultaneously in *Drugs & Society* (The Haworth Press, Inc.) Vol. 13, No. 1/2, 1998, pp. 193-212; and: *Women and Substance Abuse: Gender Transparency* (ed: Sally J. Stevens, and Harry K. Wexler) The Haworth Press, Inc., 1998, pp. 193-212. Single or multiple copies of this article are available for a fee from The Haworth Document Delivery Service [1-800-342-9678, 9:00 a.m. - 5:00 p.m. (EST). E-mail address: getinfo@haworthpressinc.com].

SUMMARY. Experience and research have affirmed that treatment works for drug-involved offenders. Nonetheless, adapting these treatment models for drug-involved women offenders remains a challenge. One treatment modality, the therapeutic community (TC), has proven effective for women. This article discusses the adaptations necessary to the TC model to make it appropriate and effective for drug-involved women. Several themes are discussed including the staffing structure, staff-client interactions, the safety of the treatment environment, characteristics of the residential community, programming, and the treatment program's relationship with various social service agencies. In addition, the program elements specific to effective TCs for women in the criminal justice setting are also discussed. The experiences of developing, implementing and operating a specific TC for drug-involved female offenders provide examples of establishing an effective TC for women. *[Article copies available for a fee from The Haworth Document Delivery Service: 1-800-342-9678. E-mail address: getinfo@haworthpressinc.com]*

INTRODUCTION

Experience and research have affirmed that treatment works for drug-involved offenders. Indeed, a variety of modalities have proven effective–from therapeutic communities (Lockwood & Inciardi 1993; Wexler, Falkin & Lipton, 1990) and methadone maintenance (Ball & Corty, 1988) to a number of compulsory treatment initiatives (Anglin, 1988; De Leon, 1988; Leukefeld & Tims, 1988). Treatment Alternatives to Street Crime (TASC) programs across the United States have demonstrated that it is possible to combine treatment and correctional management in a number of environments (Cook & Weinman, 1988; Hubbard, Collins, Rachal, & Cavanaugh, 1988). Research within prison settings has also shown success for various treatment approaches (Chaiken, 1989; Forceir 1991; Wexler et al., 1990).

Nonetheless, adapting these treatment models for drug-involved women offenders remains a challenge. Following the National Institute on Drug Abuse's development of research protocols in 1974, numerous studies have demonstrated that women's treatment needs and treatment experiences differ markedly from those of men (Center for Substance Abuse Treatment, 1994; Winick, Levine, & Stone 1992). Women, for example, encounter a variety of gender-specific barriers that often discourage their efforts to enter treatment. Barriers to entering treatment involve such obstacles as a woman's role as primary caregiver to children, limited access to treatment programs, and pregnancy.

Once in treatment, many women face barriers to successful completion. The availability of women-only treatment facilities is extremely limited.

Most women enter co-ed programs in which staff members are predominately male and male residents outnumber female residents by ratios of 10 to 1 and higher. Furthermore, treatment regimens and services are designed for male clients and generally fail to address correlates of women's substance abuse. This situation serves to further marginalize women, and aggravates, rather than alleviates, issues surrounding low self-esteem, self-blaming and learned helplessness. The result is that many women leave treatment prematurely (Beschner, Reed & Mondanaro, 1981; Ramsey, 1980; Reed, 1987; Zankowski, 1988).

The 1980s brought concerns regarding treatment for women to the forefront. The cocaine and crack epidemics produced new profiles of drug abusing women: young, African-American, with several children, from low income neighborhoods, limited educational attainment, little to no vocational experience or skills, extensive sexual abuse victimization, and histories of trading sex for drugs and money (Inciardi, Lockwood, & Pottieger, 1993). Many of these women have flooded the criminal justice system. Drug Abuse Forecasting (DUF) statistics indicate that as many as 88% of female arrestees in some metropolitan areas test positive for illicit drugs (Wish & Gropper, 1991). In addition, the number of women in prisons increased by 200% in some jurisdictions with as many as 80% of incarcerated women in need of drug treatment.

Despite the limited treatment resources available to women, there has been some progress in addressing their treatment needs. The fundamental treatment components essential for effective and appropriate treatment for women have been identified, and a variety of programs have been successful in adapting modalities to incorporate these components. One treatment modality, the therapeutic community (or *TC*), which was originally designed for and by men, has proven effective both for male offenders (Lockwood & Inciardi, 1993; Wexler et al., 1990) *and* for women (Stevens, Arbiter & Glider, 1989).

The success of the TC modality for treating women is attributable to its unique philosophy and programmatic structure (for a more general description of therapeutic communities see De Leon & Ziegenfuss, 1986; Yablonsky, 1989). Specifically, treatment in TCs is based on the idea that substance abuse is a disorder of the whole person. This approach invites clients and practitioners to explore the many issues and experiences that frame the client's substance use, thereby ensuring that gender-specific issues facing women clients will be addressed. Second, TCs seek to improve interpersonal skills and coping strategies so that clients may better handle the problematic situations they encounter in their everyday lives. This theme is particularly salient for women, since many women's psychiatric disorders are triggered by interpersonal relationships (Jack, 1991;

Kessler & McLeod, 1984). In addition, through job assignments and other program activities, TCs teach prevocational and vocational skills, including responsibility and sound work habits. This aspect is of enormous practical importance for drug-involved women, since few have experience in legal jobs. Finally, the rituals and ceremonies which mark rehabilitative progress are easily reformulated to include those specific to the growth and development of women (Stevens et al., 1989).

This article provides an overview of those program elements necessary for the treatment of women substance abusers, and examines the process through which such elements can be successfully implemented into the TC. In addition, we explore the conditions under which a TC for women can prove an effective option for treating incarcerated women offenders. Our analysis is based on data collected during a three-year process evaluation of BWCI Village, a prison-based TC for women in New Castle, Delaware.

ADAPTING THE THERAPEUTIC COMMUNITY MODEL FOR WOMEN

Over the past two decades, a variety of treatment modalities have restructured their programming to better serve women (Ramsey, 1980; Stevens et al., 1989; Wellisch, Anglin & Prendergast, 1993; Zankowski, 1988). Several themes have emerged from these adaptations that appear essential to the development of gender-sensitive treatment. These themes include: the structure of staffing and the nature of staff-client interactions; the "safety" of the treatment environment; characteristics of the residential community; the content of programming; and the treatment program's relationship with various social service agencies.

First, the structure of staffing is important in TCs because staff members serve as role models for the resident community. Staff members that are unaware of, or minimize women's treatment needs are likely to foster a treatment environment that is insensitive (and occasionally hostile) to female clients. Preliminary research indicates that having a woman director appears to significantly increase the success of both co-ed and women-only programs (Ramsey, 1980; Stevens et al., 1989). Further, due to multiple and varied treatment concerns for women clients, staff with experience from other professional fields is also essential (Stevens et al., 1989; Zankowski, 1988). Staff with expertise in women's health care is necessary not only for health reasons, but for educational purposes as well. Many drug-involved women are at high risk for health complications and have little knowledge about health issues, particularly in regard to gynecological care, sexually transmitted diseases, and prenatal care (Inciardi et al., 1993). Staff with knowledge and experience in working with clients on parenting, childhood abuse, and sexual abuse are also essential in providing appropriate and comprehensive treatment to women (Stevens et al., 1989; Zankowski 1988).

Not only is it important to staff programs appropriately, but specialized training is also fundamental. Treatment providers must be cognizant of women's experiences on the "street," and their involvement in prostitution, predatory crime, drug networks, and violent relationships. In addition, training on drug-abusing women's relationships with their children is beneficial (Stevens et al., 1989; Zankowski, 1988). Educating staff in these areas aids counselors in gaining the perspective of their clients, allowing them to better work with the client from "where she is" when she enters the TC. Counselor familiarity and sensitivity to life on the street lessens the chances of clients feeling alienated or hostile toward treatment. Sensitivity training also decreases the risk of staff inadvertently perpetuating or condoning hierarchical or otherwise problematic interactions between women and men within the TC. A trained staff prevents the formation of unhealthy relationships and teaches male and female clients how to interact with one another in ways that encourage mutual respect and understanding.

Second, treatment providers must work to promote a safe environment for women to engage and progress in treatment. One of the first steps is to ensure that program policies encourage a supportive treatment environment. For instance, many TCs use coercion, rewards, and punishment to ensure participation in program activities. Inappropriate use of punishment and/or excessive use of coercion to encourage participation may only serve to alienate women, particularly since decreased participation may be the result of inappropriate activities or an environment that is otherwise hostile to women clients. Punishing women for non-participation without examining the causes of such behavior may perpetuate feelings of alienation, low self-esteem, and lack of trust. A "safe" treatment environment is one that encourages women's participation through the scheduling of appropriate activities and supportive rewards.

The third requirement for gender-sensitive treatment involves the nature of the community. Much of the TC treatment model is based on group activities and group counseling. Successful group counseling relies on bonding and trust among members. Many women who have been involved in drug use and criminal activity do not trust other women and may find it difficult to trust and bond with others, more generally (Ramsey, 1980). Treatment interventions such as gender specific groups (segregated by sex), individual counseling, leisure activities and seminars may be necessary to teach women to bond in positive ways and develop a sense of trust.

In addition, TCs are characterized by a structured hierarchy in which clients gain increased authority as they progress through treatment. Many women involved in drugs and criminal activity are not accustomed to positions of authority and many male clients are not accustomed to women holding positions of power. Seminars, role-taking groups, and staff role models are essential for encouraging women clients to assume positions of authority and in assisting male clients to interact in positive ways with women who are above and below them in the program hierarchy.

Creating a safe equitable environment based on mutual respect between men and women is greatly dependent on establishing the first cohort of female residents who have progressed through the TC process. Establishing this cohort is difficult, primarily because until this is accomplished women residents have no peer role models. Staff may need to implement safeguards and interventions to ensure that the first cohort is established. Two methods of ensuring a stable and strong first cohort are targeted recruiting and over-recruiting. Through targeted recruiting, clients most ready for treatment are selected. This process increases the likelihood that the women will engage in and progress through treatment as a group, eventually becoming role models for newer clients. After the first cohort is recruited, a broader range of clients can be included in the recruitment criteria. Over recruiting ensures that a sufficient number of women enter treatment together to create a critical mass necessary for group acitivities. In this instance, new recruits enter treatment as a group rather than one at a time. Once a cohort is established, clients can enter the program one at a time.

In addition, staff must also be attuned to the development of this cohort and withdraw as soon as the older women residents are promoted into positions of authority. This cohort ensures that women are integrated into the TC structure. It also enables the program to pair older and newer female residents so that the older residents can assist the newer residents in treatment engagement (Stevens et al., 1989).

The fourth condition for successful treatment of women is providing gender specific programming (Reed, 1987). As noted earlier, women's addiction experiences differ from men's, and often involve issues surrounding abusive relationships, role overload, and self-derogation. Within TCs, gender specific programming is essential to all treatment interventions including seminars, branch groups, encounter groups, and individual counseling. Focused attention must be paid to developing relationship skills for women. In addition, activities aimed at increasing contact with children and developing parenting skills are necessary. As with men, experience with leisure activities and appropriate use of free time must be addressed in treatment. Ensuring that leisure activities are enjoyable and compatible with women's interests and talents is another aspect of appropriate programming. As noted earlier, health care, particularly gynecological care, and health education for women are essential (Reed, 1987; Stevens et al., 1989; Zankowski, 1988).

The fifth condition for successful programming is coordination with social welfare agencies. One of the barriers to treatment for women is their involvement with other services and agencies, and their child care responsibilities. Extricating themselves from other services may threaten sources of income and destabilize child care arrangements. Treatment programs for women must be aware of these potential barriers and coordinate services within the existing network of social welfare agencies. Coordination and sound working relationships with courts, child protective services, and other social service agencies during treatment is essential to women's progress in treatment (Reed, 1987; Zankowski 1988).

In sum, adapting therapeutic communities for women is not merely a task of admitting women into an existing TC. Rather, it requires intentional planning and development with regard to staffing, programming, services, and the overall treatment environment.

THERAPEUTIC COMMUNITIES IN CORRECTIONAL SETTINGS

The TC modality has functioned primarily as a community-based, co-ed treatment option. During the past twenty years, however, the TC model also has been adapted for treating male offenders in prison settings and has been effective in reducing recidivism and relapse rates (Field, 1989; Holland, 1978; Inciardi & Lockwood, 1994; Wexler et al., 1988). Similar to adapting the therapeutic community model for women, the model must also be restructured to treat offenders and to function effectively in correctional environments.

Ideally, TC treatment for offenders is comprised of three stages, with the first stage–primary treatment–beginning in prison. In this setting, TC residents are segregated from the negative prison environment in which drug use, drug dealing, violence and manipulation are routinized aspects of inmate life. During primary treatment, residents are inducted into the TC culture and learn prosocial ways of behaving and interacting with others. The second stage of treatment is transitional, in which residents move from the prison to a community-based work release center or halfway house. Here, the TC process emphasizes community reintegratation. Residents seek and maintain employment as well as reunite with their families. The final or tertiary stage of treatment is an aftercare phase. In this stage, graduates live and work in the community and continue their involvement with the TC. They begin the lifelong process of recovery through involvement with 12-Step support groups such as AA (Alcoholics Anonymous) and NA (Narcotics Anonymous) and maintain ties to the TC through support groups and volunteered time (Inciardi, Lockwood & Hooper, 1994).

This continuum of TC treatment has proven successful for offenders (Inciardi et al., 1994; Wexler et al., 1990). Nonetheless, the relative success of prison-based TCs is contingent upon several conditions. First, surveillance and custodial responsibilities of the institution must be separate from, but coordinated with, the treatment program. When things are operating as expected and residents are conforming to program policies, custodial mandates and treatment goals do not conflict. On the other hand, when residents deviate from behavioral guidelines, correctional reaction usually conflicts with preferred treatment policies. In order to avoid conflict between treatment and correctional staff in these situations, TC and prison administrators must clearly delineate which behaviors and actions are to be addressed by treatment staff and which are to be addressed by correctional staff (Inciardi & Lockwood, 1994; Wellisch et al., 1993; Wexler, Blackmore & Lipton, 1991).

Further, cross-training involving correctional and treatment staff is essential (Inciardi & Lockwood, 1994). Both groups need to understand and respect the others' responsibilities and goals. Greater exchange of information and training, leads to more coordinated efforts and stronger communication. Some prison based TCs are able to hire correctional officers who are trained in the TC model (Jones, 1980). Such staffing reduces the risk of conflict and enhances compatibility of goals. Including treatment administrators in the selection of correctional officers can also reduce potential conflict. Unfortunately, these types of staffing arrangements are rare.

Appropriate, trained, experienced treatment staff is integral to the success of TCs (Lockwood & Inciardi, 1993; Wellisch et al., 1993). Traditionally, TCs have been staffed primarily by TC graduates. More recently, a heterogeneous staff with both TC graduates and counselors with formal education and credentialing has proven effective (Inciardi & Lockwood, 1994). In the prison setting, it is difficult to hire TC graduates despite successful employment histories and training, because of their histories of criminal activity. Nonetheless, having TC graduates on staff provides residents with necessary role models, staff who fully understand their position and history, as well as staff who are able to quickly identify manipulative behaviors and deceptive practices. Many prison administrators are willing to accommodate these staffing needs by making allowances in the hiring procedures and criteria (Inciardi et al., 1992).

Cooperation with hiring appropriate TC staff is one of many forms of support and endorsement from correctional authorities essential in successful treatment for offenders (Wellisch et al., 1993). Lack of support, even from mid-level administrators, will undermine the development of the TC (Inciardi & Lockwood, 1994). Just as the correctional officers must be educated and trained on the philosophy and operation of a TC, so must prison administrators. Most have been promoted through the ranks of the correctional system and adhere to the traditional philosophy of surveillance and custody. Informing administrators of the benefits of a TC, particularly in regard to the management of inmates, will increase cooperation and success.

There are several key steps in ensuring cooperation and coordination between the prison administrators and the TC staff. The first and most obvious is to obtain official written endorsement and agreements to cooperate and coordinate with establishing the TC. The second is to establish formal communication channels between the TC and the correctional authorities (Wellisch et al., 1993). Strong communication is not only necessary for planning and implementing the TC, but also for the day to day management of clients. Ensuring that there is a liaison who understands therapeutic and custodial goals, and who is respected and has authority within both organizations greatly enhances the efficient and timely implementation of the TC as well as continued development (Inciardi & Lockwood, 1994).

Although coordination between the correctional system and the TC is required, it is also essential that the TC is separate and independent of the prison system (Inciardi, Martin, Lockwood, Hooper & Wald, 1992; Jones, 1980; Wellisch et al., 1993). In other words, TC staff and residents need to maintain autonomy with regard to managing the program. Ideally, the TC residents should be separate from other inmates in order to limit their exposure to the negative prison environment where street values are condoned (Field, 1989; Levinson 1980; Wexler & Lipton, 1993). TC staff must be allowed to respond to rule violations with treatment strategies rather than correctional sanctions. Additionally, rewards, like punishments, should be distributed at the discretion of TC staff based on program guidelines as opposed to "good time" standards used for other inmates.

Coordinating treatment completion with release from the correctional institution as specified by the sentencing order is one of the most difficult tasks of integrating treatment with corrections. However, making the transition from the prison TC to the community is fundamental to the success of any prison-based treatment program (Inciardi & Lockwood, 1994; Wellisch et al., 1993). Here, again, the difference between treatment and punishment emerges. Within the treatment framework, completion of treatment is marked by client development and progress. On the other hand, release from prison or correctional supervision is predetermined by the sentencing order from the court. This situation creates a double-bind for treatment staff. On the one hand, clients who have successfully completed the program but are unable to obtain early release often become alienated and begin to regress. At the other extreme are offenders who are released prior to successful program completion due to sentencing requirements. Often, these offenders are at risk for recidivism and relapse. A strategy to coordinate treatment completion and prison release is a necessary part of the planning process. In fact, it often becomes part of the intake and orientation process. TC staff must begin to coordinate with the correctional authorities, release boards, the parole board and the courts, as soon as the resident enters treatment (Inciardi et al., 1992; Lockwood & Inciardi, 1993)

Release from prison and graduation from the TC are not the final steps in developing effective treatment for offenders. Implementing viable transitional and aftercare programs in the community to complete the continuum of treatment is a key factor (Wellisch et al., 1993). This is particularly so for offenders graduating from a TC. For instance, TC graduates from an in-prison TC who were released to the community with no transitional or aftercare provisions quickly relapsed and returned to crime (Inciardi et al., 1992).

BWCI VILLAGE: A PRISON-BASED TC FOR WOMEN

Despite the success of prison-based TCs for reducing recidivism and relapse among male offenders, efforts to incorporate this model to treat women have been limited. The remainder of this paper describes the development and implementation of BWCI Village, a promising new TC designed to meet the treatment needs of substance-abusing women offenders. The case of BWCI demonstrates that treatment for women begins with gender-specific adaptations to the therapeutic framework; however, the success of the program is ultimately determined by the program's relationship with the surrounding correctional environment.

In January 1994, through funding from the Center for Substance Abuse Treatment (CSAT), BWCI Village accepted its first cohort of women residents. BWCI Village is a 42-bed program and occupies a separate building on the campus of the only women's correctional facility in Delaware–Baylor Women's Correctional Institution (BWCI). The program is operated by an independent treatment and medical provider, Correctional Medical Services, Inc., which also operates corrections-based drug treatment programs elsewhere in Delaware and numerous other jurisdictions.

The program requires that for entry, potential residents have six to eighteen months remaining on their sentence and no diagnoses of severe mental disorders. As of January 1996, a total of 134 women had been admitted to BWCI Village; 30 had graduated from the program, with the vast majority of these moving on to a transitional, work-release TC and or some other form of community aftercare support.

The program has several unique characteristics that distinguish it from a traditional, male-oriented TC. First, the treatment staff is comprised solely of women. While the decision to hire a female-only staff was not an intentional one, the program found that this particular adaptation assisted in the development of a "safe" environment for residents, allowing them to explore issues they might avoid in the presence of men. The absence of men on the treatment staff has generated a need for counselors to seek out positive male role models for clients to interact with. Currently, the program has trained two male correctional officers for duty in the facility and invites other positive male figures (prison psychiatrists, teachers, and volunteers) to interact regularly with clients.

Like other TCs, the counselling staff members come from a variety of backgrounds. The director and two counselors have formal education combined with work experience in co-ed, community-based TCs. A third counselor is a TC graduate, another is a former correctional officer, and the final counselor has experience working with substance-abusing clients in a non-TC treatment setting. All counselors participate in group therapy and individual counselling sessions, but each has an area of treatment specialization. The aftercare counselor, for example, maintains a caseload of all clients who are preparing to exit the program. She assists residents in developing an aftercare plan, accessing resources (including continued treatment and housing), and preparing for release from prison and graduation from the TC. Other specialty areas include organizing leisure activities and recreation, HIV education and awareness, addiction education, spirituality sessions, multicultural awareness, parenting sessions, and domestic violence/abusive relationships.

In regard to the correctional staff, BWCI Village's experience has been much like other prison-based TCs. Many of the correctional officers originally selected for the program were uncomfortable with the TC approach. It took over a year to identify correctional officers who understood the philosophy and were able to effectively participate in it, in addition to fulfilling their responsibilities to the prison. Typically, officers found to be ineffective in the program tended to have an authoritarian style of interaction with residents and were uncomfortable with "inmates" having authority in the treatment setting. The program currently maintains a roster of five trained officers who supervise the program in shifts. Each of these officers is an active participant in the community and in one case, an officer accepted an offer from the program staff to become a counselor.

The second characteristic of BWCI Village that distinguishes it from traditional TCs is the content of programming. It has successfully incorporated a variety of services deemed essential in treating women. The program provides medical and health education which focuses on general health and gynecological care, pregnancy, body image, nutrition, the effects of drug use on the body, and stress reduction. In addition, the program is expanding health care education to include accessing medical resources in the community. The program provides all residents with anonymous HIV and TB testing, and holds HIV education seminars twice a month.

An outside provider conducts an eight week parenting course with all program residents. Women must complete this course of instruction prior to having their children stay with them at the program. In this regard, BWCI Village is not able to accommodate a full-time children's program but has created space for a children's room in the facility. Women who have progressed in treatment and who have completed the parenting program are able to have their children stay overnight in the TC once every two months. Additionally, most women are able to visit with their children during the prison's regular visiting hours. The program also provides job readiness and job seeking skills. BWCI Village residents are encouraged to participate in the educational and vocational training provided by the prison. Treatment schedules are adapted to allow for training courses. Courses include GED, food services, clerical, nurse's aid, and computer training.

Through the TC process women learn assertiveness skills, goal setting skills, stress and crisis management, communication and interpersonal skills, and relationship skills. In addition, BWCI Village has developed a component where women learn to reduce stress and increase self control through meditation and other relaxation techniques. The TC counselors address sexuality and intimacy issues, including emotional dependency and co-dependency on an individual basis as needed. Following the program's first year, it became clear that it was necessary to supplement programming with a stronger emphasis on domestic violence and abusive relationships. The vast majority of BWCI residents have extensive histories of sexual victimization, violence, and abuse which are coterminous with addiction experiences. Since none of the original staff had specialty training in these areas, a counselor who had experience treating battered and sexually victimized women was hired. The addition of domestic violence programming has strengthened the program considerably and has better prepared staff to effectively respond to unique features of women's substance abuse.

BWCI, like other TCs, teaches residents how to use and understand the 12-Step model. Women are expected to participate in AA and NA meetings and to begin to develop a support system which includes AA and NA groups. These groups are the initial component of an aftercare plan. All women graduating from BWCI Village leave the program with a plan and resources to continue treatment. Most will go on to a work release TC, but others will be released to halfway houses and directly into the community. The women who do not continue TC treatment are transferred to outpatient programs as their aftercare plan. In sum, through the TC process and added services, BWCI Village has evolved into a comprehensive treatment program which includes a continuum of care designed specifically for women.

While these adaptations have proven effective for meeting the treatment needs of drug-abusing, female offenders, the success of any prison-based program is largely contingent on the program's relationship with the correctional environment in which it operates. The power of the institution to allocate resources, foster a pro or antitreatment correctional culture, influence program intake and discharge, and provide security is extremely influential in determining the effectiveness of the program. BWCI Village's first two years were marked by many of the common barriers to implementing TCs in prison settings (Inciardi et al., 1992; Inciardi & Lockwood, 1994). These center primarily around working with the prison system. Although it has been well documented that coordinating with prison administrators as part of the planning process is integral to developing successful treatment for offenders, the only focused planning occurred during the preparation of the BWCI Village grant application.

Prison administrators and staff involved in the planning process were pro-treatment in their efforts to endorse the proposal, allocate resources (including the separate facility), and in pledging support and cooperation. When the women's TC was proposed, TC's had been well-established and accepted by the Department of Correction in both male and co-ed institutions. This positive attitude toward treatment masked how little was actually known about treatment, particularly treatment in a TC setting. In reality, the institution's familiarity and experience with treatment was largely limited to occasional group sessions conducted by community-based outpatient providers and AA/NA meetings. As a result, no provisions were made for educating the correctional staff on the TC model and the implementation process. While the structure and challenges presented for clients in the TC were understood and accepted fairly readily by the security staff, the support and services staff had much more difficulty in understanding and accepting the TC model. The consequences of this proved crucial to the program's growth and development over the two year period.

One of the primary barriers to program implementation for BWCI Village was hostile actions undertaken by some prison staff members. Correctional counselors, administrators, and officers are frequently responsible for selecting residents from the general prison population for the TC. Early recruitment efforts were hampered when several of these individuals discouraged inmates from entering the program, encouraged current residents to prematurely leave the program, and otherwise validated unfounded rumors regarding the program's harsh treatment of clients. In addition, confusion regarding release policies led a few officials to promise some recruits early release for their participation in the program. This information was misleading in that release from prison is entirely contingent on the discretion of courts and parole boards. These early promises, however, left many clients resenting the program and caused them to regress in their treatment.

The lack of training for correctional personnel dampened recruiting efforts during the first twelve months. Ambiguity regarding who (treatment vs. corrections staff) had primary responsibility for recruiting clients into treatment made intake of new residents slow and, at times, stagnant. Slow intake and inappropriate referrals resulted in delayed development of the first cohort of senior residents. Of the first sixteen BWCI Village clients, only five remained in the TC. Four ultimately graduated and moved to the work release TC, with the fifth still at BWCI Village. The remaining women in the first cohort were returned to the prison population without completing treatment.

Coordination between the institution and the program improved markedly during the second year of operation. In large part, this was attributable to the desire of both parties to clarify organizational boundaries and improve treatment services for women. Additionally, both parties recognized the need to redress existing deficiencies regarding TC training for all correctional staff. In January 1995, CSAT sponsored cross training for TC and correctional staff. This would have undoubtedly been more effective had it been held during the program's initial start-up; however, the session allowed both parties to air grievances, express perceptions of the program and its progress, ask questions, and coordinate recruiting, placement, and security efforts.

The cross-training session did not solve many of the organizational conflicts between the program and the correctional facility, but it did establish several important ground rules for coordinating services and setting precedents for future communication. Several solutions to recruiting and retention efforts have emerged over the course of time. First, the warden and several other high ranking administrators publicly announced their support for the program and refused to tolerate staff members who attempted to undermine it. Second, a member of the program staff was appointed to the classification board to review placement of incoming inmates. In addition, names of all inmates with histories of drug and alcohol use and appropriate sentence lengths are now forwarded to the program. Third, the director of the program regularly attends meetings with correctional supervisors. This allows her to combat anti-treatment philosophies among correctional staff. Fourth, a manual outlining security policies for program residents was jointly produced by treatment and correctional staff. This manual details procedures, policies, and organizational boundaries for all treatment and corrections staff. Fifth, the warden opened prestigious institutional jobs to senior residents of the program. This assisted in developing a pro-treatment correctional environment by reserving institutional privileges for women in treatment. With these changes, recruiting and retention efforts have improved dramatically.

Nonetheless, problems still remain that inhibit organizational communication and impact on program effectiveness. There continues to be a lack of a strong, authoritative liaison. The director of the treatment program has periodically assumed the role of liaison but has limited effect due to her position and alliance to the TC. Lack of a neutral liaison continues to generate territory disputes between treatment and corrections staff (McCorkel & Gluck, 1995). Further, while communication channels have improved, there is no established routine structure for interactions between treatment and corrections staff.

Second, although BWCI Village staff work with the prison administration in selecting appropriate candidates for the program, new residents continue to experience a culture shock as they enter the TC and progress through the orientation phase. Participating in a TC requires engagement, accountability, responsibility and a high level of activity, creating a very different setting than the typical prison. In general, residents find that they do not have the same degree of autonomy that they were able to maintain in the general prison population. Perhaps like other institutions, BWCI sees itself as a caregiving institution. Staff has had difficulty recognizing that recovery is often a very difficult process; at times it is perceived by clients to be more difficult than life as a drug addict on the streets. Failure to create an environment that is truly "pro treatment" often leads incoming residents to perceive treatment as being a harsh form of punishment, increases attrition rates, and encourages staff to support clients to pursue less demanding and less effective activities.

Many of the new residents experience another type of transition when they enter the TC. A significant proportion of the women in the general prison population have been prescribed sedatives or other psychotropic medications. Women who enter BWCI Village are assessed on several dimensions, including current prescription drug use. It is the policy of the TC to run a drug-free environment. Although concessions are made for residents who truly need psychotropic medications, most prescription drug use is terminated upon entering the TC. Weaning new residents from unnecessary medication has required another level of coordination and communication between BWCI Village staff and the medical providers in the prison system. The consequences of withdrawing drugs also create treatment issues that must be addressed. Allowing women to act out in response to emotional issues, internal conflicts, anger and stress rather than sedating them is frequently a point of contention between treatment staff on the one hand, and the medical provider and prison administrators on the other. Fortunately, the TC is structured to address these situations by resolving the underlying issues causing the behavior.

Third, the prison continues to foster competition among treatment providers within the institution. The result is that many programs are interested in recruiting a specified number of clients to maintain external funding support. The BWCI Village program, because it involves nearly one-sixth of the prison population, was viewed as a threat to the existence of other service programs. Classification of inmates was often made on the basis of program numbers rather than actual treatment need. BWCI Village has attempted to mitigate this problem by allowing residents (following graduation from the orientation phase) to participate in other programs. While this has alleviated some of the problems of recruitment, the institution continues to foster competition among service providers.

The case of BWCI Village is extremely informative because it demonstrates that even programs which are modified to treat women offenders often face difficulty in recruiting and keeping them. Ultimately, this is the result of the program's relationship and coordination with the correctional institution of which it is a part. Failure to clarify organizational boundaries and establish effective communication channels threatens to jeopardize recruiting efforts, retention, and individual treatment progress.

DISCUSSION

Although BWCI Village has faced many of the common barriers to implementing a TC, it has persevered and after its second year shows potential as a successful prison-based TC for women. The experiences at BWCI Village as well as other TCs for offenders provides beneficial lessons for others contemplating developing prison-based TCs. Some struggles of implementing a new TC can not be avoided. For instance, establishing the first cohort of experienced TC residents comes only with time and continuous effort in teaching novices the TC process. It is expected that many of the first admissions will not succeed in the TC and that it may take as long as a year before the first residents have progressed to a level of truly taking the responsibility of "running the house."

However, most of the barriers to implementation can be eliminated or at least diminished through careful and thorough planning. Planning and coordination are particularly important when developing a TC for offenders. Defining TC eligibility criteria, establishing the selection process, meshing prison release and treatment completion, and delineating between correctional tasks and treatment tasks must be beneficial and agreeable to both the prison and the TC. A strong authoritative liaison who understands both corrections and TCs is essential in both the planning and implementation phases. Cross-training between the TC staff and the correctional staff, including administrators, is integral to the success of a TC for offenders. Sufficient planning will also ensure that appropriate and necessary services, especially for women, are included in the TC program. And finally, hiring TC experienced staff and staff with a formal education whose experiences and training are complimentary is central to the success of the TC. The more the staff understands and has had experience with TCs the more quickly the TC will evolve.

Over the past several decades, the TC model has been adapted to serve women. During the same time period, the TC has been developed for offenders in a variety of criminal justice settings. And as the BWCI Village example demonstrates, the TC is also an appropriate model for women offenders. In establishing a TC for women in prison, both the adaptations necessary to serve women and the planning and coordination necessary for offenders must be accomplished to produce a viable and successful TC.

AUTHOR NOTE

This research was supported, in part, by HHS Grant Number 1 TI00676-010001, "WCI Village: A Therapeutic Community for Women Inmates," from the Center for Substance Abuse Treatment.

REFERENCES

Anglin, M.D. (1988). The efficacy of civil commitment in treating narcotic addiction. In F. Tims and C. Leukefeld (Eds.) *Compulsory Treatment of Drug Abuse: Research and Clinical Practice* (pp. 8-34). Rockville, MD: National Institute on Drug Abuse.

Ball, J.C. and Corty, E. (1988). Basic issues pertaining to the effectiveness of methadone maintenance treatment. In F. Tims and C. Leukefeld (Eds.) *Compulsory Treatment of Drug Abuse: Research and Clinical Practice* (pp. 81-98). Rockville, MD: National Institute on Drug Abuse.

Beschner, G.M., Reed, B.G., and Mondanaro, J. (Eds.). (1981). *Treatment Services for Drug Dependent Women.* Rockville, MD: National Institute on Drug Abuse.

Center for Substance Abuse Treatment. (1994). *Practical Approaches in the Treatment of Women Who Abuse Alcohol and Other Drugs.* Rockville, MD: Department of Health and Human Services, Public Health Service.

Chaiken, M.R. (1989). *In-Prison Programs for Drug-Involved Offenders.* Washington, D.C.: National Institute of Justice.

Cook, L.F. and Weinman, B.A. (1988). Treatment alternatives to street crime. In F. Tims and C. Leukefeld (Eds.) *Compulsory Treatment of Drug Abuse: Research and Clinical Practice* (pp. 99-105). Rockville, MD: National Institute on Drug Abuse.

De Leon, G. (1988). Legal pressure in therapeutic communities. In F. Tims and C. Leukefeld (Eds.) *Compulsory Treatment of Drug Abuse: Research and Clinical Practice* (pp. 160-177). Rockville, MD: National Institute on Drug Abuse.

De Leon, G. and Ziegenfuss, J.T. (Eds.). (1986). *Therapeutic Communities for Addictions: Readings in Theory, Research, and Practice.* Springfield, IL: Charles C. Thomas.

Field, G. (1989). The effects of intensive treatment on reducing the criminal recidivism of addicted offenders. *Federal Probation* (December), 51-56.

Forcier, M.W. (1991). Substance abuse, crime and prison-based treatment: Problems and prospects. *Sociological Practice Review* 2, (2), 123-131.

Holland, S. (1978). Gateway Houses: Effectiveness of treatment on criminal behavior. *International Journal of the Addictions* 13, (3), 369-381.

Hubbard, R.L., Collins, J.J., Rachal, J.V. and Cavanaugh, E.R. (1988). The criminal justice client in drug abuse treatment." In F. Tims and C. Leukefeld (Eds.) *Compulsory Treatment of Drug Abuse: Research and Clinical Practice* (pp. 57-79). Rockville, MD: National Institute on Drug Abuse.

Inciardi, J.A., Lockwood, D., and Pottieger, A.E. (1993). *Women and Crack-Cocaine*. New York: Macmillan Publishing Company.

Inciardi, J.A. and Lockwood, D. (1994). When worlds collide: Establishing CREST Outreach Center. In B.W. Fletcher, J.A. Inciardi and A.M. Horton (Eds.) *Drug Abuse Treatment: The Implementation of Innovative Approaches* (pp. 63-78). Westport, CT: Greenwood Presses.

Inciardi, J.A., Lockwood, D. and Hooper, R.M. (1994). Delaware treatment program presents promising results." Corrections Today (February), 34-42.

Inciardi, J.A., Martin, S.S., Lockwood, D., Hooper, R.M., and Wald, B.M. (1992). Obstacles to the implementation and evaluation of drug treatment programs in correctional settings: Reviewing the Delaware KEY experience. In C. Leukefeld and F. Tims (Eds.) *Drug Abuse Treatment in Prisons and Jails* (pp. 176-191). Rockville, MD: National Institute on Drug Abuse.

Jack, D.C. (1991). *Silencing the self: Women and depression*. New York: Harper Perennial.

Jones, M. (1980). Desirable features of a therapeutic community in a prison. In H. Toch (Ed.) *Therapeutic Communities in Corrections* (pp. 34-39). New York: Praeger.

Kessler, R.M. and McLeod, J.D. (1984). Sex differences in vulnerability to undesirable life events. *American Sociological Review* 49, 620-631.

Leukefeld, C. and Tims, F. (1988). Compulsory treatment: A review of the findings." In F. Tims and C. Leukefeld (Eds.) *Compulsory Treatment of Drug Abuse: Research and Clinical Practice* (pp. 236-250). Rockville, MD: National Institute on Drug Abuse.

Levinson, R.G. (1980). TC or not TC? That is the question. In H. Toch (Ed.) *Therapeutic Communities in Corrections* (pp. 50-52). New York: Praeger.

Lockwood, D. and Inciardi, J.A. (1993). CREST Outreach Center: A work release iteration of the TC model." In J.A. Inciardi, F.M. Tims, and B.W. Fletcher (Eds.) *Innovative Approaches in the Treatment of Drug Abuse: Program Models and Strategies* (pp. 61-69). Westport, CT: Greenwood Presses.

McCorkel, J. and Gluck, L. (1995). Territory, Power, and the revolving door: The struggle for hegemony between treatment and corrections staff in a women's prison. Presented at the 47th Annual Meeting of the American Society of Criminology, November 15-18, 1995, Boston, Massachusetts.

Ramsey, M.L. (1980). Special features and treatment needs of female drug offenders. *Journal of Offender Counseling* 44 (4/Summer), 357-367.

Reed, B.G. (1987). Developing women-sensitive drug dependence treatment services: Why so difficult?" *Journal of Psychoactive Drugs* 19 (2/April-June), 151-164.

Stevens, S., Arbiter, N., and Glider, P. (1989). Women residents: expanding their role to increase treatment effectiveness in substance abuse programs. *The International Journal of the Addictions* 24 (5), 425-434.

Wellisch, J. Anglin, M.D., and Prendergast, M.L. (1993). Treatment strategies for drug-abusing women offenders. In J.A. Inciardi (Ed.) *Drug Treatment and Criminal Justice* (pp. 5-29). Newbury Park, CA: Sage Publications.

Wexler, H.K., Blackmore, J., and Lipton, D.S. (1991). Project REFORM: Developing a drug abuse treatment strategy for corrections. *Journal of Drug Issues* 21 (2), 473-495.

Wexler, H.K., Falkin, G.P., and Lipton, D.S. (1990). Outcome evaluation of a prison therapeutic community for substance abuse treatment. *Criminal Justice and Behavior* 17 (1), 71-92.

Wexler, H.K. and Lipton, D.S. (1993). From REFORM to RECOVERY: Advances in prison drug treatment. In J.A. Inciardi (Ed.), Drug Treatment and Criminal Justice (pp. 209-227). Newbury Park, CA: Sage Publications.

Winick, C., Levine, A., and Stone, W.A. (1992). An incest survivors' therapy group." *Journal of Substance Abuse Treatment* 9(4), 311-318.

Wish, E.D., and Gropper, B.A. (1990). Drug testing by the criminal justice system: Methods, research and applications. In M. Tonry and J.Q. Wilson (Eds.) *Drugs and Crime* (pp. 321-391). Chicago, IL: University of Chicago Press.

Yablonsky, L. (1989). *The Therapeutic Community: A Successful Approach for Treating Substance Abusers*. New York: Gardner Press.

Zankowski, G.L. (1987). Responsive programming: Meeting the needs of chemically dependent women." *Alcoholism Treatment Quarterly* 4 (4/Winter), 53-66.

Residential Treatment for Women:
Behavioral and Psychological Outcomes

Harry K. Wexler, PhD
Mary Cuadrado, PhD
Sally J. Stevens, PhD

SUMMARY. Treatment outcomes are reported for a therapeutic community for women which provided substance abuse treatment. The 83 residents had a mean age of 28.3 years. Overall, the women had long histories of substance abuse and criminal activity, and high levels of psychological disturbance. Their main drug of choice was cocaine and crack. Differences between women with and without children during treatment were examined. Women without their children were older, more often white, had more severe drug and crime histories, showed more signs of psychological disturbance, and were more likely to use sedative type drugs. Major 6 and 12 month post treatment improvements included increases in employment and decreases in criminality, substance abuse, and psychological disturbance. Women who remained over 3 months in treatment were significantly more likely to be employed and less likely to commit crimes or use drugs at 6 and 12 months post treatment. Remaining in treatment

Harry K. Wexler is affiliated with the Center for Therapeutic Community Research at National Development and Research Institutes, Inc., Two World Trade Center, New York, NY 10048. Mary Cuadrado is affiliated with the University of South Florida at Sarasota, Department of Criminology, Sarasota, FL 34243. Sally J. Stevens is affiliated with the National Development and Research Institutes, Inc., University of Arizona, 3910 South 6th Avenue, Tucson, AZ 85714.

This research was supported by DHHS grant 5 HD8 T100383, 4 HDS T110339 and U01 DA07470.

[Haworth co-indexing entry note]: "Residential Treatment for Women: Behavioral and Psychological Outcomes." Wexler, Harry K., Mary Cuadrado, and Sally J. Stevens. Co-published simultaneously in *Drugs & Society* (The Haworth Press, Inc.) Vol. 13, No. 1/2, 1998, pp. 213-233; and: *Women and Substance Abuse: Gender Transparency* (ed: Sally J. Stevens, and Harry K. Wexler) The Haworth Press, Inc., 1998, pp. 213-233. Single or multiple copies of this article are available for a fee from The Haworth Document Delivery Service [1-800-342-9678, 9:00 a.m. - 5:00 p.m. (EST). E-mail address: getinfo@haworthpressinc.com].

was also related to decreases in psychopathology. Similar outcomes were found for women who had their children with them during treatment. *[Article copies available for a fee from The Haworth Document Delivery Service: 1-800-342-9678. E-mail address: getinfo@haworthpressinc. com]*

INTRODUCTION

Data from the 1993 National Household Survey on Drug Abuse indicates that an estimated 77 million people ages 12 and older living in the United States (US) have used an illicit drug, alcohol or cigarettes at some point during their life and an estimated 12 million used at least one of these substances in the month prior to the survey (Substance Abuse and Mental Health Administration, 1994 a). Results from this same survey indicate that an estimated 48.9% of all US women of childbearing age (15-44 years) used an illicit drug, alcohol or cigarettes sometime during their life and 14.1% used at least one of these substances during the previous year.

The negative effects of alcohol and other drugs (AOD) on women who use drugs, her fetus, and her children are numerous. For the woman, AOD use may result in negative health-related consequences such as overdose, infections, human immunodeficiency virus (HIV) and other sexually transmitted diseases (STDs). Furthermore, prolonged drug use can result in social and psychological problems such as employability, criminality, depression and aggression (Bureau of Justice Statistics, 1992; Bowden, 1996). Babies exposed to drugs in the womb may be born addicted and/or experience other physical problems. Children of addicted mothers are at greater risk of accidents, illness, abuse, and neglect (Zuckerman, Frank & Brown, 1995).

Prior to 1990 most drug treatment programs were developed and facilitated by men for a predominately male population (Stevens, Arbiter and Glider, 1989). Specialized gender specific curriculum, daycare facilities, and housing for children at residential centers were offered by only a few programs nationwide (Stevens & Glider, 1994). Advocates for female substance abusers argued for implementation of services that met the needs of AOD using women and their children. By the early 1990s, federal funding for demonstration grants that addressed the needs of female substance abusers was approved and numerous programs nationwide were funded to implement such services.

In Tucson, Arizona, Amity, a not-for-profit therapeutic community (TC) was funded by the Center of Substance Abuse Treatment (CSAT) to provide long-term residential treatment for addicted women with children. The sample of women used in this study were pregnant or had children under 7 months of age. While Amity had already modified their TC to more adequately fit the needs of women and children (Stevens, Arbiter and Glider, 1989) further modifications were made to meet the needs of the 20 women and 40 children who were funded by the CSAT grant. Facility renovations were made at Amity's 23 acre Desert Willow Ranch so that appropriate family style housing for the mothers and children was possible and an on-site therapeutic nursery for the children under the age of three could be provided. Changes in the TC program were also made to include parenting classes, family sessions with a developmental specialist, after school programs for the preschool and school aged children, a full time registered nurse, additional focus on nutrition and health especially for the pregnant women, and so on. Additionally, the schedule for curriculum and other daily activities was adjusted to balance the women's treatment needs with her parenting responsibilities.

In accord with the more classical TC model, women were expected to stay a minimum of 15-18 months in residence at Desert Willow (De Leon, 1989). Treatment was divided into four phases: Basic Interface (orientation, 0-3 months), Community Class (primary treatment, 3-12 months), Senior Class (re-entry readiness, 12-18 months) and Continuance (aftercare, 18-24 months). The major program components included: case management and referral, counseling and education, support groups, seminars, two day intensive workshops on various topics, parenting education, GED classes, pre-vocational and vocational training, and family and significant other programming.

With the exception of one early study by De Leon and Jainchill (1981), very little is known about the effectiveness of long term residential (TC) treatment for women. The prior study, which evaluated outcomes for a community TC that served both sexes, showed improvements in crime, drug use and psychological status, for males and females at 2 years after treatment. Since almost no outcome information is available on TCs designed specifically for women or for women with their children, the current study represents a pioneering effort. Treatment effects are studied for both women in treatment with their children and women in treatment without their children. Information on employment, criminal behavior, substance abuse, and mental health are provided.

The main research questions addressed by the study include: (1) Who comes to treatment? (2) What client outcomes are obtained at 6 and 12 months post program? and, (3) Does time in program impact community outcomes?

METHOD

Recruitment of substance abusing women who were either pregnant and/or who had young children began in October of 1992. Staff at the Desert Willow ranch worked with personnel at other treatment facilities, Child Protective Services and various criminal justice agencies (i.e., courts, probation, jail). Entrance criteria for the Desert Willow program included women who were 18 years of age or older, had used alcohol or drugs for at least one year, were either pregnant or had children under 7 months of age, and who were not taking prescribed psychiatric medication for a diagnosed mental illness. The Desert Willow staff encouraged the referral of women whose background and life situation made them unable to access treatment elsewhere. This included women with numerous years of substance abuse, those with histories of relapse, violence and/or criminality, and those with difficult life histories and situations (i.e., years of prostitution, history of violence).

In addition to the CSAT funded women, the Desert Willow program also provided treatment for 20 women who did not have children or had children but were unable to secure custody of them. The same entrance criteria applied to those women except for the requirement of being pregnant or having a child under 7 months who could enter treatment with his/her mother.

Within two weeks of entry into Desert Willow the pregnant women and women with children as well as women who did not have children with them in treatment were given a baseline assessment which included a consent form, a locator form for follow-up purposes and numerous standardized instruments. In-treatment data was gathered quarterly and post treatment assessment were administered at six, 12 and 24 months after discharge from the program. All assessments were facilitated in private individual sessions with trained research assistants. To encourage honesty the clients were assured that the research data would be kept confidential and only aggregated data would be reported to the clinical staff. For the purpose of this paper, data from the Addictions Severity Index (ASI), the Beck Depression Inventory (BDI), and the Symptoms Checklist (SCL-90-R) which measures dimensions of psychopathology were analyzed.

Included in the analysis is data from the first 83[1] women who entered the Desert Willow program (44 women with children and 39 women

---

1. An additional 11 women with baseline information were not included in the analysis because of refusal to participate at follow-up (8 with children and 1 without children), death (1 woman without children) and being out of reach because of participation in a witness protection program (1 woman without children).

without children) for whom data was collected both at admission and at 6 and 12 months post program. This outcome report provides information on: (1) who comes into treatment; (2) six and 12 month post treatment behavioral and psychological outcomes; and, (3) effects of length of stay in treatment (LOS) on six month outcomes.

RESULTS

Who Comes into Treatment?

Background information on women residing at Desert Willow, with and without children, are compared in Tables 1 and 2. Percentage differences between groups were tested with Chi-square while mean differences between groups were tested using T-test. The mean age of the entire group was 28.3 years with the women without children being significantly older (30.3 years) than the women with children (26.5 years). The total group of women were primarily Caucasian with the women without children being more likely to be Caucasian (72%) than the women with children (48%). The overall, education level was relatively high (11.8 years) with the two sub groups having similar levels of education. Over half the women were never married and 41% had been employed during the year prior to treatment. While both groups of women were similar in terms of marital status, the women without children were significantly more likely to have been employed.

Although both groups of women were highly criminal with 78% reporting ever having been charged with a crime, women with children were significantly more likely to have ever been charged (86% vs. 69%). This may be attributed to charges of child abuse or neglect which was the charge in which a significant difference was found between both groups of women. No differences were found among the groups on number of charges–the women were charged a mean number of 6.3 times. Women without children spent significantly more time incarcerated than women with children (26.3 months vs. 11.5 months, respectively). Over half the women were on probation or parole when admitted to the program and 52% reported entering the program at the suggestion of the criminal justice system.

The women at Desert Willow had severe substance abuse histories. Almost 100% of them had used alcohol and drugs and had used drugs regularly for 11.3 years. Women without children had used significantly longer which may be related to them being older. Table 1 shows that the

TABLE 1. Background Information at Program Intake for Women with 6 Month Follow-Up

Demographics	Total N = 83	Group 1 Women with Children N = 44	Group 2 Women without Children N = 39
Mean Age:	28.3	26.5	30.3**
Race:	%	%	%
Caucasian	59	48	72
African American	22	23	20
Native American	6	9	3
Hispanic	13	20	5
Mean Years of Education:	11.8	11.6	11.9
Marital Status:	%	%	%
Married	24	18	31
Divorce/Separated/ Widowed	23	25	20
Never Married	53	57	49
Employed (during prior year)	41%	27%	56%**
LEGAL HISTORY			
Ever Charged with a Crime:	78%	86%	69%*
Mean # of Charges, Ever:	6.3	5.3	7.3
Mean # of Months Incarcerated (for those ever incarcerated):	17.8	11.5	26.3*
On Probation or Parole (at intake):	53%	52%	54%
Entered Program at Suggestion of CJS:	52%	57%	46%

Substance Use	Total N = 83	Group 1 Women with Children N = 44	Group 2 Women without Children N = 39
Mean Years of Regular **Drug Use (excluding alc.)**	11.3	9.6	13.2*
Substances Ever Used:	%	%	%
Any Alcohol	95	93	97
Any Drugs	99	98	100
Marijuana	96	96	97
Cocaine/crack	90	91	90
Heroin	42	23	64***
Hallucinogens	48	46	51
Inhalants	22	16	28
Methadone	16	2	31***
Other Opiates	27	9	46***
Barbiturates	16	7	26**
Sedatives	36	21	54***
Amphetamines	49	50	49
Primary Problem Substance **(self report):**	%	%	%
No Problem	6	5	8
Alcohol	12	14	10
Marijuana	7	7	8
Cocaine/crack	46	52	39
Heroin	13	2	26***
Amphetamines	16	21	10
Mean Length of last voluntary **abstinence from primary** **problem substance (months):**	9.22	5.5	13.4**
Mean Times in **Prior Treatment:**	Alc. Drugs	Alc. Drugs	Alc. Drugs
	1.17 1.76	.66 1.52	1.74 2.03

NOTE: Mean differences tested with T-Test; percentage differences tested with Chi Square.
*Differences between groups significant at p. < .05.
**Difference between groups significant at p. < .01.
***Differences between groups significant at p. < .001.

TABLE 2. Comparison of Psychological Scores at Intake for Women with Follow-Up

	Total	Group 1 Women with Children	Group 2 Women without Children
	N = 64†	N = 35	N = 29
Beck Depression	17.09	16.56	17.84
SCL-90-R			
Somatization	0.99	0.95	1.04
Depression	1.48	1.29	1.71*
Phobic Anxiety	0.49	0.49	0.50
Obsessive-Compulsive	1.10	1.00	1.21
Anxiety	0.95	0.73	1.20**
Paranoid	1.33	1.18	1.50
Interpersonal Sensitivity	1.23	1.04	1.45*
Hostility	1.01	0.75	1.31*
Psychoticism	0.83	0.71	0.95

NOTE: Mean differences tested with T-Test; percentage differences tested with Chi Square.
† Nineteen of the women with baseline and follow-up interviews had missing psychological tests.
* Difference between groups significant at $p < .05$.
** Difference between groups significant at $p < .01$.

women used a variety of drugs during their lifetime. Differences in drug use pattern were detected, with significantly greater use of heroin, methadone, other opiates, barbiturates, and sedatives by the women without children. The primary drug of abuse for both groups was cocaine/crack followed by amphetamines and heroin. The single significant difference between the subgroups on the primary drug of choice was the greater likelihood for women without children to identify heroin as their primary drug.

As shown in Table 2, the women had high levels of depression as measured by the Beck Depression Scale as well as elevated SCL-90-R scales. Significant differences were found with the SCL-90-R. Women without children scored as more pathological on the Depression, Anxiety, Interpersonal Sensitivity, and Hostility scales. The group of drugs that the women without children were significantly more likely to have used (heroin, methadone, other opiates, barbiturates, and sedatives) all have sedating effects and may reflect attempts at self medication for their greater levels of psychological disturbance.

In summary, the women came into treatment with long histories of substance abuse and crime, and high levels of psychological disturbance. Their main drugs of choice were cocaine and crack. Women without their children were older, more often white, had more severe drug and crime histories, and more signs of psychological disturbance. The differences in drugs and crime histories may have been age related.

Six and Twelve Month Outcomes

Table 3 shows the comparison of intake and 6 months post program information. Differences between pre/post responses were tested with McNemar. An important and consistent finding in the TC outcome literature is that positive client outcomes are related to time spent in program and positive effects are often found for residents who remain in TCs for 9 to 12 months (De Leon, Wexler and Jainchill, 1982; Simpson and Sells, 1982). Table 3 shows the average time in treatment for Desert Willow women was 9 months with almost no difference between the women with and without children.

Table 3 shows differences in levels of functioning prior to program and at 6 months post program. Overall, the groups showed increases in employment, decreases in crime, decreases in drug use (except for opiates), and improvements in serious self reported depression. Employment for the total Desert Willow women group significantly increased 14% and crime significantly decreased 37% at six months post treatment. The women with children and the women without children showed similar increases in employment, but women with children had a greater decrease in crime. While at intake women with children were almost 1.5 times more likely to have engaged in illegal activities, at follow-up the percentage reporting crimes was lower than women without children.

Overall, there were large significant decreases in the number of women who reported any drug use and any alcohol at six months post treatment (72% and 16% respectively). The total group showed significant reductions in alcohol and drug use for all drugs except for opiates at 6 months post treatment discharge. Women with children showed significant reduc-

TABLE 3. Comparison of Intake and 6 Months Post Program Information

	Total N = 83	Group 1 Women with Children N = 44	Group 2 Women without Children N = 39
Mean Months in Program	8.99	8.55	9.49
Employed	%	%	%
Intake	41	27	56
6 mo. post	<u>55</u>	<u>43</u>	<u>68</u>
Difference	14*	16	12
Committed Illegal Acts			
Intake	78	86	69
6 mo. post	<u>41</u>	<u>39</u>	<u>44</u>
Difference	−37***	−47***	−25**
Substance Use **(30 days prior)**			
Any Alcohol			
Intake	41	30	54
6 mo. post	<u>25</u>	<u>18</u>	<u>33</u>
Difference	−16**	−12	−21*
Any Drugs			
Intake	100	100	100
6 mo. post	<u>28</u>	<u>25</u>	<u>31</u>
Difference	−72***	−75***	−69***
Marijuana			
Intake	25	21	31
6 mo. post	<u>12</u>	<u>11</u>	<u>13</u>
Difference	−13**	−10	−18**
Cocaine/crack			
Intake	45	36	54
6 mo. post	<u>15</u>	<u>15</u>	<u>14</u>
Difference	−30***	−21**	−40***
Opioids/Opiates			
Intake	12	2	23
6 mo. post	<u>12</u>	<u>9</u>	<u>15</u>
Difference	--	07	−08

	Total N = 83 %	Group 1 Women with Children N = 44 %	Group 2 Women without Children N = 39 %
Substance Use (30 days prior)			
Sedative/Tranq.			
Intake	72	84	59
6 mo. post	3	0	5
Difference	− 69***	− 84***	− 54***
Amphetamines			
Intake	60	57	64
6 mo. post	7	3	11
Difference	− 53***	− 54***	− 53***
Psy/Emotional Problems in past 30 days (includes drug induced)			
Serious Depression			
Intake	61	61	62
6 mo. post	38	42	33
Difference	− 23**	− 19	− 29**
Serious Anxiety or Tension			
Intake	63	59	67
6 mo. post	57	58	56
Difference	− 06	− 01	− 11
Hallucinations			
Intake	10	9	10
6 mo. post	9	7	10
Difference	− 01	− 02	00
Confusion			
Intake	45	45	44
6 mo. post	46	54	39
Difference	01	09	− 05
Psy/Emotional Problems in past 30 days (includes drug induced)			
Trouble Control. Violent Beh.			
Intake	26	23	31
6 mo. post	20	23	15
Difference	− 06	00	− 16*

TABLE 3 (continued)

	Total N = 83 %	Group 1 Women with Children N = 44 %	Group 2 Women without Children N = 39 %
Serious Thoughts of Suicide			
Intake	23	20	26
6 mo. post	19	21	18
Difference	− 04	01	− 08

Note: Significance in difference between pre and post responses tested with McNemar.
*One-tail test p. < .05. **One-tail test p. < .01. ***One-tail test p. < .001

tions in "any drug," cocaine, sedatives and amphetamines. Women without children showed significant drops in use of alcohol, "any drug," marijuana, cocaine, sedatives and amphetamines. In addition, women with children showed an increase in opiate use, although the difference was not significant.

Table 3 also shows the incidence of self reported psychological and emotional problems, captured by the ASI, for the 30 day period prior to program admission and the 30 days period prior to the six month follow up interview. Overall there were decreases in the percentage of women who reported each of the mental health problems at time of follow-up, with the exception of "confusion." However, the decreases were generally small except for serious depression which decreased a significant 23%.

Table 4 shows the comparisons of test scores that assess psychological disturbance at admission and at six months post treatment measured by the Beck Depression Inventory and the SCL-90-R. Improvements were found for all groups on all scales at six months post treatment with 9 of the 10 differences reaching significance for the combined group. Over half of the improvements for the women with children and the women without children groups reached significance. Thus, it appears that participation in the Desert Willow TC had a positive impact on the mental health of the women.

Of the 83 women with 6 month follow-up, 77 had been out of treatment long enough to allow for 12 months post data to also be collected. Sustained post treatment improvements were found for the women on increased employment and decreased criminal activities, drug use and self-reported pathologies during the 30 days prior to interview. In addition, the

TABLE 4. Comparison of Psychological Scores at Intake and 6 Months Post Program

	Total N = 64	Group 1 Women with Children N = 35	Group 2 Women without Children N = 29
Beck Depression			
Intake	17.1	16.56	17.84
6 mo. post	12.3	10.39	14.88
Difference	− 4.8***	− 6.01***	− 2.96
SCL-90			
Somatization			
Intake	0.99	0.95	1.04
6 mo. post	0.72	0.67	0.78
Difference	− 0.27**	− 0.28*	− 0.26*
Depression			
Intake	1.48	1.29	1.71
6 mo. post	1.03	0.84	1.26
Difference	− 0.45***	− 0.45**	− 0.45**
Phobic Anxiety			
Intake	0.49	0.49	0.50
6 mo. post	0.39	0.33	0.45
Difference	− 0.10	− 0.16	− 0.05
Obsessive-Compulsive			
Intake	1.10	1.00	1.21
6 mo. post	0.85	0.77	0.93
Difference	− 0.25**	− 0.23*	− 0.28*
Anxiety			
Intake	0.95	0.73	1.20
6 mo. post	0.67	0.56	0.80
Difference	− 0.28**	− 0.17	− 0.40**
Paranoid			
Intake	1.31	1.16	1.50
6 mo. post	0.87	0.68	1.10
Difference	− 0.44***	− 0.48**	− 0.40**
Interpersonal Sensitivity			
Intake	1.23	1.05	1.45
6 mo. post	0.85	0.69	1.05
Difference	− 0.38***	− 0.36**	− 0.40**

TABLE 4 (continued)

	Total	Group 1 Women with Children	Group 2 Women without Children
	N = 64	N = 35	N = 29
Hostility			
Intake	1.01	0.75	1.31
6 mo. post	0.73	0.58	0.91
Difference	−0.28**	−0.17	−0.40**
Psychoticism			
Intake	0.83	0.71	0.95
6 mo. post	0.55	0.44	0.67
Difference	−0.28**	−0.27*	−0.28**

Note: Significance in difference between pre and post scores tested with T-test.
* One Tail Test, p. < .05.
** One Tail Test, p. < .01.
*** One Tail Test, p. < .001.

women maintained their psychological improvements at 12 months post treatment and showed further significant improvements as indicated by lower scores on the SCL-90-R. Women without children showed larger decreases in SCL-90-R scores, but it should be noted that their scores were more elevated than the women without children at baseline, and the women in both groups reached similar test levels at 12 months.

Impact of Time in Program on Six Month Outcomes

Because previous research on TC outcomes has demonstrated that positive treatment effects are present after 3 months length of stay (LOS) in treatment, a preliminary examination of time in program effects for Desert Willow participants was done by comparing outcomes for women who dropped out prior to 3 months and women who stayed longer than 3 months. Table 7 shows the mean number of months in program for the less than 3 month Dropouts was 1.5 months and 12.0 months for the more than 3 months Remains. In general, women who remained in treatment had far better outcomes than those who dropped.

There were some differences between Dropouts and Remains at admission to the program (see Table 5). Overall, the residents who dropped out in less than 3 months reported more drug use and psychological disturbance at admission into the program. Although the differences were gener-

TABLE 5. Comparison of Intake and 6 Months Post Program: Dropouts (3 Mo. or Less) vs. Remains (>3 Mo.)

	Total		Group 1 Women with Children		Group 2 Women without Children	
	Dropout (N = 24)	Remain (N = 59)	Dropout (N = 13)	Remain (N = 31)	Dropout (N = 11)	Remain (N = 28)
Mean Months in Pgm	1.5	12.0	1.46	11.51	1.55	12.61
Employed	%	%	%	%	%	%
Intake	54	36	54	16**	55	57
6 mo. post	29	66***	15	55**	46	79*
Pre/post Diff	−25	30†††	−38	38††	−09	22
Committed Illegal Acts						
Intake	67	83	69	94*	64	71
6 mo. post	67	31**	69	26**	64	36
Pre/post Diff	--	−52†††	--	−68†††	--	−35††
Substance Use (30 days prior)						
Any Alcohol						
Intake	67	31**	54	19**	82	43*
6 mo. post	29	24	15	19	46	29
Pre/post Diff	−38††	−07	−39†	00	−36	−14
Any Drugs						
Intake	100	100	100	100	100	100
6 mo. post	46	20**	31	23	64	18**
Pre/post Diff	−54†††	−80†††	−69†††	−77†††	−36	−82†††
Marijuana						
Intake	38	20	39	13*	36	29
6 mo. post	17	10	15	10	18	11
Pre/post Diff	−21†	−10†	−24	−03	−18	−18†
Cocaine/crack						
Intake	63	37*	54	29	73	46
6 mo. post	17	13	17	15	18	12
Pre/post Diff	−46††	−24††	−37	−14	−55†	−34†
Substance Use (30 days prior)						
Opiods/Opiates						
Intake	29	05**	08	00	55	11**
6 mo. post	25	07*	15	07	36	07*
Pre/post Diff	−04	02	07	07	−19	−04

TABLE 5 (continued)

	Total		Group 1 Women with Children		Group 2 Women without Children	
	Dropout (N = 24)	Remain (N = 59)	Dropout (N = 13)	Remain (N = 31)	Dropout (N = 11)	Remain (N = 28)
Sedatives/Tranq.						
Intake	67	75	77	87	55	61
6 mo. post	08	00*	00	00	18	00*
Pre/post Diff	−59†††	−75†††	−77†††	−87†††	−37	−61†††
Amphetamines						
Intake	75	54	77	48	73	61
6 mo. post	13	04	00	04	27	04*
Pre/post Diff	−62†††	50†††	77†††	44†††	46	57†††
Psy/Emotional Prob. in past 30 days (includes drug induced)						
Serious Depression						
Intake	71	58	77	55	64	61
6 mo. post	48	34	42	42	55	25
Pre/post Diff	−23	−24††	−35	−13	−09	−36††
Serious Anxiety or Tension						
Intake	75	58	69	55	82	61
6 mo. post	61	56	50	61	73	50
Pre/post Diff	−14	−02	−19	09	−09	−11
Hallucinations						
Intake	25	03***	15	07	36	00***
6 mo. post	30	00***	25	00**	36	00***
Pre/post Diff	02	−03	10	−07	00	00
Confusion						
Intake	58	39	54	42	64	36
6 mo. post	61	41	67	48	55	32
Pre/post diff	03	02	13	06	−09	−04
Trouble Controlling Violent Behavior						
Intake	46	19**	31	19	64	18**
6 mo. post	26	17	17	26	36	07*
Pre/post diff	−20	−02	−14	07	−28	−11
Serious Thoughts of Suicide						
Intake	33	19	23	19	46	18
6 mo.post	30	15	33	16	27	14
Pre/post Diff	−03	−04	10	−03	−19	−04

Note: Difference between groups tested with Chi Square (*). Difference between pre and post responses tested with McNemar (†).
* p. < .05 **p. < .01 ***p. < .001.
†One-tail test p. < .05 ††One-tail test p. < .01 †††One-tail test p. < .001.

ally more pronounced for the women with children, the pattern was similar in the women without children group. The Dropouts tended to be more employed and somewhat less likely to have reported illegal acts at admission although the differences did not reach significance.

Table 5 shows the impact of remaining in program less than 3 months (Dropouts) versus more than 3 months (Remains) on differences in functioning at program admission and at 6 months post program. Table 5 includes statistical tests of significance for differences between Dropouts and Remains at intake and at 6 months as well as for intake versus 6 month post program differences.

The women who remained in program over 3 months showed a 30% increase in employment at follow up as compared to a 25% decrease in employment found for the Dropouts. Additionally, the Remains showed a 52% decrease in illegal activity at follow up versus no change for Dropouts. For Remains, the pattern of employment and crime results for women with children was better than for women without children (increase in employment 39% vs. 22%, decrease in crime − 68% vs. − 35%).

Both the total Dropout and Remain groups showed significant reductions in substance abuse at follow up. Only the Dropouts showed significant reductions in alcohol abuse at follow up, which was probably related to their higher levels of alcohol abuse at admission. Significantly fewer Remains than Dropouts reported "any drug use" at follow up. The pattern of results was similar for the individual drugs reported in Table 5.

Overall, both Dropouts and Remains reported decreases in psychological problems at follow up. The results for self reported psychological and emotional problems showed few pre/post differences between Dropouts and Remains. The pattern of results for women with and without children were consistent with the total group results.

Table 6 shows the psychological test results, measured by the Beck Depression Inventory and the SCL-90-R for Dropouts and Remains. A very consistent pattern of significant improvement for Remains and a general worsening for Dropouts was found. Among the ten scales of psychological disturbance, Remains showed significant improvements in all of them while Dropouts showed none and they showed some worsening on six of the scales. Similar patterns were found for the women with children and without children with significant improvements on nine of the ten scales.

DISCUSSION

In general, the women at Desert Willow had long histories of substance abuse with the most frequently reported choice of drugs being cocaine and

TABLE 6. Comparison of Psychological Scores at Intake and 6 Months Post Program: Dropouts (3 Mo. or Less) vs. Remains (> 3 Mo.)

	Total		Group 1 Women with Children		Group 2 Women without Children	
	Dropout	Remain	Dropout	Remain	Dropout	Remain
Beck Depression	(N = 19)	(N = 42)	(N = 10)	(N = 25)	(N = 9)	(N = 17)
Intake	22.21	14.84	23.40	13.92	20.89	16.23
6 mo. post	18.84	9.37	14.70	8.73	23.44	10.35
Difference	−3.37	−5.47***	−8.70*	−5.19**	2.55	−5.88*
SCL-90	(N = 17)	(N = 47)	(N = 8)	(N = 27)	(N = 9)	(N = 20)
Somatization						
Intake	1.06	0.97	1.13	0.89	0.99	1.07
6 mo. post	1.13	0.57	1.14	0.53	1.12	0.63
Difference	0.07	−0.40***	0.01	−0.36**	0.12	−0.44**
Depression						
Intake	1.53	1.47	1.22	1.31	1.80	1.67
6 mo. post	1.43	0.89	1.22	0.73	1.62	1.10
Difference	−0.10	−0.58***	0.00	−0.58***	−0.18	−0.57**
Phobic Anxiety						
Intake	0.53	0.48	0.48	0.49	0.57	0.47
6 mo. post	0.59	0.31	0.62	0.25	0.56	0.40
Difference	0.06	−0.17*	0.14	−0.24*	−0.01	−0.07
Obsessive-Compulsive						
Intake	1.03	1.11	0.95	1.01	1.11	1.25
6 mo. post	1.23	0.70	1.18	0.65	1.27	0.77
Difference	0.19	−0.44***	0.23	−0.36**	0.16	−0.48**
Anxiety						
Intake	0.99	0.93	0.87	0.70	1.08	1.25
6 mo. post	1.05	0.54	0.88	0.47	1.18	0.63
Difference	0.06	−0.39***	0.01	−0.23	0.10	−0.62***
Paranoid						
Intake	1.43	1.28	1.02	1.19	1.75	1.38
6 mo. post	1.28	0.74	1.14	0.56	1.38	0.98
Difference	−0.15	−0.54***	0.12	−0.63***	−0.37	−0.40*
Interpersonal Sensitivity						
Intake	1.24	1.23	0.81	1.12	1.61	1.38
6 mo. post	1.16	0.74	1.06	0.58	1.23	0.97
Difference	−0.08	−0.49***	0.25	−0.54***	−0.38*	−0.41*

	Total		Group 1 Women with Children		Group 2 Women without Children	
	Dropout	Remain	Dropout	Remain	Dropout	Remain
Hostility						
Intake	1.25	0.93	0.47	0.82	1.85	1.07
6 mo. post	1.31	0.53	1.02	0.46	1.53	0.63
Difference	0.06	−0.40***	0.54	−0.36**	−0.31	−0.44**
Psychoticism						
Intake	0.94	0.79	0.68	0.72	1.13	0.88
6 mo. past	1.02	0.38	1.02	0.28	1.02	0.52
Difference	0.08	−0.41***	0.34	−0.44***	−0.11	−0.36**

Note: Significance in differences between pre and post scores test with T-test.
* One Tail Test, p. < .05.
** One Tail Test, p. < .01.
*** One Tail Test, p. < .001.

crack. Most of the women had experienced prior treatment failures. They also reported extensive criminal histories which included many arrests and lengthy periods of incarceration. High levels of depression were observed at baseline as well as elevated scales on the SCL-90-R which indicates greater psychopathology. The women without children were older, more often white, had used drugs significantly longer and had spent more time in prison than the women who had children. Some evidence of self medication was found for the women without children who were more likely to use sedating type drugs (heroin, methadone, other opiates, barbiturates, and sedatives) that may have been related to their greater levels of psychological disturbance.

The preliminary findings indicate that the Desert Willow is an effective program for female substance abusers. A number of improvements were found when comparing behavior reported at baseline with that reported six months after discharge from the treatment program. Major improvements included a significant decrease in substance abuse and criminal behavior and a significant increase in employment. Additionally, a very consistent pattern of significant decreases in several measures of psychopathology were found including a large and significant decrease of serious depression.

Outcomes for women who had children with them in treatment did not differ from the outcomes for women who did not have children. This finding is contrary to that reported by Stevens and Patton (this volume), perhaps due to the differences in the comparison groups (e.g., women without children) of each of the respective studies. In this study, the women without children included women who were either childless, had adult-aged children, or had no hope of ever obtaining custody of their children. Consequently, having one's children was not a factor at treatment entry. In the Stevens and Patton study, *all* the women had the possibility of obtaining custody of their children. As Stevens and Patton point out, treatment outcomes may not be as good for those who have the opportunity for custody of their children but are not allowed to bring their children into treatment with them.

While this study did not include a "no treatment control group," the positive outcomes shown by the residents with over 3 months of treatment (mean of 12 months) compared to those with less than 3 months of treatment are impressive. Consistent with results of other TC studies, the women who remained in treatment at Desert Willow had, in general, better outcomes than those who dropped out of treatment. The comparison of Dropouts and Remains shows that women who remained in treatment for more than 3 months were significantly less likely to use drugs and commit crimes, and significantly more likely to be employed. The study findings essentially replicate the earlier positive female TC results reported by De Leon and Jainchill (1981).

The findings in this study suggest that women's TC substance abuse treatment programs can be effective for women with extensive histories of drug use, criminal behavior and psychopathology. Both groups of women (women with children and women without children) demonstrated equally positive outcomes indicating that a treatment environment that includes children may be beneficial for both groups. Having children in the treatment environment may not only be good for women who have children, but may also be good for women who are childless, have adult-aged children, or who have lost custody of their children. Living with and helping with other women's children may provide a sense of shared responsibility and community; important concepts in a healthy TC milieu. Moreover, for women who have lost custody of their children due to their drug use and other related negative behaviors, helping with other women's children may provide an opportunity to make amends; yet another important concept in the TC treatment process. And, finally, having children in the environment may trigger unresolved painful childhood memories, opening opportunities for in-depth introspection and healthy transformation of the entire person; a primary goal for those enrolled in a TC.

REFERENCES

Bowden, K. (1996). *Street Drugs & Methamphetamine.* Presented at the Interagency Council on Alcohol and Drug Addictions Training Conference, March 28, 1996. Tucson, Arizona.

Bureau of Justice Statistics. *Drugs, Crime, and the Justice System: A National Report From the Bureau of Justice Statistics.* NCJ-133652. Washington, DC: U.S. Govt. Print. Off., December 1992.

De Leon, G. and Jainchill, N. (1981) Male and female drug abusers: Social and psychological status 2 years after treatment in a therapeutic community. *American Journal of Alcohol Abuse,* 8(4) 465-497.

De Leon, G. (1989). Therapeutic communities for substance abusers: Overview of approach and effectiveness. *Psychology of Addictive Behaviors*, 3,140-149.

De Leon, G., Wexler, H.K., and Jainchill, N. (1982) Success and improvement rates 5 years after treatment in a therapeutic community. *Int. J. Addic.* 17:703-747.

Simpson, D.D. and Sells, S.B. (1982). Effectiveness of treatment for drug abuse: An overview of the DARP research program. *Advances in Alcohol and Substance Abuse,* 2 (1), 7-29.

Stevens, S.J., Arbiter, N., and Glider, P. (1989). Women residents: Expanding their role to increase treatment effectiveness. *International Journal of Addictions,* 24 (5), 425-434.

Stevens, S.J. and Glider, P. (1994). Therapeutic communities: Substance abuse treatment for women. In F. Tims, G. De Leon, and N. Jainchill (Eds.), *National Institute on Drug Abuse Research Monograph Series; Therapeutic Community: Advances in Research and Application. Technical Review on Therapeutic to Communities, NIDA Research Monograph 144, U.S. DHHS.*

Substance Abuse and Mental Health Services Administration. *National Household Survey on Drug Abuse: Population Estimates, October 1994.* DHHS Pub. No. 94-3017. Washington, DC: U.S. Govt. Print Off., 1994a.

Watters, J., & Biernacki, P. (1989). Targeted sampling: Options for the study of hidden populations. *Social Problems*, 36, 416-430.

Zuckerman, B., Frank, D., and Brown, E. Overview of the effects of abuse and drugs on pregnancy and offspring. In: *Medications Development for the Treatment of Pregnant Addicts and Their Infants.* NIDA Research Monograph 149. NIH Pub. No. 95-3891. Washington, DC: U.S. Govt. Print. Off., 1995. pp. 16-38.

Residential Treatment
for Drug Addicted Women
and Their Children:
Effective Treatment Strategies

Sally J. Stevens, PhD
Tara Patton, BS

SUMMARY. Concern regarding the health of female drug users and the well being of her children or fetus have prompted researchers and service providers to look for effective treatment strategies for this population. This study examined the differential effectiveness of providing residential treatment for drug using women and their children with residential treatment for women alone (with child housing and care provided elsewhere). Results of the study indicated that the women who were assigned to have their children live with them in treatment reported better outcomes six months after discharge from the program compared to those who did not have their children with them in treatment. A greater percentage of the women who had their children live with them reported abstaining from alcohol and drugs, being employed, having custody of their children, not being arrested or incarcerated and being involved in aftercare or support groups. Implications of the research findings are discussed. *[Article copies available for a fee from The Haworth Document Delivery Service: 1-800-342-9678. E-mail address: getinfo@haworthpressinc.com]*

Sally J. Stevens and Tara Patton are affiliated with the University of Arizona, Southwest Institute for Research on Women.

This research was funded by the National Institute on Drug Abuse, Research Demonstration Grant 1 R18 DAO6918.

[Haworth co-indexing entry note]: "Residential Treatment for Drug Addicted Women and Their Children: Effective Treatment Strategies." Stevens, Sally J., and Tara Patton. Co-published simultaneously in *Drugs & Society* (The Haworth Press, Inc.) Vol. 13, No. 1/2, 1998, pp. 235-249; and: *Women and Substance Abuse: Gender Transparency* (ed: Sally J. Stevens, and Harry K. Wexler) The Haworth Press, Inc., 1998, pp. 235-249. Single or multiple copies of this article are available for a fee from The Haworth Document Delivery Service [1-800-342-9678, 9:00 a.m. - 5:00 p.m. (EST). E-mail address: getinfo@haworthpressinc.com].

235

INTRODUCTION

The number of women of childbearing age who use drugs is troubling. In 1990, it was estimated that of the 9.5 million drug users in the United States, over 5.5 million were women (*New York Times*, 1990). With recent increases in the number of young women who have begun to use drugs, the population of drug using women has continued to increase (National Institute on Drug Abuse [NIDA], 1994). Concern regarding the increase in the number of female drug users, her health, and the potential negative effects on her children or her fetus has prompted funding officials and service providers to offer more treatment opportunities for women (Stevens, Arbiter & McGrath, in press).

Drug using women have reported numerous barriers to entering drug treatment. Past research has shown that two major barriers to seeking drug treatment or other health related interventions and services include transportation difficulties and the unavailability of adequate childcare (McBride et al., 1996; Stevens & Glider, 1994; Wechsberg, 1995). In an attempt to reduce these reported barriers funding officials and service providers began to provide substance abuse treatment services for pregnant women and women with children that included childcare components. Day treatment programs began to have on-site therapeutic nurseries for the children of the women enrolled in treatment (D'Amore & Glider, 1992) and residential programs began to enroll and house drug using pregnant women and women with their children (Glider et al., 1996; Stevens, Arbiter & McGrath, in press; Stevens & Glider, 1994).

While it can be assumed that providing services and daycare for children while their mothers participate in treatment would be helpful in engaging women in treatment, little research has been conducted on how this would effect treatment outcomes. This research study attempted to help fill this knowledge gap. In particular, this study sought to understand how having one's children living in residential treatment would effect post treatment outcomes in the areas of alcohol and drug use, employment, child custody, and criminal justice involvement.

The Addicted Mothers and Offspring in Recovery (AMOR) project was funded by the National Institute on Drug Abuse. It was funded for five years, beginning in September of 1990. Amity, a not-for-profit drug prevention and treatment agency provided the service component and the University of Arizona, Department of Psychology conducted the research. The target population was addicted women who had children 6 months to 10 years of age. The program targeted women living in Arizona, primarily those living in either Phoenix or Tucson. Phoenix is located in central Arizona in Maricopa County while Tucson is located in southern Arizona in Pima County. Pima County is a large county which approximates the size of the state of Connecticut. Given its size, the county includes large undeveloped pieces of land which cross the U.S./Mexico border providing a corridor for large amounts of high quality inexpensive drugs. Most of these drugs are routed into Phoenix or Tucson where they are often cut with other substances and then sold or moved on to other locations.

The AMOR program was a modified therapeutic community (TC). The TC emerged in the 1960s as a self-help alternative to existing conventional treatments and was first applied to the treatment of male heroin addicts. The foundations or roots of the TC are not from a medical model but rather are based in the tradition of the Alcoholics Anonymous Twelve Step Self-Help Model. Therapeutic communities provide a microcosm of a healthy society in which people who have problems with alcohol, drugs, and other alienating behaviors can learn to deal with the many facets which have driven their behavior (De Leon, 1984). A basic assumption of the TC is that addiction cannot be cured but only put into remission (Yablonsky, 1965). If remission is to be achieved, all aspects of the addict's lifestyle must be changed, and such change requires a 24 hour community (De Leon and Rosenthal, 1979). Traditional TCs have a planned duration of stay of 15 to 24 months. Treatment in most TCs are divided into three phases; (1) induction and orientation, (2) primary treatment, and (3) re-entry (De Leon, 1989). The AMOR program included these same three phases of treatment which were modified to serve women with children. They are briefly described below:

1. Introduction and Orientation (approximately three months): In this first phase the AMOR participants were assimilated into the community and into full participation in all of the activities; social, educational, vocational and therapeutic. The women were challenged to gain an understanding of their underlying problems, and learn to use the encounter groups, peer structure, and other TC basics. They parented their child(ren), and were assigned work and social duties in the community including helping the other women with their children.
2. Primary Treatment (approximately nine to 12 months): In this phase of treatment the main objectives included personal growth, socialization and psychological awareness. The women were challenged to use self disclosure in the therapeutic groups to facilitate deeper understanding of themselves. They were encouraged to build positive and supportive relationships with the other women in the program. The women learned appropriate parenting skills in classes on parenting and through participation in an ongoing weekly family session with a family interventionist.

3. Re-entry (approximately three to six months): During re-entry the women were encouraged to strengthen skills for autonomous decision making and management for themselves and their children. All women participated in the relapse prevention curriculum and preparation for moving back into the wider community began. Re-entry plans included tasks for the mother (i.e., employment, housing, transportation, support groups) and making plans for their children (i.e., school, daycare, therapy/special services).

PROCEDURES

To study the question of how having one's children in treatment affects treatment outcomes, the AMOR program design randomly assigned half of the women coming into treatment to *not* have their children live with them in treatment. The children stayed with relatives or friends or in foster care and had day or week-end visits with their mother. The other half of the women were randomly assigned to have their children live in residential treatment with them at the AMOR facility. While this assignment process appears "tough," the program sought to enroll women who were losing permanent custody of their children due to their drug use and related negative behavior. Consequently, having their children's "severance and adoption" process put on hold while they were in treatment was appealing and having a 50% chance of also having their children living in residential treatment with them was, for most women, additionally attractive. The AMOR treatment facility housed forty women (20 with children) at one time. A therapeutic nursery on property was provided by the AMOR program staff for the younger pre-school children. The older pre-school children (ages 3 to 5 years) attended a Department of Economic Security (DES) approved day care in the wider Tucson community. The school aged children attended public school at the local elementary school. Entrance criteria for the AMOR project included:

1. drug use, regardless of frequency or type of drug used, for at least one year prior to entry; and
2. at least one child 6 months to 10 years of age who could join his/her mother for a minimum of a 15 month treatment period at AMOR.

It was anticipated that over a five year period a total of 120 women would participate in the study; 60 in the Control group (women randomly assigned *not* to have their children in treatment with them) and 60 in the Experimental group (women randomly assigned to have their children in treatment with them). Additionally, a third group of women, the "Seed" group, participated in treatment at AMOR. The Seed group was composed of women with children who had already been in treatment and were given the opportunity to start the AMOR program and serve as role models for the new women entering AMOR. Finally, at any given time two of the treatment slots could be allocated as "Compassionate" slots for women who had particularly difficult circumstances (i.e., HIV positive). Those in the compassionate slots bypassed the random assignment and were allowed to have their child(ren) in treatment with them.

Eligible women were interviewed by the Enrollment Coordinator and, if possible, visited the program prior to an entrance decision on the part of AMOR staff and the woman seeking enrollment. Once the decision was made to enter the study, a consent form which outlined the basic components of the project was completed. The baseline assessment was administered within two weeks of treatment entry. Thereafter, in-treatment assessments were administered at 3, 6, 12, 18, and 24 months. Follow-up assessments were administered at 6, 12, and 24 months after discharge from the program. Numerous assessment instruments were administered at each assessment point. Data analyzed for this paper included self report data from the Addiction Severity Index (ASI) administered at baseline (intake) and self report data from the ASI administered six months after discharge from the program.

RESULTS

A total of 120 baseline interviews were collected; 46 Control women, 49 Experimental women, 12 Seed women, 6 Compassionate women, and 7 Non-randomized "Splits." For the purpose of this paper data for only the Control, Experimental, and Seed groups were analyzed (N = 107). As shown in Table 1, the average age of the study sample was 28.7 years. The average age for each subgroup was similar (Control = 29.1; Experimental = 28.7; Seed = 27.6 years). The mean educational level for the total sample was 11.2 years. Again, the mean educational level for the subgroups was similar (Control = 11.0; Experimental = 11.4; Seed = 11.3 years). The average number of convictions for the total sample was 3.7 (Control = 3.0; Experimental = 4.7: Seed = 2.3). For those who reported spending time in jail/prison, the average number of months for the total of sample was 11.9 (Control = 13.3; Experimental = 9.5; Seed = 15.3 months). Lifetime drug use could only be calculated on the Control and Experimental women because this question was not included in an earlier version of the Addictions Severity Index (ASI) that was used during the first six months of the project. Lifetime drug use for the total sample was 10.8 years (Control = 9.0; Experimental = 12.5 years).

Table 2 shows that the largest ethnic group represented in the study sample was Caucasian (37.7%). While the Control and Experimental groups had approximately the same percent of Caucasians (41.3% and 38.8% respectively), the percentage of Caucasians in the Seed group was much smaller (18.2%). Close to half (48.1%) of the women were never married. The percent of Control and Experimental women that were never married was similar (44.4% and 46.9% respectively), while the percentage of Seed women who were never married was much higher (66.7%). With regard to typical employment pattern the year prior to entry into the AMOR project, almost half (49.5%) of the total sample reported being unemployed. Again, data from the Control and Experimental groups were similar with 47.8% of the Control and 59.2% of the Experimental groups reporting being unemployed. Only 16.7% of the women in the Seed group reported being unemployed the year prior to entry. Primary drug use varied somewhat by group assignment, however cocaine was reported as being the primary drug most frequently used by all three groups (Control = 34.8%; Experimental = 42.9%; Seed = 50.0%). Substantially more Seed group women were coerced into treatment by the criminal justice system or Child Protective Services (91.7%) compared to the Control (54.3%) and Experimental (51.0%) participants. In part, this might have been due to the greater percentage of Seed women (83.3%) who were on probation or parole compared to those in the Control (63.0%) and Experimental (42.9%) groups. However, it should be noted that over three quarters of all three groups had been arrested/incarcerated and had been convicted of at least one crime. Having been raped sometime during lifetime was reported by 62.2% of the women (Control = 57.1%; Experimental = 66.7%).[1] When looking at suicide attempts and use of psychiatric medication a greater percentage of Seed group (58.3%) had attempted suicide compared to the Control (44.4%) and Experimental (38.8%) groups. Yet, prescribed psychiatric medication for all three groups was approximately the same (Control = 35.6%; Experimental = 38.8%; Seed = 33.3%) (see Table 2).

Six month outcome data was analyzed for five variables: (1) *any* AOD use, (2) stable part-time or full-time employment, (3) custody of children, (4) arrest data, and (5) involvement in aftercare or support groups. As length of stay (LOS) in treatment has often been associated with treatment outcomes, the mean LOS for each group was also calculated. Two separate analyses were conducted. First a comparison of women who did not have their children in treatment with them (Control) with those women who did have their children in treatment with them (Experimental + Seed) was

---

1. Percentage of the seed group who experienced rape is not provided since an earlier version of the ASI was used which did not include this question.

TABLE 1. Baseline Means: Age, Educational Level, Lifetime Drug Use, Convictions, Jail/Prison Time, and Rape by Assignment Group

	Total		Control		Experimental		Seed	
	M	*N*	*M*	*N*	*M*	*N*	*M*	*N*
Age (yrs)	28.7	107	29.1	46	28.7	49	27.6	12
Education (yrs)	11.2	107	11.0	46	11.4	49	11.3	12
Convictions (#)	3.7	107	3.0	46	4.7	49	2.3	12
[1]Jail/Prison time (mo)	11.9	86	13.3	38	9.5	38	15.3	10
[2]Lifetime drug use (yrs)	10.8	93	9.0	44	12.5	49	—	—

1 The mean jail/prison time was calculated for only those women who reported jail or prison time.
2 Sample size is smaller for this variable because this question was not included in the earlier version of the Addictions Severity Index.

TABLE 2. Baseline Percentages: Ethnicity, Marital Status, Employment, Primary Drug Use, Criminal Justice Involvement, Suicide Attempt and Psychiatric Medication

	Total		Control		Experimental		Seed	
	%	N	%	N	%	N	%	N
Ethnicity								
Caucasian	37.7	40	41.3	19	38.8	19	18.2	2
Hispanic	28.3	30	28.3	13	30.6	15	18.2	2
African Am.	25.5	27	17.4	8	28.6	14	45.5	5
Native Am.	8.5	9	13.0	6	2.0	1	18.2	2
Marital Status								
Married	16.0	17	17.8	8	18.4	9	0.0	0
Separated	10.4	11	4.4	2	12.2	6	25.0	3
Divorced	20.8	22	28.9	13	16.3	8	8.3	1
Widowed	4.7	5	4.4	2	6.1	3	0.0	0
Never Married	48.1	51	44.4	20	46.9	23	66.7	8
Employment Pattern								
Full Time	18.7	20	15.2	7	14.3	7	50.0	6
Part Time	15.0	16	17.4	8	10.2	5	25.0	3
Stud/Home/Disabil	6.5	7	6.5	3	8.1	4	.0	0
Unemployed	49.5	53	47.8	22	59.2	29	16.7	2
Controlled Envir	10.3	11	13.0	6	8.2	4	8.3	1

[1]Primary Drug Use	%	n	%	n	%	n	%	n
Alcohol	23.4	25	34.8	16	18.4	9	0.0	0
Heroin	14.0	15	15.2	7	14.3	7	8.3	1
Cocaine	40.2	43	34.8	16	42.9	21	50.0	6
Amphetamines	10.3	11	8.7	4	14.3	7	0.0	0
Opiate, Pot, Halluc	5.6	6	2.2	1	10.2	5	0.0	0
Alcohol and Drugs	6.5	7	4.3	2	0.0	0	41.7	5
Coerced into Tx	57.0	61	54.3	25	51.0	25	91.7	11
On Probation/Parole	56.1	60	63.0	29	42.9	21	83.3	10
Been Arrested/Incarcer	80.4	86	84.4	38	77.6	38	83.3	10
Convicted ≥ One Crime	77.6	83	76.1	35	77.6	38	83.3	10
[2]Rape	62.2	56	57.1	24	66.7	32	--	--
Attempted Suicide	43.4	46	44.4	20	38.8	19	58.3	7
Psychiatric Medication	36.8	39	35.6	16	38.8	19	33.3	4

1   Results of this question differ because the "alcohol and drugs" response was only included in the earlier version of the Addictions Severity Index.
2   Sample size is smaller for this variable because this question was not included in the earlier version of the Addictions Severity Index.

completed. Second, a comparison between all three groups was completed (Control vs Experimental vs Seed) for examination of differences between the groups. Results of the analyses are shown on Table 3. Results from the first analysis shows substantial differences on all five of the outcome variables with women who had children living with them in the program (Experimental and Seed) demonstrating better outcomes. Over fifty-five percent (55.6%) of those in the Experimental and Seed groups remained *completely* AOD free compared to 42.9% of the Control group. A greater percentage of those in the Experimental and Seed groups (74.1%) were employed compared to those in the Control group (57.1%) despite the fact that the Experimental and Seed group women more frequently had child-care responsibilities because they had custody of their children (74.1% Experimental and Seed vs 38.1% Control). With regard to arrest/incarceration which includes probation revocations for previous–before treatment arrests), 74.1% of those in the Seed and Experimental groups were not rearrested compared to 61.9% of the Control group. Over eighty-one percent (81.5%) of the Experimental and Seed group women were involved in aftercare compared to 71.4% of those in the Control group. Finally, the average length of stay for the Experimental and Seed group women was 10.8 months compared to an average of 8.8 months for the Control group.

Comparing data for the three groups under study is also shown on Table 3. A greater percent of the Experimental group evidenced positive outcomes compared with the Control group on all five variables. Moreover, the Seed group evidenced even better outcomes than either the Control or the Experimental groups. Seventy percent of the Seed women reported *not* using *any* alcohol or other drugs compared with 47.1% of the Experimental and 42.9% of the Control women. Ninety percent of the Seed women reported steady employment compared to 64.7% of the Experimental and 57.1% of the Control women. One hundred percent of the Seed women had custody of all or some of their children six months after discharge compared to 58.8% of the Experimental and 38.1% of the Control women. When looking at outcome data for arrest/incarceration, 80% of the Seed women had *not* been arrested compared with 70.6% of the Experimental and 61.9% of the Control women. Involvement in aftercare or support groups was reported by 90.0% of the Seed women compared with 76.5% of the Experimental and 71.4% of the Control women. The average length of stay was 11.7 months for the Seed group, 10.2 months for the Experimental group, and 8.5 months for the Control group.

DISCUSSION

The results of the study indicate that, in general, the women in the AMOR project had extensive drug use histories, had substantial involve-

TABLE 3. Six Month Follow-Ups: Alcohol and Drug Use, Employment, Custody of Children, Arrest or Incarcerations, Aftercare, and Length of Stay by Control, Experimental, Seed, and Experimental + Seed Groups

	Total		Control		Experimental		Seed		Experimental + Seed	
	%	N	%	N	%	N	%	N	%	N
Percent										
No AOD Use	50.0	24	42.9	9	47.1	8	70.0	7	55.6	15
Employed	66.7	32	57.1	12	64.7	11	90.0	9	74.1	20
Custody of Children	58.3	28	38.1	8	58.8	10	100.0	10	74.1	20
Not Arrested/Incarc	68.8	33	61.9	13	70.6	12	80.0	8	74.1	20
In Aftercare/Support	77.1	37	71.4	15	76.5	13	90.0	9	81.5	22
	M	*N*	*M*	*N*	*M*	*N*	*M*	*N*	*M*	*N*
Means										
Length of Stay (mo.)	9.9	24	8.8	9	10.2	8	11.7	7	10.8	15

ment in the criminal justice system, and had experienced traumatic life experiences such as rape and suicide. Less than half were employed and only a small proportion were married. The three groups under study were similar in age, education, drug use and psychiatric medication. Additionally, over half of the women in the Experimental and Control group experienced rape sometime during their life. Differences between the three groups also existed, particularly between the Seed group women and the two randomized groups. The women in the Seed group were more often from a minority background, unmarried, employed and had attempted suicide more often. They had fewer criminal convictions but were more often on probation/parole, had spent more months in jail or prison and were more often coerced into treatment; perhaps indicating that their crimes were more serious. Differences between the Control and Experimental groups also existed. The women in the Control group reported fewer years of lifetime drug use. Conversely, they spent more months in jail or prison and were more often on probation/parole.

The background characteristics and life experiences reported by the AMOR women indicate that the women in all three groups experienced substantial dysfunction and the severity of their drug use and life situation warranted long term residential treatment. However, because of the noted difference between the groups (i.e., lifetime drug use, attempted suicide), caution must be used when making conclusions about the observed outcome differences between groups. Differences in outcomes may, in part, be due to differences in the baseline characteristics and behaviors of the women who comprised each group.

Of the 107 women, 71 were eligible for a six month follow-up. A total of 48 follow-ups were completed (Control = 21; Experimental = 17; Seed = 10). The six-month follow-up rate was 66.7% for the total sample, 72.4% for the Control, 56.7% for the Experimental, and 83.3% for the women in the Seed group. While a higher follow-up rate is more desirable, the follow-up sample did include both those who had negative outcomes and those who were doing well. AMOR staff worked closely with Child Protective Services, Probation/Parole, and the Department of Corrections to follow-up on the former participants. The AMOR participants who re-entered the system were the easiest to follow-up because many of those who were mandated to treatment by the criminal justice system and left the program early (against staff advice) returned to jail or prison. Conversely, those who were involved in aftercare and kept in contact with the program were also likely to complete their follow-up. Consequently, those who were not doing well (rearrested or Child Protective Services involved) and those who were doing well were the easiest to engage in follow-up.

Outcome data comparing the Control group with women who had their children in treatment with them (Experimental + Seed) shows that a greater percentage of women with children evidenced better outcomes, indicating that having one's children in treatment is an important element for treatment success. Perhaps part of the differential successfulness of the women with children might be due to the greater percentage of them who were involved in aftercare/support groups at the time of follow-up. This higher percentage of women with children attending aftercare/support groups was a surprising positive finding given that so many of them also had childcare responsibilities. Additionally, as prior research has demonstrated that LOS is positively correlated with desired treatment outcomes (Glider, Mullen, Herbst, Davis and Fleishman, in press; Simpson and Sells, 1982; Wexler, Falkin & Lipton, 1990), the differential successfulness of the women with children might, in part, be a result of their substantially longer length of stay (LOS) in treatment. Perhaps living with one's children in treatment increases women's awareness of the need for aftercare/support, while having physical custody of their children may be one important reason for why they stay longer.

Having children in treatment keeps families together. The women who had their children in treatment with them were almost twice as likely (74.1% Experimental + Seed vs 38.1% Control) to have custody of their children six months after discharge from treatment. Despite their childcare responsibilities a greater percentage of these women were also more frequently employed, adding financial stability for them and their children.

The outcomes comparing the Control group with the Experimental and Seed groups combined indicates better outcomes for women who had children living in treatment with them. The percentage of those who were "successful" on the five outcome variables was the greatest for the Seed group, followed by the Experimental group, and finally followed by the Control group. Why the Seed group women demonstrated such superior positive outcomes could again be associated with LOS and involvement in aftercare/support groups. However, there existed important differences in the treatment that the Seed group received compared with the Control and Experimental groups which might have also contributed to the Seed groups elevated positive outcomes. First, the women in the Seed group participated in a treatment center which served a smaller number of women. Consequently, their treatment was directed and facilitated by staff who had many years of experience. Previous research on TC treatment has noted the importance of having "Senior Professors" directly involved in the day to day treatment experience (De Leon, 1983; De Leon, 1991). Secondly, the women in the Seed group had several months to address their substance abuse problem and related dysfunctional behavior prior to having their children join them in treatment. Third, in accord with the therapeutic community (TC) model, residents who have remained in treatment longer acted as role models for those who are newer to the treatment community. When the AMOR project opened the women in the Seed group had already been in treatment for several months. They were challenged to "teach" the new AMOR enrollees and serve as their role models. Expectations for this group were notable. As in other learning environments it is often the teacher that learns the most. Finally, in preparation for the AMOR project, the women in the Seed group were told that if they worked diligently in their own recovery process, they might be given the opportunity to "seed" the new program and bring their children to live with them in treatment. In other words, having their children with them in treatment was not an "entitlement" nor was it the fate of a random selection process. The Seed women had to demonstrate by their efforts in their recovery process their fitness for the opportunity to have their children with them in treatment. Perhaps they were either more internally motivated or more motivated from the external pressure of having to "work" for the opportunity to have their children with them in treatment. In other words, being "entitled" to one's children when the mother's behavior (AOD use, criminal activity, neglect/abuse of children) has resulted in inadequate parenting may not provide the needed external pressure to address one's drug addiction and related behaviors. Similarly, allowing random selection to decide whether children are allowed to join the mother in treatment may not encourage or motivate women to address their addiction and related behavior. In fact, random selection on such an important factor may foster the idea that the women are not in control of their own lives. If one of the most important aspects of their lives (their children) is perceived to be out of their control, perhaps other important aspects (i.e., AOD use) will also be perceived to be beyond their control.

REFERENCES

D'Amore, L., & Glider, P.J. (1992). Embracing Families at Risk. Workshop presented at the Annual Meeting of the National Association of Perinatal Addiction Research Education, Chicago, IL., December.

De Leon, G. (1983). Predicting Retention and Follow-up Status. Final Report of Project Activities, National Institute on Drug Abuse Grant No. DA-02741.

De Leon, G. (1984). The therapeutic community: Study of effectiveness. NIDA Monograph, DHHS Publication No. (ADM) 84-1286.

De Leon, G. (1989). Therapeutic communities for substance abuse: Overview of approach and effectiveness. *Psychology of Addictive Behaviors, 3*, 140-149.

De Leon, G. (1991). Retention in drug free therapeutic communities. In R.W. Pickens, C.G. Leukefeld & C.R. Schuster (Eds.), *Improving Drug Abuse Treat-*

ment, National Institute on Drug Abuse Research Monograph, No. 106, Rockville, MD: National Institute on Drug Abuse.

De Leon, G. and Rosenthal, M. (1979). Therapeutic communities. In: R. DuPont, A. Goldstein and J. O'Donnel (Eds.) *Handbook on Drug Abuse*.

Glider, P., Hughes, P., Mullen, R., Colletti, S., Sechrest, L., Renner, B., & Sicilian, D. (1996). Two therapeutic communities for substance-abusing women and their children. In E. Rahdart (Ed.), *Treatment for Drug-Exposed Women and Their Children: Advances in Research Methodology*, Rockville, MD: National Institute on Drug Abuse Monograph 165, pp. 32-51.

Glider, P., Mullen, R., Herbst, D., Davis, C., & Fleishman, B. (in press). Substance abuse treatment in a jail setting: A therapeutic community model. In G. De Leon (Ed.), *Community as Method: Modified Therapeutic Communities for Special Populations in Special Settings*. NY: The Greenwood Publishing Group.

McBride, D.C., Mutch, P., Kilcher, C., McCoy, V., Inciardi, J.A., & Pottieger, A. (1996). Treatment barriers for drug using women. In D.D. Chitwood, J.E. Rivers & J.A. Inciardi (Eds.), *The American Pipe Dream: Crack Use in the Inner City*. Fort Worth, TX: Harcourt Brace.

National Institute on Drug Abuse (1994). *National Survey Results on Drug Use from the Monitoring the Future Study, 1975-1993, Volume II*, NIH Publication No. 94-3810. Washington, D.C.: U.S. Govt. Printing Office.

New York Times, (January 1990). Ideas & Trends: Drug Treatment is scarcer than ever for women, pp. 26-27.

Simpson, D.D. and Sells, S.B. (1982). Effectiveness of treatment for drug abuse: An overview of the DARP research program. *Advances in Alcohol and Substance Abuse*, 2 (1), 7-29.

Stevens, S.J. Arbiter, N. and McGrath, R. (in press). Women and children: Therapeutic community substance abuse treatment and outcome findings. In G. De Leon (Ed.), *Community as Method: Modified Therapeutic Communities for Special Populations in Special Settings*. NY: The Greenwood Publishing Group.

Stevens, S.J., & Glider, P.J. (1994). Therapeutic communities: Substance abuse treatment for women. In F. Tims, G. De Leon, & Nancy Jainchill (Eds.), *National Institute on Drug Abuse Research Monograph Series; Therapeutic Community: Advances in Research and Application. Technical Review on Therapeutic Communities, NIDA Research Monograph 144, U.S. DHHS*.

Wechsberg, W. (1995). Strategies for working with women substance abusers. In B.S. Brown (Ed.), *Substance Abuse Treatment in the Era of AIDS*.

Wexler, H.K., Falkin, P. and Lipton, D. (1990). Outcome evaluation of prison TC's for substance abuse treatment *Criminal Justice and Behavior, 17*, 71-72.

Yablonsky, L. (1965). *The Tunnel Back: Synanon*, New York: Macmillan.

Gender Differences in the Economic Impacts of Clients Before, During and After Substance Abuse Treatment

Henrick Harwood, BA
Douglas Fountain, MPA
Sharon Carothers, MA
Dean Gerstein, PhD
Robert Johnson, MS

SUMMARY. Gender differences in substance abuse treatment have been a topic of increasing importance for over 10 years. This study analyzes the publicly-supported California treatment system using a representative sample of 1825 clients from five modalities. An economic framework is used to compare outcomes of women and men, concluding that: (1) on average, treatment of women is strongly cost-beneficial, but (2) cost-benefit ratios are materially lower among women compared with men in some modalities. In the year before treatment, women imposed less economic burden than men, mostly due to less criminal involvement. Women were somewhat more likely to be seen in outpatient settings than in 24 hour care settings (residential and social model programs) and had significant-

Henrick Harwood, Douglas Fountain, and Sharon Carothers are affiliated with The Lewin Group, 9302 Lee Highway, Suite 500, Fairfax, VA 22031. Dean Gerstein and Robert Johnson are associated with the National Opinion Research Center, Washington, DC.

[Haworth co-indexing entry note]: "Gender Differences in the Economic Impacts of Clients Before, During and After Substance Abuse Treatment." Harwood, Henrick et al. Co-published simultaneously in *Drugs & Society* (The Haworth Press, Inc.) Vol. 13, No. 1/2, 1998, pp. 251-269; and: *Women and Substance Abuse: Gender Transparency* (ed: Sally J. Stevens, and Harry K. Wexler) The Haworth Press, Inc., 1998, pp. 251-269. Single or multiple copies of this article are available for a fee from The Haworth Document Delivery Service [1-800-342-9678, 9:00 a.m. - 5:00 p.m. (EST). E-mail address: getinfo@ haworthpressinc.com].

251

ly longer lengths of stay in non-methadone outpatient treatment but only modestly different lengths of stay in other types of treatment. Economic savings from the treatment of men and women are four to twelve times greater than the cost of treatment, depending on the type of treatment setting studied. However, savings from treatment are estimated to be 4.3 times the cost of treatment for women, and 9.3 times the cost of treatment for men. Moreover, total savings during treatment and in the year following treatment exceeded costs for both men and women regardless of the treatment setting. *[Article copies available for a fee from The Haworth Document Delivery Service: 1-800-342-9678. E-mail address: getinfo@haworthpressinc.com]*

INTRODUCTION

The California Alcohol and Drug Abuse Treatment Assessment (CAL-DATA) study has provided the most rigorous and most recent examination of a major substance abuse treatment system in the United States (Gerstein et al., 1994) and builds on prior large scale studies of treatment effectiveness (Hubbard et al., 1989). This representative study of treatment provided to 146,000 persons treated in California in 1991 found that the benefits of treatment outweigh costs by 7 to 1, in large measure due to declines in crime by two thirds and hospitalizations by about one third in the year following treatment.

Not surprisingly, women comprise a larger proportion of the treatment population than ever before. The CALDATA study estimated that, in four major modalities of treatment, 38 percent of the publicly-subsidized California treatment population in 1992 were women. This affords an opportunity to rigorously compare and contrast the women and men that are receiving services in terms of their pre-treatment behaviors, and the impacts on those behaviors during and following the treatment episode.

Making more and better treatment available for women has been a major issue for the substance abuse treatment system. This attention has been particularly fueled by concerns about the potential of adverse fetal effects from perinatal use of alcohol and psychoactive drugs as well as fear for the well being of infants and children in the care of substance abusers. Consequently, public treatment systems have invested increasing proportions of financing in provision of services focused on women, and there have been major investments in federal research on and demonstrations of treatment for women.

A particular goal of this paper is to examine the performance of the California public system in treating women and men, respectively. Recognizing that the treatment system and various treatment protocols were developed to treat what was once a predominately male population, there have been concerns that women might not be well-served by the larger system, but would benefit more from therapeutic approaches which are oriented to address therapeutic needs more prevalent among women. This study unfortunately can neither address whether such approaches are more effective for women, nor provide data about the availability of such treatment services. However, this study does attempt to provide a snapshot of the relative performance of the California public treatment system for women and men in general.

This study employs an economic framework to characterize and analyze women treated for substance abuse in the California public system, and to contrast them with males. The great utility of an economic framework is that it allows a variety of otherwise disparate behaviors and impacts to be summarized in what is best characterized as an index. The components of the index are the tangible behaviors and impacts of concern—e.g., various types of crime, impacts on victims, the costs of correctional services, various health problems, and receipt of social welfare benefits. These components are then essentially weighted by the application of economic theory and appropriate market prices. The final value of the index is in dollars, which can be compared and contrasted to factors such as the cost of providing treatment, or of undertaking other interventions. This construct is the foundation of benefit-cost analysis.

Following a discussion on the background of gender differences in substance abuse treatment, this paper describes the methodology employed in the CALDATA study and salient characteristics of women and men that accessed treatment services from the California public system. The economic model used in this study is briefly summarized. Basic findings are presented about the estimated economic impacts of female and male substance abusers prior to their entry into treatment. This is followed by data concerning the types of treatment and expenditures on services utilized by women and men. The analysis then proceeds to examine the economic value of treatment impacts for women and men, by treatment modality, and to contrast this with the cost of the treatment services. The final issue examined is the proportion of women and men that appear to improve, or get worse, following treatment, and by how much.

BACKGROUND

Society's concern with substance abuse problems largely stems from the health, crime, and other sequelae associated with substance abuse and addiction. These social effects exact a substantial cost on society at large (Gerstein and Harwood, 1990; Hubbard et al., 1989; Hser, Anglin, & Liu, 1991; Rice, Kelman, Miller, and Dunmeyer, 1990). Substance abusing men and women are affected differently by substance abuse and therefore impact society in disparate manners. Research points to several important differences between men and women, including access to treatment, appropriateness of alternative treatment models, and individual characteristics such as psychology and abuse experience, family and social support, work and welfare, and crime. These are discussed below.

Access to treatment. A considerable body of research indicates that women have different treatment needs and outcomes than men. Women in general underutilize the formal substance abuse treatment system (Weisner and Schmidt, 1992). Examples of barriers identified previously include social and cultural barriers, as well as a lack of: child care, finances, transportation, family treatment, gender-sensitive treatment programs, information regarding services, outreach to women, and affordable services. Some women do not enter treatment for fear of losing custody of their children, and some women simply have too many responsibilities, which prevents them from receiving needed treatment services (Schliebner, 1994).

Pregnant and parenting women with substance abuse problems have unique problems in accessing treatment. In general, there is a lack of resources specifically designed for pregnant women and their newborn infants. Where programs exist that do accept pregnant women, they are often not equipped to accept the women with their other children or accept them back into treatment with their newborn (Finnegan, 1991).

Appropriateness of Recovery Models. Some treatment programs may not be appropriately designed for the needs of women. Many treatment programs that started in the 1970s and early 1980s were based on male-oriented recovery models focused on confrontational "individual change" processes that excluded family and other system factors from recovery (Finkelstein, 1993). Failure rates of women in traditional drug treatment programs (Nelson-Zlupko, Kauffman, & Dore, 1995) contributed to the development of new treatment models that incorporate family and other system factors, build on individual strengths, rely on nurturance and empowerment and relationships, and use client's experiences as learning tools rather than as a source of grief and shame (Nelson-Zlupko et al., 1995; Schliebner, 1994).

Psychology and Abuse Experience. Women are more likely to have experienced physical, sexual, or emotional abuse as children or adults than men (Fountain, Caddell, Roig, Auwers, and Ginsburg, 1995) and are more likely to have comorbid psychiatric symptoms such as depression and anxiety. About one half to two thirds of women presenting for substance abuse treatment have a history of childhood physical or sexual traumas. Initiation of substance use began for many women after traumatic events such as incest, rape, physical illness, accidents, or disruption in family life (Nelson-Zlupko et al., 1995). Treatment programs that do not address childhood sexual experiences may seriously impede progress in recovery for women (Pearce & Lovejoy, 1995). Survivors of abuse are also at increased risk of suffering from anxiety, depression, and other psychological problems.

Family and Social Support. Most substance abusing women come from families in which drugs were abused by one or more family members (Nelson-Zlupko et al., 1995). Women who abuse substances are more likely than men to be in relationships with drug-using partners or spouses (Reed, 1985). Substance abusing women often have a history of having too much responsibility in their families of origin (Bepko, 1989) and some studies have indicated that women have experienced greater disruption in their families than their male counterparts (Blume, 1990). These women are likely to have the primary responsibility for child care and the care of other family members and they are less likely than their male counterparts to have someone actively supporting them in treatment (Reed, 1985). Primary responsibility for child care often interferes with women's access to substance abuse treatment and earning capacity (Karuntzos, Caddell, & Dennis, 1994).

Work and Welfare. Substance abusing women in general have less education, fewer work experiences, lower vocational readiness, and fewer financial resources than substance abusing men (Nelson-Zlupko et al., 1995; Karuntzos et al., 1994; Yang, 1990) and typically are unemployed or had not been employed in the year preceding treatment admission. Women may have been less inclined to use and benefit from vocational services provided in substance abuse treatment settings compared with men (Karuntzos et al., 1994). Substance abusing women are more likely than male counterparts to be receiving public assistance or depending on a family member in order to live.

Crime. Substance abusing men are more likely to commit crimes such as robbery, con games, and burglary than substance abusing women. Shoplifting and prostitution are more common among substance abusing women who have any criminal history (Nelson-Zlupko, Kauffman, & Dore, 1995). Women who are participating in a substance abuse treatment program are more likely to be involved in civil actions such as child custody, separation and divorce, and landlord-tenant disputes than in criminal proceedings (Reed, 1985).

This paper builds on prior analyses by focusing on the economic impacts of client status and behaviors. The following questions guided the analysis presented below.

- What differences exist between men and women in their economic impacts before treatment–including crime, employment, and health-care utilization;
- Do economic impacts change differently for men and women during and/or following treatment?
- What are the differences in costs of care, lengths of stay, readmission rates, and economic benefits between men and women in different modalities?

METHODOLOGY

Data Collection

The California Drug and Alcohol Treatment Assessment (CALDATA) was the first-ever representative study of client outcomes in a large substance abuse treatment system. The State of California's Department of Alcohol and Drug Programs launched an initiative to study the epidemiology of substance abuse and outcomes of treatment among its funded treatment providers. CALDATA was the first component in this initiative. The National Opinion Research Center (NORC) at the University of Chicago conducted this study for the CADP and Lewin-VHI conducted the economic analyses of the data.

NORC employed a multi-tier sampling strategy to accomplish this study. Counties were randomly selected, then providers within counties, then treatment participants within each provider. Providers were sampled to represent residential, social model, outpatient non-methadone, and methadone programs. Social model programs are somewhat unique to California: they provide non-medical model residential services. Of the 110 providers sampled, 83 programs agreed to participate in the study. Over 90 percent of residential and social model programs and over 75 percent of outpatient non-methadone programs participated in the study. Just under 75% of the methadone programs selected were willing to participate, due mostly to blanket noncooperation by owners of two large chains of for-profit methadone facilities.

Of 3,000 clients sampled, professional interviewers successfully located and recruited 1,825 clients at 15 months, on average, following treatment (or during treatment for continuing methadone clients). The overall response rate was about 61 percent, though 76.5 percent of methadone maintenance clients participated in the study. Participant non-response in the study was attributable to failure to locate the client rather than to the client's refusal to participate. A comparison of clients who participated versus those who did not was made using clinical records–no systematic difference between groups was detected. Structured interviews with the treatment participants lasted about 75 minutes and covered a person's behaviors and status from before, during, and after treatment on diverse topics including substance abuse, criminality, employment/income, and health status. The result of this study is an outcome database representative of over 146,000 persons treated in publicly funded treatment programs in the State of California during 1991-1992.

As shown in Table 1, there were over 55,761 women and 90,833 men treated in California's publicly-funded programs during the study period. Compared to men, women were younger (34.6 years versus 36.7 years old), were more likely to be Caucasian rather than Hispanic, and had about the same education level. In the year before treatment, women were less likely to have been employed either full or part time, were more likely to have experienced depression or attempted suicide, and were less likely to have been engaged in illegal activities or to have been arrested. Overall, more than 40 percent of the CALDATA population reported heroin as the main drug which led to treatment, 31 percent cited alcohol, and about 25 percent cited stimulants (split with little overlap between amphetamines, cocaine, and crack). All other drugs accounted for about 5 percent of the treatment admissions. Heroin's predominance as the main drug reflects the fact that just under 40 percent of the treatment population in California's state-funded modalities are in methadone treatment, rather than an underlying trend in substance use in California. The proportion of women versus men citing each type of drug was generally consistent; though women were slightly more likely than men to have reported amphetamines and slightly less likely than men to have reported heroin and alcohol.

Economic Analysis

Data is available and increasingly being cited concerning the cost of treatment, but very few large scale studies have examined the economic benefits of substance abuse treatment. The approach used in this study is similar to that used in prior analyses (e.g., Hubbard et al., 1989). Following is a summary of this study's approach to estimate the costs and economic benefits of treatment.

TABLE 1. Characteristics of the Population Studied in CALDATA

	Women	Men
Weighted Population (total 146,594)	55,761	90,833
Average Age	34.6	36.7
Black or African American	13%	14%
Hispanic	29%	38%
White, not Hispanic	53%	41%
Other	6%	6%
Less than high school education	38%	36%
High school diploma or equivalent only	12%	15%
Education or training beyond high school	49%	49%
In Year Before Treatment:		
Employed full time at any time	31%	47%
Employed part time at any time	16%	23%
Received substance abuse treatment	47%	46%
Depressed	74%	61%
Attempted suicide	9%	6%
Received outpatient mental health services	30%	21%
Hospitalized for mental health problems	8%	7%
Pregnant	23%	
Engaged in any illegal activities	68%	75%
Arrested, booked, or taken into custody	41%	47%

The cost of treatment for each of the 146,000 clients represented in the CALDATA study was established by obtaining provider responses to the annual National Alcohol and Drug Treatment Unit Survey (NDATUS). The State of California provided information to link provider identifiers with NDATUS identifiers; 80 of the 83 participating providers were matched. NDATUS data on program revenues for single modality providers was divided by annual program clients to obtain cost per client day in treatment; this was then applied on a case by case basis to the CALDATA sample. In all, it is estimated that over $209 million was spent on the treatment of the 146,000 clients represented in CALDATA. An episode of care ranged from $404 for about 60 days of methadone treatment to $4,405 for about 69 days of residential treatment.

Estimating economic "benefits" of treatment entails comparing the economic costs imposed by participants before treatment with the economic costs imposed during and after treatment. Essentially, *avoided costs equal benefits.* When economic impacts either during or following treatment are lower than the baseline costs, a "benefit" is said to exist. Benefits take on a negative value if economic costs are greater during or after treatment compared to before treatment.

The economic impacts of the CALDATA population was estimated using standard "cost of illness" methods employed in previous estimates of the cost of substance abuse on society (Rice et al., 1990; Harwood et al., 1984). In particular, this study takes the view that the salient economic impacts are those imposed on "taxpayers" or other individuals beyond the substance abuser and their immediate family. For example, the types of economic impacts analyzed here are crime, healthcare, and income transfers (receipt of welfare and disability).

CALDATA used a single interview to collect data on participant behaviors during the year before and after treatment as well as the period during treatment. This study then assigned average values for specific crimes, healthcare episodes, and used participant-reported welfare and disability receipts. Crime and healthcare expenditure data are available at the national level and, in some cases, for California for the study period (see the original CALDATA report for a discussion of information sources). Values were inflated to 1992 levels if expenditure information was only available for prior years. Healthcare costs were estimated by applying national averages of per day costs for hospitalization, outpatient physician care, mental health hospitalization, outpatient mental health care, and emergency room care to participant reported healthcare service use.

Components of the cost of crime include police protection; prosecution, adjudication and sentencing; corrections; victim costs; and theft costs. Police protection costs were assigned by applying the average cost per arrest times the likelihood of arrest for each type of crime to participant self-reported engagement in specific crimes. Average adjudication and sentencing expenditures, incarceration expenditures, and probation/parolee expenditures were applied respectively to the number of participant-reported arrests, days incarcerated, and days on parole/probation. The value of victim costs, such as time lost from work and property damage, and the value of property and cash stolen were derived from analysis of the National Criminal Victimization Survey data and applied to participant-reported specific crimes.

RESULTS

Economic Impacts in the Year Before Treatment

Women imposed generally lower costs on taxpayers in the year before treatment than did men. These economic impacts in the year before treatment constitute a "baseline" against which subsequent estimates during and following treatment may be compared. As shown in Figure 1, total costs attributed to crime, healthcare use, welfare, and disability in the year before treatment averaged $18,072 for women and $25,311 for men. Criminal justice expenditures (including police protection, adjudication, and correction) and victim costs were lower for women than for men. Theft costs, or the value of property and cash stolen, constituted the greatest difference between women ($2,861) and men ($7,590) in the year before treatment. The costs associated with crime reflect lower engagement by women in crime relative to men.

Healthcare costs and welfare receipts were not lower among women than men. Healthcare costs were virtually the same, averaging about $3200 per year. Women, who are more likely to be categorically eligible for some cash assistance programs like AFDC, reported more from welfare than men ($1,771 versus $544). Disability payments to women were somewhat lower compared with men ($602 versus $1,044).

The pre-treatment economic impacts presented here are consistent with our understanding of general differences between male and female sub-

FIGURE 1. Economic Impacts of Women and Men in the Year Before Treatment

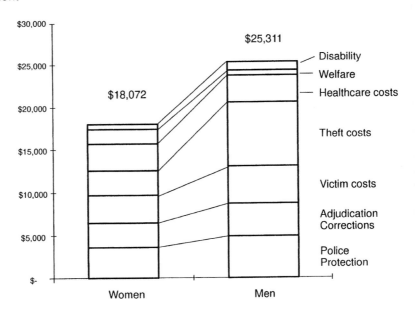

stance abusers who present for treatment. Women are less likely to have engaged in crime and are more likely to be eligible for welfare.

Characteristics of Treatment Provided in California

The CALDATA survey represents 146,000 treatment episodes in the publicly-subsidized California substance abuse treatment system, at an estimated cost of $206 million. Women constituted 38 percent of clients, at a cost of over $77 million or $1,381 per client. Men constituted 62 percent of clients, and per client spending of $1,424 was almost identical to that for women (Table 2).

Women were more likely to be seen in outpatient non-methadone settings than 24-hour care settings and have longer lengths of stay than men. While women make up 42.4% of outpatient non-methadone treatment clients and 42.5% of continuing methadone clients, women only account for 34.7% of the residential treatment population and 29.1% of California's social model treatment population.

Across all modalities, women tended to have significantly longer lengths of stay than men, but this mostly reflects outpatient non-methadone treatment. Women in outpatient non-methadone treatment stayed substantially longer in treatment than men (187 days versus 122 days, p = .0004). Modest differences in length of stay in residential and social model programs were not statistically different. Among the population receiving methadone, women who were discharged had modest but not significantly longer lengths of stay than men but women who were still receiving methadone had been in treatment for a significantly shorter period than men (p = .0043).

As discussed, this study relied on annual revenues and clients treated as reported by providers to NDATUS to estimate the cost per day of care. Estimates reported in the original CALDATA report are comparable to other estimates of the cost per day of care (e.g., Harwood, Thomson, and Nesmith, 1994) with the exception that methadone treatment costs in California on average are $6 to $7 dollars per day (or about $2,500 per year), whereas national estimates place the value closer to $11 per day (about $3,900 per year).

Cost per day of treatment was calculated based on total program revenues divided by average daily census: no allocation could be made between the actual cost associated with treatment for women verus men. Instead, averages reported here are based on the average cost per day for any client in the program. The cost per day of treatment was generally lower for women than men ($10.53 versus $14.53 across all types of care). While this is primarily attributable to women making less use of more

TABLE 2. Type, Length, and Cost of Treatment for Women and Men

	Women	Men
Type of Treatment **		
Residential	34.7%	65.3%
Social Model	29.1%	70.9%
Outpatient Non-Methadone	42.4%	57.6%
Methadone, Discharged	35.8%	64.2%
Methadone, Continuing	42.5%	57.5%
Average, All Modalities	**38.0%**	**62.0%**
Average Length of Stay (days)		
Residential	72	67
Social Model	74	81
Outpatient Non-Methadone	187**	122
Methadone, Discharged	64	57
Methadone, Continuing	304*	338
Average, All Modalities	**131*****	**98**
Cost per Episode		
Residential	$4,433	$4,391
Social Model	$2,523	$2,794
Outpatient Non-Methadone	$1,033	$959
Methadone, Discharged	$423	$395
Methadone, Continuing	$1,980	$2,115
Average, All Modalities	**$1,381**	**$1,424**
Cost per Day		
Residential	$61.48	$65.34
Social Model	$34.22	$34.31
Outpatient Non-Methadone	$5.51	$7.88
Methadone, Discharged	$6.56	$6.95
Methadone, Continuing	$6.51	$6.26
Average, All Modalities	**$10.53**	**$14.53**

Significance of women/men difference: * .05, ** .001, *** .0001.

intensive residential modalities, the cost per day in residential services for women was about 6% less than for men, and outpatient non-methadone services for women cost about 30% less than for men. Again, this means that women are more likely to receive treatment in less expensive residential and outpatient programs, not that their actual treatment costs less in the same facility or type of facility. Cost per day for social model and methadone treatment were about the same for men and women. The lower cost per day for women in outpatient non-methadone mitigated their longer lengths of stay so that, on average, an episode of care costs about the same for men and women ($1,381 versus $1,424). No significant differences were found in the cost of an episode in any of the 5 types of treatment.

Savings from Reduced Crime, Healthcare Utilization, and Welfare/Disability Use

This analysis of CALDATA essentially split the CALDATA population into men and women and analyzed their costs–and savings–independently. This study estimated "savings" that accrued during, as well as in the year following, a person's treatment episode. Savings have not been projected or estimated beyond one year following discharge from treatment, although clearly successful treatment yields a lifetime of benefits. Thus, these estimates should be considered only the first installment in repayment to tax paying citizens for providing subsidized substance abuse treatment.

Savings, as described above, are equal to the economic value of reductions in crime, healthcare, and welfare and disability reliance from what was expected based on the year before treatment. Table 3 presents savings during treatment and savings in the year following treatment for men and women in all modalities. These savings are then divided by the cost of the treatment episode to produce the benefit to cost ratio.

A finding from the original CALDATA report is that treatment "pays for itself on the day in which it was delivered." What this means is that the savings from changed behaviors *during* treatment surpasses the cost of providing that treatment. While this finding generally holds when examining women and men separately, Table 3 shows that among women in social model and residential treatment programs, economic benefits of treatment do not finish "paying off" costs until several months after leaving treatment.

Benefits during and following treatment are estimated at 4.3 for women and 9.3 for men relative to the cost of that treatment. Women generally had lower benefit to cost ratios than men. For example, while the cost of an episode of treatment for women compared to men was equivalent in outpatient and residential treatment, savings among men were over 2.5 times greater for residentially treated men than women (p = .008) and almost 2 times greater for outpatient men compared with women (p = .0565). These results warrant further attention since we have also shown that length of stay is longer in residential and outpatient programs for women compared with men.

The findings for methadone present interesting contrasts. Women and men had very similar results in long term/continuing treatment. However, among short term/discharged clients, women achieved smaller benefits–

TABLE 3. Savings During and Following Treatment and the Benefit/Cost Ratio by Type of Treatment, for Women and Men

	Residential		Social Model		Outpatient Non-Methadone		Methadone, Discharged		Methadone, Continuing	
	Women	Men	Women	Men	Women	Men	Women	Men	Women	Men
Savings During Treatment	$3,273	$4,475	$2,408	$3,404	$2,383	$2,393	$741	$1,081	$10,418	$11,637
Savings Following Treatment	$7,228	$22,618	$7,619	$9,031	$5,228	$10,910	$822	$5,977	n/a	n/a
Total Savings	**$10,501**	**$27,093**	**$10,027**	**$12,435**	**$7,611**	**$13,302**	**$1,563**	**$7,057**	**$10,418**	**$11,637**
Savings as Percent of Pre-Treatment Cost	54%	77%	56%	59%	51%	64%	7%	27%	57%	58%
Episode Cost	$4,433	$4,391	$2,523	$2,794	$1,033	$959	$423	$395	$1,980	$2,115
Benefits Divided by Costs	**2.4**	**6.2**	**4.0**	**4.5**	**7.4**	**13.9**	**3.7**	**17.9**	**5.3**	**5.5**
significance of difference ($* p < .05$, $** p < .01$):	**						*			

both absolutely and relatively–than men. While women and men dis-charged from methadone treatment had comparable lengths of stay (64 versus 57 days), savings among men exceeded $7,000 compared to over $1,500 among women. Benefit to cost ratios were therefore 3.7 for women and 17.9 for men (p = .0206). Exploring this difference further, we ob-served that half of the discharged methadone clients had been in treatment 21 days or less. These clients either simply dropped out or were using methadone for detoxification only. Not surprisingly, economic benefits for clients who stayed less than 21 days were half those for clients who stayed over 21 days ($3226 versus $7517).

Only modest and non-significant differences in savings are observed between men and women who continue to receive methadone. However, benefits for these clients are substantially greater than for clients who were discharged from treatment, presumably due to their stabilization after sub-stantially more time in treatment.

The original CALDATA report found that observed benefits of treat-ment do not diminish over time. This finding was based on the fact that clients on average were not interviewed until 15 months after discharge, and some were not interviewed until over 21 months after discharge. While savings reported in the original report as well as Table 3 here are annualized, it is possible to analyze savings generated regardless of when participants were interviewed. Figure 2 shows the savings per unit of time for women and men at different points in time after discharge from treat-ment. Costs before treatment are always higher than the costs after treat-ment, regardless of when the person was interviewed, and the ratio of these two values did not appear to diminish over the period this sample was observed.

Finally, as reported in the original CALDATA report, treatment may not have been successful for all clients. While savings on average and in total are positive and substantially greater than the cost of treatment, it is clear that some people actually get worse in the year after treatment. Figure 3 shows the distribution of men and women across four categories: those who worsened (increased costs after treatment) by more than 50%, those who worsened between 0 and 50%, those who improved (reduced costs after treatment) between 0 and 50%, and those who improved over 50% (which includes a number of persons who totally eliminated costs after treatment). Worsening implies that these clients increased their criminal activity, healthcare use, or welfare/disability receipt in the year after treat-ment compared with the year before; improvement implies the reverse.

Almost a third of men and women worsened in the year after treatment compared with the year before (Figure 3). Moreover, women were more

FIGURE 2. Savings in the Year After Treatment for Men and Women Discharged from Treatment

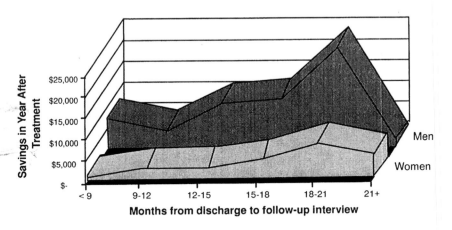

FIGURE 3. Relative Changes in Economic Impacts Among Men and Women, from Before to After Treatment

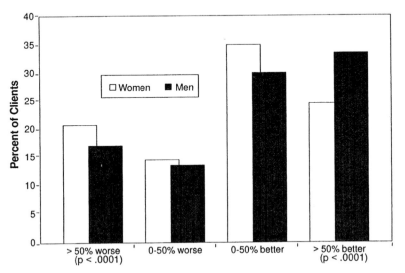

likely than men to have been in the group with the worst results (worsened more than 50%, p < .0001). Conversely, women were less likely than men to be in the best category (improved more than 50%, p < .0001). This distribution of improvement/decline among the CALDATA population is presented for all clients discharged from treatment in total. We also examined similar data for all four modalities and found virtually identical patterns, comparing women to men.

DISCUSSION

As with the main CALDATA report, this paper found substantial benefits accruing from the treatment of both men and women in California's publicly funded treatment system. Benefits outweighed costs regardless of the modality and regardless of when a person was interviewed after treatment.

While outcomes were strongly positive overall, it is also evident that women fared less well than men. Benefit to cost ratios for women (4.3) were generally lower than those for men (9.3) in all modalities, and were significantly lower for women discharged from residential treatment and from methadone treatment. Moreover, evidence suggests that more women worsened after treatment than men.

Introducing gender differences to the analysis of CALDATA may stimulate additional research questions. Additional investigation into specific causes of treatment failure would undoubtedly provide a basis for system planners and service providers to identify deficits in treatment regimens and seek to ameliorate those deficits. Quality of treatment can always be improved. Moreover, data were not available concerning the gender-sensitivity and appropriateness of services for women. We do not know which programs had attempted to tailor their programming to the needs of women. It is therefore not possible to conclude that gender-sensitive treatment is more or less effective from this analysis. This will be an important area for further exploration.

The economic perspective of the benefits and cost of treatment is certainly not the only perspective one may take. Such estimates do provide a means of comparing the relative impact of different benefits that accrue from treatment. For example, economic benefits from reductions in crime can be compared with the value of healthcare used or the amount of welfare and disability payment received. Other economic data could also be examined. For example, the original CALDATA report analyzed differences in expected versus actual earnings, from the standpoint of economic self sufficiency.

Other economic impacts that were not the focus of the CALDATA study also warrant further study. For example, data are not available here on the value of improvements in family and social functioning which may differentially impact women because they tend to bear greater responsibilities than men. The study did not examine the need or use of such services nor fertility or birth outcomes of women treated. Additional data on the costs associated with foster care, child protective services and caseworkers, medical costs and special intervention costs for perinatal exposure of children to drugs or alcohol or to related medical conditions such as HIV infection would provide additional important insights into the benefits and costs associated with treatment of women.

Additionally, there are caveats to this analysis. Foremost among them is that this study could not control for "regression to the mean" (improvement that might have occurred even without treatment). Therefore, these estimates probably over-estimate the benefits of treatment to some degree. This is always a contentious issue for which there is no single answer. Moreover, these analyses do not "net out" for re-entry to treatment. Many CALDATA clients did return to treatment after their primary "CALDATA" episode. However, it is worth noting that almost half of the clients had been treated in the year before their "CALDATA" episode. The field needs to address and model the concept of "treatment careers" in order to understand the impact and relationship of multiple treatment episodes, building off the pioneer work of Douglas Anglin and his colleagues at UCLA. Research on regression to the mean and the cumulative economic impact of multiple treatment episodes is needed. Explicit examination of the differences between men and women will be a necessary component of such exploration.

REFERENCES

Bepko, C. (1989). Disorders of power: Women and addiction in the family. In M. McGoldrick, C. Anderson, & F. Walsh (Eds.), *Women in families* (pp. 406-426). New York: W.W. Norton.

Blume, S.B. (1990). Chemical dependency in women: Important issues. *American Journal of Drug and Alcohol Abuse, 16*(3&4), 297-307.

Finkelstein, N. (1993). Treatment programming for alcohol and drug-dependent pregnant women. *The International Journal of the Addictions, 28*(13), 1275-1309.

Finnegan, L. (1991). *The clinical management of the pregnant, drug dependent woman.* Workshop presented at the NIDA National Conference on Drug Abuse Research and Practice, an Alliance for the 21st Century, Washington, D.C., January 12-15.

Fountain, D.L., Caddell, J.M., Roig, E.R., Auwers, L., & Ginsburg, S. (1994).

Child abuse before addiction: The role of child abuse trauma in substance abuse problems and recovery. Fairfax, VA: Lewin-VHI.

Gerstein, D., & Harwood, H., (Eds). (1990). *Treating drug problems.* Washington DC: National Academy Press.

Gerstein, D., Johnson, R., Harwood, H., Fountain, D., Suter, N. & Malloy, K. (1994). *Evaluating recovery services: The California Drug and Alcohol Treatment Assessment (CALDATA).* [Publication ADP 94-629.] Sacramento, CA: California Department of Alcohol and Drug Programs.

Harwood, H., Napolitano, D., Kristiansen, P., & Collins, J. (1984). *Economic Costs to Society of Alcohol and Drug Abuse and Mental Illness: 1980.* Research Triangle Park, NC: Research Triangle Institute.

Harwood, H.J., Thomson, M., & Nesmith, T. (1994). *Healthcare reform and substance abuse treatment: The cost of financing under alternative approaches.* Fairfax, VA: Lewin-VHI.

Hser, Y., Anglin, M.D., & Liu, Y. (1991). A survival analysis of gender and ethnic differences in responsiveness to methadone maintenance treatment. *International Journal of the Addiction, 25*(11A), 1295-1315.

Hubbard, R., Marsden, M.E., Rachal, J.V., Harwood, H., Cavanaugh, E., & Ginzburg, H. (1989). *Drug abuse treatment: A national study of effectiveness.* Chapel Hill, NC: University of North Carolina Press.

Karuntzos, G.T., Caddell, J.M., & Dennis, M.L. (1994). Gender differences in vocational needs and outcomes for methadone treatment clients. *Journal of Psychoactive Drugs, 26*(2), 173-180.

Nelson-Zlupko, L., Kauffman, E., & Dore, M.M. (1995). Gender differences in drug addiction and treatment: Implications for social work intervention with substance-abusing women. *Social Work, 40*(1), 45-54.

Pearce, E.J., & Lovejoy, F.H. (1995). Detecting a history of childhood sexual experiences among women substance abusers. *Journal of substance abuse treatment, 12*(4), 283-287.

Reed, B.G. (1985). Drug misuse and dependency in women: The meaning and implications of being considered a special population or minority group. *International Journal of the Addictions, 20*, 13-62.

Rice, D.P., Kelman, S., Miller, L., & Dunmeyer, S. (1990). *The economic costs of alcohol and drug abuse and mental illness: 1985.* Washington, DC: U.S. Department of Health and Human Services.

Schliebner, C.T. (1994). Gender-sensitive therapy: An alternative for women in substance abuse treatment. *Journal of Substance Abuse Treatment, 11*(6), 511-515.

Weisner, C., & Schmidt, L. (1992). Gender disparities in treatment for alcohol problems. *Journal of the American Medical Association, 268*, 1872-1876.

Yang, S.S. (1990). The unique treatment needs of female substance abusers in correctional institutions: The obligation of the criminal justice system to provide parity of services. *Medicine and Law, 9*(4), 1018-1027.

Index

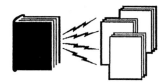

Haworth
DOCUMENT DELIVERY
SERVICE

This valuable service provides a single-article order form for any article from a Haworth journal.

- *Time Saving:* No running around from library to library to find a specific article.
- *Cost Effective:* All costs are kept down to a minimum.
- *Fast Delivery:* Choose from several options, including same-day FAX.
- *No Copyright Hassles:* You will be supplied by the original publisher.
- *Easy Payment:* Choose from several easy payment methods.

Open Accounts Welcome for . . .
- Library Interlibrary Loan Departments
- Library Network/Consortia Wishing to Provide Single-Article Services
- Indexing/Abstracting Services with Single Article Provision Services
- Document Provision Brokers and Freelance Information Service Providers

---

MAIL or *FAX* THIS ENTIRE ORDER FORM TO:

Haworth Document Delivery Service
The Haworth Press, Inc.
10 Alice Street
Binghamton, NY 13904-1580

or **FAX:** 1-800-895-0582
or **CALL:** 1-800-429-6784
9am-5pm EST

PLEASE SEND ME PHOTOCOPIES OF THE FOLLOWING SINGLE ARTICLES:

1) Journal Title: _____

    Vol/Issue/Year: _____ Starting & Ending Pages: _____

Article Title: _____

_____

2) Journal Title: _____

    Vol/Issue/Year: _____ Starting & Ending Pages: _____

Article Title: _____

_____

3) Journal Title: _____

    Vol/Issue/Year: _____ Starting & Ending Pages: _____

Article Title: _____

_____

4) Journal Title: _____

    Vol/Issue/Year: _____ Starting & Ending Pages: _____

Article Title: _____

(See other side for Costs and Payment Information)

COSTS: Please figure your cost to order quality copies of an article.

1. Set-up charge per article: $8.00
   ($8.00 × number of separate articles)   _____

2. Photocopying charge for each article:
   1-10 pages: $1.00   _____

   11-19 pages: $3.00   _____

   20-29 pages: $5.00   _____

   30+ pages: $2.00/10 pages   _____

3. Flexicover (optional): $2.00/article   _____

4. Postage & Handling: US: $1.00 for the first article/
   $.50 each additional article   _____

   Federal Express: $25.00   _____

   Outside US: $2.00 for first article/
   $.50 each additional article   _____

5. Same-day FAX service: $.50 per page   _____

   GRAND TOTAL: _____

METHOD OF PAYMENT: (please check one)

❑ Check enclosed   ❑ Please ship and bill. PO # _____
   (sorry we can ship and bill to bookstores only! All others must pre-pay)

❑ Charge to my credit card: ❑ Visa; ❑ MasterCard; ❑ Discover;
   ❑ American Express;

Account Number: _____ Expiration date: _____

Signature: ✗ _____

Name: _____ Institution: _____

Address: _____

_____

City: _____ State: _____ Zip: _____

Phone Number: _____ FAX Number: _____

MAIL or *FAX* THIS ENTIRE ORDER FORM TO:

Haworth Document Delivery Service   **or FAX:** 1-800-895-0582
The Haworth Press, Inc.   **or CALL:** 1-800-429-6784
10 Alice Street   (9am-5pm EST)
Binghamton, NY 13904-1580

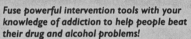

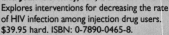